BY PRECISION
INTO POWER

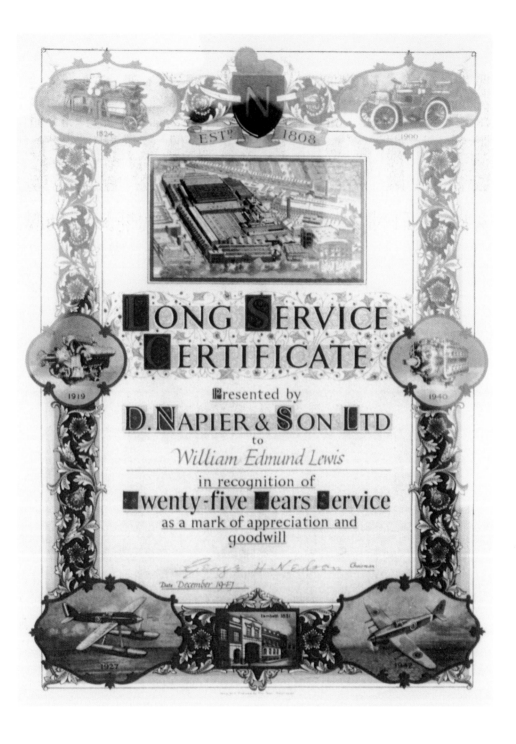

LONG SERVICE
CERTIFICATE

Presented by

D. NAPIER & SON LTD

to

William Edmund Lewis

in recognition of

TWENTY-FIVE YEARS SERVICE

as a mark of appreciation and
goodwill

George H. Nelson Chairman

Date *December 1947*

BY PRECISION INTO POWER

A BICENTENNIAL RECORD OF D. NAPIER & SON

ALAN VESSEY

TEMPUS

Dedicated to

Daphne my wife and tandem bicycle 'stoker'

during fifty years of shared endeavour

First published 2007

Tempus Publishing Limited
The Mill, Brimscombe Port,
Stroud, Gloucestershire, GL5 2QG
www.tempus-publishing.com

British Library Cataloguing in Publication Data.
A catalogue record for this book is available from the British Library.

ISBN 978 0 7524 3888 7

Typesetting and origination by Tempus Publishing Limited
Printed in Great Britain

CONTENTS

ACKNOWLEDGEMENTS

Initially, the seeds of an idea to write the story of the wide-reaching achievements of D. Napier & Son, from 1808 until the early twenty-first century, were sown within the company itself. For me, the spellbinding influence that Napier imparted over the four years of a student apprenticeship at Acton works in the 1950s left an indelible mark that has lasted my entire technological career. I had, in fact, during those years up to 1960, become a Napierian!

Firstly, I must thank members within the Napier Power Heritage Trust who, over the last twelve years, have passed to me much vital information and memories of their Napier colleagues, along with the technical developments they played a part in. Also, thanks are due for the encouragement to go on gathering, often literally from 'the four winds', archive records of innovative Napier projects that had been tackled at Acton, Luton and Liverpool during the last century while I also viewed many of the records from the nineteenth century at Napier's Vine Street works, Lambeth.

It is hard now to see how I had even proposed to start writing this Napier story back in 1990, following a short spell as an editor with *Model Engineer*. At that time I was not aware of much of the pioneering history of D. Napier & Son during the early twentieth century, let alone that going back to its formative days at the beginning of the nineteenth. After much research with Napier Power Heritage Trust friends, which has, of necessity, delayed the compilation of this Napier story, I can confidently say that our greatly increased knowledge of the company is attributable to them, for which I cannot give enough thanks. Only now has it become possible to pass on much of this previously unpublished company technical information, as freshly extracted with the Trust's full blessing, from those recently retrieved Napier archives.

There have been many new sources of information kindly offered during the preparation of this book by engineering institutions, museums and libraries. Firstly, however, I must thank the present day, as well as former, executives of the Napier Turbocharger works in Lincoln (now Siemens owned), and of the GKN Aerospace Transparency Systems works (formerly Napier) in Luton, for making available material and for their continued assistance. Secondly, I must give special thanks to Keith Moore – former senior librarian and archivist at the Institution of Mechanical Engineers – for his always willing help and advice given at the Institution HQ, where the Napier Company Archives are now housed and displayed, some within their 'Napier Room' at 1 Birdcage Walk, Westminster. My thanks for all their co-operation over the years also go to patient curators at the RAF Museum Hendon, the Brooklands Museum, the Motor Boat Museum at Pitsea, the Science Museum, 'Solent Sky' at Southampton, the National Maritime Museum Greenwich, the Birmingham Museum of Science & Discovery and York National Railway Museum.

Additional sources of data used in this current Napier story have been many and varied, from popular books and magazine articles by well-known authors, to some little known and seldom read antiquarian histories. Many important key records have been extracted from, and numerous dates, facts and figures cross checked contained within the following major publications, for which their authors and publishers are hereby acknowledged.

Boddy, W., *Aero Engined Racing Cars at Brooklands* (1992)
Boyle, B.R., *The Napier Way* (2000)
Cardell, W.P., *Drafts on the Memory of a Septuagenarian Plain Man* (1912)
Cantrell & Cookson, *Henry Maudslay and the Pioneers of the Machine Age* (2002)
Cheverton, B., *Portrait of a Unique Aviation Establishment – DNS at Luton* (1998)
Desmond, K., *Power Boat Speed* (1988)
Edge, S.F., *My Motoring Reminiscences* (1933)
Holtham, T., *RAF Marine Craft Directory* (2000)
Lumsden, A., *British Piston Engines and their Aircraft* (1994)
Marsden, C.J. & Fenn, G.B., *British Main Line Diesel Locomotives* (1988)
Marshall, A.W., *D. Napier & Son Engineers, London: A History* (1922)
Nevard, L.A., *Gas Turbine Design, Research & Development at Napiers* (1998)
Rance, A., *Fast Boats and Flying Boats – a biography of Hubert Scott-Paine* (1989)
Tagg, A.E. & Wheeler, R.L., *From Sea to Air – heritage of Sam Saunders* (1989)
Venables, D., *NAPIER – The first to wear the Green* (1998)
Wheeler, R.L., *From River to Sea – heritage of Sam Saunders* (1990)
Wilson, C. and Reader, W., *Men and Machines* (1958)

JANES Fighting Ships, All the World's Aircraft, and World Railways (various years)
Various authors. *PUTNAM Aeronautical Books* – (1957 to 1987)

For his insight and translations referring to early Napier printing machines, from both French and German sources, my grateful thanks go to Alan D. Jones.

My very special appreciation, for readily sharing their knowledge over many years, goes to three outstanding Napierians whom it has been my privilege and pleasure to know throughout my research for this present Napier review.

Firstly, to Derek Grossmark for his help regarding Napier Motors and for information readily offered from the original Napier Motor Carriage Archives he has held since 1963.

My thanks are also due to late Trust member Ronald Humphrey, who had prepared a fine manuscript on Napier aero-engines; this passed to NPHT before his sudden death in 2001.

Finally, heartfelt thanks go to my good friend Geoff McGarry, a fellow researcher of 'all things Napier' who, having a full fifty years of Napier Company service to his credit, now holds the position of President of the Napier Power Heritage Trust. Geoff's eagerness to discover new sides to the D. Napier & Son story never tires, and so to him I record my appreciation for his constant support, help and inspiration since 1990 and the formation of the present-day Trust, of which he was for eight years the founder Chairman.

Alan F. Vessey, C.Eng.
Sunnymead,
Aston Clinton,
Buckinghamshire, November 2006

FOREWORD

It is my privilege to provide a Foreword to this remarkable volume containing two histories. Firstly, to the long-awaited complete and detailed history of that most famous engineering company D. Napier & Son Ltd, a history once feared lost, but now safely restored and preserved due to the years of stirling research by the Napier Power Heritage Trust, founded and guided by its dedicated archivist Alan Vessey. Secondly, the searching story of the NPHT itself, now also included, which is so worthy of being recorded.

There can be few engineering companies able to boast of a history bordering on 200 years of continuous precision engineering; passing through eight reigns, wars and peace, industrial unrest, booms and slumps. Commenced by David Napier as a family business, he was followed by his son James Murdock, and later by grandson Montague. Their total engineering products were legion; printing presses, delicate gold coin and massive gold bullion weighing machines, and projects diverse as steam engines to stamp perforating machines, all dealt with in revealing detail in the Victorian chapter. We move on to Montague Napier's motor carriages – leaders in the field at the birth of motoring in the UK – securing the first British International Motoring victory in the Gordon Bennett race of 1902. From 1917 Napier aero engines followed, firstly the enduring 'Lion', to be in the forefront for the Schneider Trophy races, and then adapted for world speed records on land and water in turn for Sir Malcolm Campbell, Sir Henry Segrave and John Cobb.

When I entered the Napier arena, I gained experience on Lions and Daggers before meeting the top secret Sabre engine, eagerly absorbing all its complexities and engaged in a seven-day-week war effort in a prime war target, confident on youthful pride as 'Our mighty Sabre' powered Hawker 'Typhoons and Tempests' to famous wartime triumphs. That is a distant memory now, but still my secret pride. I was THERE, and there I remained in peacetime as the company's policy changed from piston engines to modern gas turbines.

Napier, reaching a pinnacle of success in the 150th Anniversary Year of 1958, then saw disrupting changes in the 1960s decade with sudden withdrawal of ministry contracts, and when I narrowly escaped redundancy by wisely transferring my allegiance to our turbo-chargers. They proved Napier's saviour, and mine too, as I progressed to Servicing and then to Sales, gladly travelling the world as a Napier representative from London, when Napier had moved to Liverpool and then on to Lincoln. Even after retirement I was still employed in London till final separation, having completed over fifty years Napier service.

This vital engineering history, the fabric of Napier mechanical heritage, has been steadily preserved since Alan set up shop for NPHT in 1991, and through those years he has faithfully collected, housed and catalogued the vast archive collection. Finally, and to realise his life's ambition, he has written this Napier Company engineering history. There is no other person so well suited to complete such a daunting task, for it has been my great pleasure to work alongside Alan throughout theses interesting and challenging years.

We must heartily congratulate Alan Vessey on his work in this fine volume, which is a monument to his dedication to the engineering wonders of D. Napier & Son Ltd, now preserved for all time.

Geoff McGarry
President of the Napier Power Heritage Trust

INTRODUCTION

Engineering Precision, Performance and Reliability are now irrefutably linked in our modern technological world, based on quality assurance for the twenty-first century. This same trilogy of priorities was fundamental to the engineering success, over a span of 200 years, of the British Company – D. Napier & Son – which can now enjoy its Bicentenary with due pride in 2008. This book is intended to bear testimony to the company's great achievements.

David Napier set about founding a general engineering works in central London in 1808, off the Charing Cross Road, where he undertook the accurate construction and repair of printing presses, firstly for others, and then to his own patented designs, until the start of the Victorian era in 1837. By then, working from new, enlarged premises in Lambeth, he began diversification of this precision work, while he appointed his son James as his apprentice. Thus, to those far-off days, can be traced the ingredients of the formula for 'Engineering Excellence' that became, and would remain, the hallmark of the long-lasting family company of D. Napier & Son. Thousands of satisfied apprentices of relatively modern times testify that the training they received through the precise and progressive hands of Napierians has been invaluable to them during their subsequent technical careers.

Today's 'remnant' company groups, stemming from that initial formulation, still bear the marks of the 'Old Master', based on precision giving performance with reliability, be it in the field of diesel-engine turbocharging or the manufacture of fine aircraft transparencies.

The author himself saw the Napier organisation at work within Acton works from 1952, soon after the company's employment peaked at just over 19,000 in 1945, spread within works in London, Luton and Liverpool. After the Second World War, D. Napier & Son, by then already a part of the English Electric Group from 1943, assumed the mantle of 'an experimental establishment', while still retaining its former high standard of design and that capability for accurate manufacture. To maintain these skills, the need for highly qualified, in-house trained engineers and craftsmen was given a high priority in these three Napier works.

The author, being a 'bit of an all-rounder' when an apprentice, whether working in R&D, the D.O. or on the shopfloor, found when he finally vacated this 'young engineer's haven' as a graduate of the Institution of Mechanical Engineers, a welcome in most spheres of industry or technical education that relied on sound engineering training and background.

Differences of personal opinion will always exist between former company staff as to their degree of success achieved at D. Napier & Son but, finally, most seem agreed that working at Napier was the best period of their career. While comparing his personal achievements within that widespread organisation with that of a colleague, a senior staff member has remarked, 'Yours doesn't sound like the same Napier Company for which I worked!' Hence, within this Napier-based account of the life and times of the company, the writer has not only drawn from well established technical histories from a great variety of authors, but uses the later records and experiences of both senior and junior technical staff, plus those of many engineers and craftsmen of modern times, in order to present a representative record of this 'old surviving company', even to the present day.

For today's mechanical enthusiasts, no doubt the elegant machines contrived by David and James Napier with such immense skill during the Victorian era at Lambeth, will still hold a fascination in our modern automated world. But also for them there remains, even today, the 'magical sound' of a Napier Deltic Diesel at full power, either powering a Hunt Class Mine Counter Measures vessel of the Royal Navy in coastal waters, or hard at work in a Class 55 Deltic Heritage Locomotive travelling upgrade at a steady 100mph. Either of these experiences could engender a spellbinding effect in any observer. This, the last Napier piston engine designed and constructed sixty years ago, is herein described, as are its predecessors on land, sea and in the air during the expansive twentieth century at Napier's Acton works. From there also, many high-performance car engines were forerunners of the leading aircraft power units to appear after the First World War. Then, after the Second World War, with the additional research and productive strength within the Napier Liverpool plant, plus the flight development skills and innovative aerospace engineering at Napier Luton, a time of richly varied and vibrant aero engineering was to follow. The telling of this story in depth has been long awaited, and can now be done as this historic company's bicentenary approaches.

Essentially, this book sets out to reveal and describe the outstanding influence of the personalities and products of the Napier Company over two centuries, in as much detail as our factual knowledge and space permit. Stories of the many racing trophies and world records gained for Great Britain while utilising the power of Napier engines, whether by air, land or water, are verified and retold. Descriptions of these 'super-powered transports' are given, with mentions of their courageous drivers or pilots, some of whom went on to earn national fame and awards, or even a knighthood, as recognition of their bravery.

The large section of appendices at the rear now provide the fullest ever references to Napier products and their achievements, and will also yield up fresh information regarding most Napier engines and applications. Some have long been forgotten, but others have just been mistakenly placed with time, within the records of our British engineering heritage.

So deep are the roots of D. Napier & Son within the history of printing, of the financial institutions and of the transport industry over the last two centuries worldwide, that it is crucially important that public awareness of the many technological innovations by Napier should be revived. This is particularly relevant as we approach 2008, when the record will appear in new illustrated book form, so ensuring that Napier's heritage remains accessible for future generations.

1

FORTH TO THE THAMES: IN SEARCH OF PRECISION 1808–1835

It is often said that 'Mighty oaks from little acorns grow'. That was certainly true for David Napier's 'Scottish acorn' when planted deeply within England's soil during the reign of George III. From its germination there grew up a mighty 'English oak' whose branches, by the year 2008, will span two centuries. This, in down-to-earth engineering terms, means that David Napier brought south to London's industrial scene of 1808, from a very different, but sound, Scottish industrial background, his own inherent mechanical abilities. Once in technically fertile London, he showed a determination to establish himself as the master of progressive design and precision manufacture in his chosen engineering field.

Even before 1808, the talent of this engineering family had been recognised, they were well established in central Scotland and had provided young David Napier (one of three David Napiers from Clydebank and all with engineering interests) with his full apprenticeship within their metalworking plant at Dumbarton, on the north shore of the Firth of Clyde, near Glasgow. There David was trained, and became proficient as a blacksmith by his early twenties. But neither the processes of plastic deformation of wrought iron under a forge hammer, or the intricate casting of molten metals in a foundry could ever satisfy his ambition to be a designer and manufacturer of precision, power-worked machinery. To fulfil that object, David Napier would need to remove himself south to some newly created 'centre of excellence'.

The background to that branch of young David's Napier Clan, of whom several shared a strong engineering aptitude like his own, will be reviewed at this point in order to see more clearly the several parallel paths that their distinguished careers eventually took.

His father was one Robert Napier (born 1760), who was appointed 'Smith and Armourer' to the 5th Duke of Argyll at Inveraray Castle, near Glen Shira at the top of Loch Fyne, that being some forty miles distant from Dumbarton's Napier family industries. His grandfather, also named Robert Napier (born 1726) and a blacksmith, had had four sons, all of whom were practising engineers or ironmasters along the banks of the Clyde. The first of these sons, John (born 1752), had a son in 1790 named David Napier, who was to become the famous Clyde steamship builder and marine engine designer. Much later on he relocated down to Millwall in London in 1836, following a disastrous marine boiler explosion at Greenock in 1835 on board one of his ships, the *Earl Grey*.

A second son of Robert was named David (born 1756), who rose to be an ironmaster near Glasgow. A third son, James (born 1764) had a son named Robert, who was also born in 1790; he became the renowned shipbuilder and engineer titled 'Robert Napier of Shandon', based in Glasgow. Now the fourth son, named Robert (born 1760), who had married a Margaret McDonald, had a son while he was the Smith at Inveraray (c. 1787), whom they named David. Young David, after completing an apprenticeship, quite soon went south to pursue his own career.

That very act in 1808, while still in his early twenties, in fact makes him the founder of the great London precision engineering company – 'D. Napier & Son Ltd'. Summing up: within his family at that time David had his two cousins, both budding shipbuilders on the Clyde (one of them having the same name as his own), plus his uncle, also with the same name, he being already established in Glasgow. Clearly, our David Napier badly needed to establish his own individual identity, and especially as a skilled precision engineer.

Now to follow the fortunes of our David Napier, the founder of D. Napier & Son in London. This young journeyman who decided prior to 1808 to come south, was to leave behind him the smithing works in Inveraray in the able hands of his officially appointed father Robert plus, also, those heavier marine-based industries that had so successfully occupied his notable family on the Clyde. This move he made in order to explore for himself the reality of those fresh claims for 'repeatable accuracy' made by some progressive precision manufacturers who were newly established in London. In particular, the highly reputed works of Henry Maudslay attracted his attention; he had read and heard about this famed engineer on Clydeside, from where he had made his prior contact. News had spread of how from Maudslay's works the Royal Navy had acquired a lot of new 'powered tooling', from which very large quantities of ships' wooden pulley blocks were now produced in Portsmouth Dockyard. These, it was reported, were of a much superior standard of finish and performance to those that, until then, had been made laboriously by hand.

David sailed that very year from Leith on the Firth of Forth, in the sailing ship, *The Czar*, for the Thames Estuary and the Port of London, past many shipyards that would come to resemble the Clyde. Having taken his lodgings in the Soho manufacturing area of central London, this itinerant young journeyman realised that in this city of 1808, by comparison with Clydeside, people would enthuse over a new mechanical novelty. He may have heard that only five years back, in 1803, the Cornish steam engineer Richard Trevithick had run his tricycle steam land carriage around London, and was still the 'talk of the town'.

Despite the effects of the renewed war against the revolutionary French from 1804, which had required more British bored cannon, some having been made by industries on the Clyde, the British and King George III were still basking in Nelson's great naval victory of 1805 off Cape Trafalgar against the French and Spanish fleets. At home, on the roads of London, the fast and direct stagecoach was still the only regular means of long distance land travel, while the well-developed canal system permitted slow movement of the majority of heavier loads required by industry on barges. Daily, up to 1,000 stagecoaches travelled in and out of the capital city, wherein individual local journeys on horseback, or by horse and cab were the norm. It would not be until 1810 that fashionable

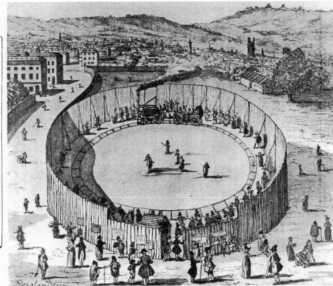

London scenery in 1808, with Trevithick's 'Catch me who can' steam locomotive at work on his demonstration railway operating near to Euston Square.

Londoners were to hear of, and then experience, their first *Velocipedes*, these being a French invention known as the foot-propelled *Draisienne*, or to Londoners simply the 'Hobby Horse'.

Then, into those entirely horse dominated days of 1808, and significantly coinciding with David Napier's arrival, there came to London a second steam-powered mechanical conveyance, this running in Torrington Square near Euston, named 'Catch-me-who-can'. It was a circular, steam locomotive operated railway, hauling one landau carriage, again a product of that innovative engineer Richard Trevithick, and was on demonstration for the more intrepid Londoner at 'One Shilling per Trip'. This pioneering steam railway exhibit carried an appropriate slogan for its time – 'Mechanical Power subduing Animal Speed'. Much of this innovation was appearing within half a mile of David Napier's lodgings in the nearby Bloomsbury area, so it is highly probable that this mechanical novelty would have been seen by him, or even possibly experienced. But for this purposeful Scottish engineer, it would have come more as a timely 're-introduction' to land steam-powered transport.

Indeed, the work of his brilliant fellow Scot, William Murdoch, who in 1799 invented the steam slide-valve gear, was now incorporated by Trevithick within the cylinders of his steam engines. Murdoch had already in 1786 demonstrated the practicability of his steam road carriage in Scotland, so was well known to most Scottish engineers. This famous name must have lodged within the memory of David Napier, as he then passed it on to his own son, James Murdoch Napier, a mere fifteen years later. But David Napier could never have imagined that 150 years ahead, just half a mile away at Kings Cross, powerful locomotives carrying his family name on their diesel engines – 'Napier Deltic' – would then speed hundreds of passengers each day to the City of Edinburgh, from where he had sailed that very year.

The task David Napier had set himself in 1808 was mainly to widen his own education and practical skills by working within the advanced workshops run by Henry Maudslay. By all accounts, these appear to have had the instructional atmosphere of a well operated and equipped toolroom, where high individual skill was required of everyone, but also where advice was readily available and given to his 'pupils'. David Napier, having his completed apprenticeship behind him from Scotland, was rapidly able to grasp and learn for himself the new machining processes and precision assembly and test techniques practised by Maudslay's craftsmen and engineers, as there he then 'worked his passage' as a short-term employee. He was involved in the construction of fast operating presses, of finely finished metal dyes for the cutlery trade, the assembly of steam table engines and, best of all, with precision-built machine tools, both for Maudslay's own use and for his customers. This variety of lathes, planing, drilling and boring machines had close fitting leadscrews and operated over scraped, well-prepared slideways. In a letter he then sent to cousin Robert in Glasgow, David, showing the thriftiness of the true Scotsman, wrote of Maudslay's latest triangular bar lathe that 'I would not recommend them to you as they are very expensive; but I would recommend a cast iron bed lathe'.

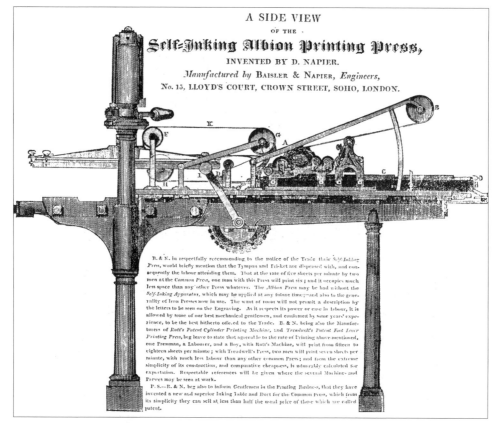

David Napier invented this Baisler & Napier 'Albion' Self-Inking Press of 1820, manufactured by that partnership at 15 Lloyds Court, Soho.

Recent research now suggests that this bright young blacksmith David Napier had, in fact, returned to Maudslay's works for a few years, while he gained more skill to achieve the best possible level of accurate workmanship and to absorb much from those 'beautiful designs' from which he worked. Certainly by 1815 having left direct employment with Maudslay; he was then occupied as a work's foreman near to Fleet Street, which was fast becoming a centre for news print. A further period was spent as the engineering partner in a stationer's business, known as Messrs Baisler & Napier Engineers, of Lloyds Court, Soho, their work being concerned with the manufacture of the Baisler Patent Paper-Plough, which was an improved paper-cutter patented in 1817. Also the new Stanhope-Lever Printing-Press that could exert a higher pressure far more rapidly than the more usual screw-type. But, while in that business, David himself became involved in producing 'engine lathes', like those used for fine ornamental turning and similar to the world-renowned Holtzapffel lathes. Privately, his mechanical designs and a steady flow of machine repair work kept him fully occupied, but when his own designs for mathematical and drawing instruments were still arousing only a little interest he had optimistically commented that it was due to 'trade being so dull' at the time, this in 1817. Commercial matters were later to much improve, particularly over his cleverly designed and precisely made 'Universal Perspectigraph'.

Manual British 'Rutt' printing presses like this were built by Napier *c.* 1819.

During much of this time David Napier had been in residence near Lloyds Court, Soho, from where, he informed his family, he taught in the Sunday school at Swallow Street Church, by St Anne's Church of Scotland in Soho. By then, needing his own workshop premises, both for design work and prototype construction, David had begun to look for a suitable property. On leaving his next recorded address at 11 Portman Buildings, Soho Square in 1818 he moved on to 3 Carlisle Street, Soho from 1820, while he worked in a larger workshop at 15 Lloyds Court, Crown Street, Soho. After 1822, then being self-employed and with his partnership dissolved, he was able to concentrate on building and developing instruments and printing machinery, which included some treadle operated printing presses patented by an appropriately named American, a Daniel Treadwell. Even more important was a Napier-built prototype of a single cylinder printing machine constructed for a Mr Rutt, its English designer, the quality and success of which was later to be much acclaimed by the print trade. This led to David's shop then producing a batch of these Rutt presses; at first these were manually driven, but later a steam engine-powered belt-driven version appeared. (See Appendix Ia.)

It was not long before a significant breakthrough occurred for David Napier in the form of his own new large 'perfecting' printing machine, to which he gave his own clever title 'The Nay-Peer'. This, devised with his Scottish astuteness and humour, proclaiming 'With no equal', became the trademark applied to some of his other products through the years.

Soon after, in 1824, commendations by the parliamentary printer Mr T.C. Hansard came to play an important part in assisting the future prosperity of the Napier printing machine business. Of a machine to 'Hansards own specification', but designed, built and proved by Napier, Mr Hansard proudly referred to it as 'his own' machine. But in fact the 'Nay-Peer' machine had in its design several original Napier features that Mr Hansard finally came to accept and for which he gave its designer full recognition. Author A. W. Marshall, in a 1922 officially commissioned book *History of D. Napier & Son*, quoted Hansard's own words in full, which applaud David Napier's machine design of 1823 as follows:

> I have now the satisfaction of bringing him forward, on my own experience, as the inventor and maker of a machine which appears to me to be more likely to succeed in all its pretensions than any which has yet been offered to us.
>
>   The motion of the machine is gained by two men turning a flywheel, which alone acts as an impelling power; and, although the same general principles prevail in this machine as in others described (that is as, printing by cylinders and inking by rollers is concerned) yet at the same time it presents some novelties which are of too great an importance to be overlooked. The first consists in a most ingenious contrivance for taking hold of each sheet of paper from the supplying board, retaining it whilst receiving the first side impression, and releasing it at the precise moment that the corresponding apparatus in the other cylinder executes the same movement for the impression of the reiteration (other side of the sheet). This beatiful mechanism is retained in the interior of the impression cylinders, which have openings along their circumference through which 'Grippers' perform their operations; and upon their action depends the 'desideratum of press work', Accurate Register, or the backing of the pages on the paper. And this purpose is so fully effected that for the many thousands of sheets which have passed through my machine, without the smallest deviation after register was made, I venture to call them infallible.

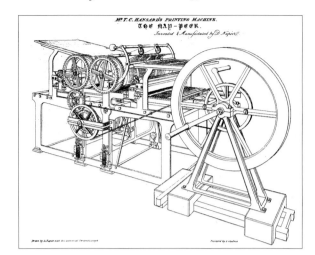

Invented, named and manufactured in 1824 by Napier, his 'Nay-Peer' cylinder press was made famous by T.C. Hansard. Napier hand-operated driving gear is shown. (Drawn by the Napier Universal Perspectigraph.)

Yet, notwithstanding the beauty and accuracy of this movement, the part of all others that reflects the highest credit upon the mechanical skill of the inventor is the rising and falling of the impression cylinders, for it is principally owing to this single contrivance that he has been able so wonderfully to compass and simplify his machine as to bring it within the capability of so small a power to produce so much work. My machine has had a trial of six months (November 1824). The ordinary speed is, according to the required quality of the work, at an average of 2000 impressions, or 1000 perfected sheets per hour… Mr Napier has also constructed several machines upon the same principle as mine for newspaper work, to print from only one 'forme', and that either with one or two cylinders; but those not requiring to reverse the sheet have none of the mechanism for perfecting.

Marshall also pointed out that the machine supplied to Hansard was a very compact early perfecting machine, having Napier's recently invented 'rising and falling cylinders' with his 'grippers' contained within the cylinder for taking hold of the sheets.

David Napier's ingenious and practical inventions had placed him in the first rank of English constructors of printing machines for his time. Napier's objective for double-side 'perfecting' machines was to enable the sheet to be passed from one cylinder to another without being dropped and so maintain its register. Koenig of Germany, who had invented the first perfecting 'stop-cylinder machine', had used a method in which the distance for passing the sheet from recto to verso was too long. Napier now shortened this, his method being widely used from then on by work-and-turn machines. He produced his first printing machine for verso-printing and using two cylinders with 'grippers' in 1830. This was improved further by various European constructors of printing machines, and was later widely used in France. Napier's single 'rocking-cylinder' machines, also with 'grippers', continued to be made for many years: the last of these was constructed by David's son James Murdoch Napier as late as 1880, and later supplied to Japan with 'our most recent improvements and inking motion for working by steam power'. James entered the business, first as an apprentice to his father David at the age of fourteen in 1837, but much of his apprenticeship was undertaken at their later Vine Street works in Lambeth.

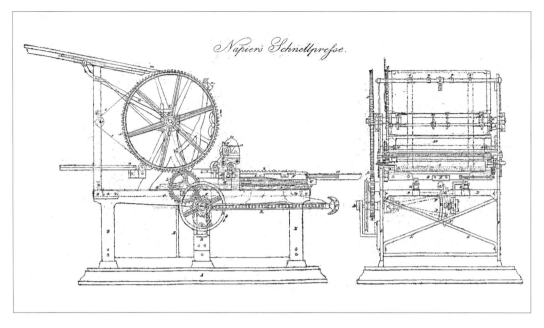

By 1827 Napier's larger 'Desideratum' single-cylinder presses were being sold to Europe. This German copy drawing shows an example for rapid steam-engine operation.

Robust and speedy David Napier-built 2-cylinder 'Perfecting Presses' of 1830 were fully equipped for steam power operation.

A.W. Marshall, himself an apprentice at Napier Lambeth works from 1881 to 1886, knew well this range of printing machines from their repair and 'the books of the firm'. He describes 'much bigger' Napier printing machines, sufficiently large to print the pages of the *Weekly Times* newspaper, these having the name of 'Desideratum' machines – that word earlier used by Hansard and chosen by David for them – that could print various sizes of sheet. This type was to become the major one of the cylinder machines produced from the Napier works. Appendix Ia lists the main output of printing machines over a full seventy-five-year period, amongst which 150 were 'Desideratum'-type machines.

Of the even larger 'Double Imperial' Presses that had been installed by the *Courier* newspaper in 1823, their proprietor later publicly stated:

> We think it right to announce to our readers that the Courier is now printed by a machine of such extraordinary power, that it is capable of throwing considerably above two thousand papers per hour; it has, indeed, on one occasion, produced at a rate of 2,880 impressions within the hour.

This appreciation seemed conclusive as to David Napier's own mastery of printing press technology, then still within the confines of his Lloyds Court workshop, with more limited machine tools and only a small number of employees. It is not surprising that the much heavier Napier 'Large Quadruple' presses had to wait for their development within his more extensive Lambeth works during the mid-1830s.

The speeding-up of machine printing in the USA, France and Germany all owed much to the work of David Napier, who in France had been described as 'an inventor of great merit who constructed a variety of printing machines'. One of these, imported to America in 1827, was the first cylinder machine ever to be used in the New World. Its design became the property of a 'Robert Hoe' by 1832, Hoe was an American gentleman who had visited Lambeth works in person, he then constructed numerous copies of it, while constantly improving them. He was in time to become the founder of the largest factory producing printing machines, presses and their equipment in America.

In 1830 Napier produced a platen press, 13ft long being larger than jobbing presses, but more easily handled than European cylinder machines of that period and well suited to short-run work. It had features in common with those of machines devised by Hopkinson & Cope of London about the same time. Both presses achieved an alternating movement of their carriage by the use of an elongated grooved drum. Napier's machine was largely used for more sophisticated tasks, producing 500-800 sheets per hour in double raisin sheet size (40in x 26in). The chief difference between the machines of Napier, and those of Hopkinson & Cope lay in the means by which the platen applied its pressure. Napier's 'toggle' method was superior and continued in use to the 1900s, notably in print runs requiring great pressure, such as in the printing of engravings, postage stamps and bank notes, where any creasing had to be avoided.

An early diversification from the workshop of David Napier was the invention and manufacture of his first Bullet Compressing Machine, which led to the bulk supply of 'lead bullets'. It was to such musket and rifle balls that the same 'Nay-Peer' trademark was applied in 1831 at the same time as supplying: 'To the Master General and Board

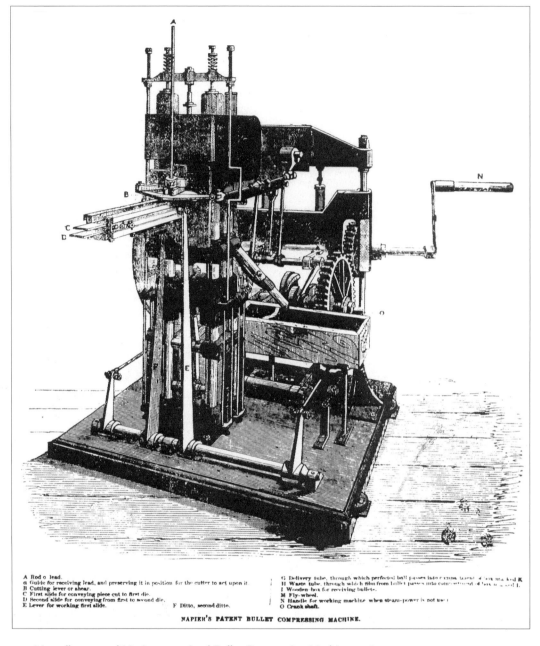

A Rod o lead.
a Guide for receiving lead, and preserving it in position for the cutter to act upon it.
B Cutting lever or shear.
C First slide for conveying piece cut to first die.
D Second slide for conveying from first to second die.
E Lever for working first slide.
F Ditto, second ditto.

G Delivery tube, through which perfected ball passes into cases turned down marked K
H Waste tube, through which film from bullet passes into compartment of box marked L.
I Wooden box for receiving bullets.
M Fly-wheel.
N Handle for working machine when steam-power is not used
O Crank shaft.

NAPIER'S PATENT BULLET COMPRESSING MACHINE.

Manually operated Napier patent Lead Bullet Compressing Machine, *c.* 1835.

of Ordnance of 'Nay-Peer balls', sold at the rate of twenty shillings per cwt.' By 1835, new bullet-making machines were being requested by ordnance factories, and an order for 300,000 rifle balls was received by Lambeth works in 1839. The chief reason for the rush to procure these 'Nay-Peer' balls for the army was due to the accuracy of their straight flight as projectiles. David Napier had, by careful inspection, found that most of the more usually as-cast lead balls contained irregularly spaced air bubbles within them, which made their flight path curve and led to their targets being missed. Those he now produced were taken from strips of lead wire which were then cut up and compressed by Napier-built machines, these balls were far closer to a spherical shape and were solid throughout, so giving them a more accurate straight flight when fired from a rifle or musket barrel. The Board of Ordnance officers at Woolwich Arsenal and the Enfield Small Arms Co. both came to rely on these Nay-Peer compressed bullets. So much so, that following the granting of a patent for this machine, Patent No. 8385 of 1840, this entitled 'The Manufacture of Projectiles', the early manually operated pressing machines were then developed and enlarged for steam power operation, being eventually adopted by the Woolwich Arsenal as their standard. By this means the way had now been opened for sales of Napier bullet-making machines at home and abroad.(see Appendix Id)

It is here, maybe, time to recall that David Napier had regularly kept in touch with the roots of his strong, innovative engineering family North of the Border, and had more than 'kept abreast' of their new developments in heavier engineering projects on land and water. Their collaboration reached public attention in 1831, when a steam land transport patent was taken out jointly in the names of David Napier in London and yet two more cousins, James and William Napier of Glasgow, Engineers. This Patent, No. 6090 of 1831, was entitled: 'Certain Improvements in Machinery for Propelling Locomotive Carriages'. This vehicle, originally invented by his Scottish cousin David in about 1826, was intended to transport passengers between Dunoon and Lock Eck. But, despite this new patent now providing for it an improved boiler and also a much smoother belt transmission, the whole venture ended in partial failure, as clearly the time was not yet ripe for steam locomotion on the poor roads of Great Britain. David, now living in Warren Street, off Fitzroy Square, Middlesex, pressed on to take out a further steam boiler patent of his own, this now based on his practical experience. It was granted him as Patent Number 9852 of 1843, entitled 'Arrangements for Preventing Priming' and was equally applicable to his small boilers manufactured in London, now used regularly with steam engine-powered presses, as to those of his family working in Glasgow with their much larger capacity marine boilers.

But the first, and so far perhaps most significant of David Napier's patents, which he had striven for alone, had been granted him back in 1828, again while he was living in Warren Street. This Patent No. 5713 on 'Letter-press Printing Machinery' in general, also covered his several innovations relating to accurate print register when perfecting sheets, as he had built into the 'Nay-Peer' machine for Hansard. This he followed up by another in 1830 – Patent No. 6010, further protecting his developments for higher speed printing presses, and economising on power used for manual and steam engine-driven operation.

Following the sixty-year reign of George III, with the wars on the continent of Europe and its slower industrial development at home, the Prince Regent George IV's uneventful, brief reign ended that same year, in 1830. Yet another new King, the easy going William IV, came to the British throne, so leading to 'times of great change and trouble in Britain' – according to Britannica – before, following the king's death in 1837, the new Victorian era commenced. A growth in world importance for Britain's industries, aided by the new countrywide faster railway system at home, was about to take place, while the colonies of the British Empire provided a reachable worldwide market through steam-powered ships.

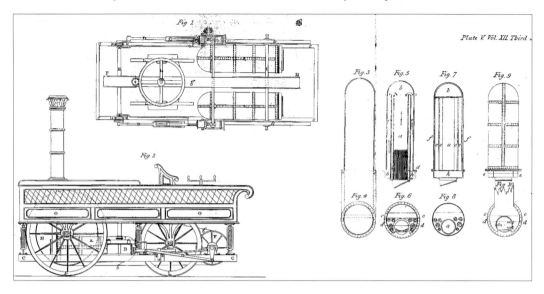

Improvements to the transmission and boiler of this steam road carriage had been the subject of a joint Napier family patent by David and two cousins in 1831.

Growth and change for the good within David Napier's company had preceded the new young Queen to her throne, for he had moved from now cramped workshops in central London north of the Thames, to a far more spacious factory site on the south bank of the Thames in Lambeth. The move to the newly opened factory (from March 1832) was accomplished (going by the surviving heavy sales ledger with steel reinforced covers) in all probability in this year. It had as its first dated entry: 'Messrs Rodgerson – To a new Desideratum Printing Machine – £440'. Rodgerson's printing works were then soon to place a follow-up order for another Desideratum machine in May 1833, but now added to it was: 'with Register Apparatus, £440', Napier wisely holding down the same price.

Any fresh start in a new premises is usually accompanied by 'new paperwork' or a recording system to be used from then on. This subsequently happened also in 1903 on opening the next new Napier works in Acton, when an entirely new system of recording engine design types was started in a new ledger register that was then used, without any break, over the next seventy years by the design office of the future 'D. Napier & Son'.

2

D. NAPIER & SON DOWN LAMBETH WAY 1836–1895

The location of David Napier's new residence was in York Road, Lambeth with his works entrance through a gateway off the narrow Vine Street, which ran down one side of it towards the river. The site was situated between the old Hungerford and new Waterloo Bridges, quite close to the present-day Waterloo Railway Terminus entrance. The land dropped away towards the river, so flood protection boards were provided, always in readiness to protect the Napier works site from unusually high Thames tides, as this was before the embankments were built from 1860 by Sir Joseph Bazelgette. All mechanical power was taken by belt drive from off a large table-type steam engine that drove, via overhead line shafting, from its engine house out into the open and thence by take-off belts into the several workshops. First, power led in to the heavy machine shops on ground level, and was then transmitted to the floors above, where lighter machines were installed.

Although some skilled, Napier-trained craftsmen had followed the moving of the works to its new site, recruitment of skilled men of European nationality into the Vine Street works proceeded steadily over the first few years, as the 1832 order book grew in size. With an autocratic yet direct management style towards his employees, David Napier succeeded in running the business economically, by paying fair rates of pay, plus overtime pay after six o'clock. Nevertheless, with no national associations to represent workers at the time, it was not long before a problem arose, in fact during 1836 over, as the men claimed, their far too low rates for overtime, so a strike ensued. This action taken by Napier men followed a similar strike at Henry Maudslay's works only a short while before. Determined to continue the work in hand, Napier engaged some new labour from Messrs Seaward in Limehouse, and by so doing inflamed the strikers even more, which then led to some violent evening scenes near to the works requiring police intervention. On this, the occasion of the first dispute, he gave way to the men, who returned to work with an overtime agreement based 'on their terms'.

By 1840 the factory had become well-established, with between 200 and 300 skilled employees, those he had recruited having the skilled trades required to operate accurate machine tools, to be fitters and press testers within the precise erecting shop of this medium-sized general engineering works. With a 'self-sufficient air', it boasted a smithy,

House of David Napier in Vine Street, Lambeth with its side works entrance, as built *c.* 1835. Here seen later in the nineteenth century with the DNS company heading.

a foundry, a first-floor pattern shop and the prototype model of the special, Napier-style, design and drawing office. It should also be noted that there was a 'small workshop for the apprentices', this ran from 1835, and it was into this shop that in 1837 the fourteen-year-old James Murdoch Napier started his own ten-year apprenticeship within his father's Lambeth works. In the course of the next ten years James was to pass through every corner of the works and offices, literally rising in skill and knowledge from the 'ground floor upwards'. There, firmly based at ground level, was the heavy machine shop that contained very large planing machines, one that was later claimed to be the biggest in the London area and capable of finishing machining beds for medium-sized lathes and the long beds for Napier's 'Large Quadruple' and 'Double Imperial – Extra Size' Printing Machines. Large gun-boring machines were later built entirely 'in-house' at Vine Street works in connection with an urgent need for Crimean War armament. Some unusual, heavy machine tools, installed from the opening, included a Robertson wheel-cutting machine, a Whitworth screw-cutting lathe, a Maudslay heavy lathe of 1817 vintage, a Fairbairn slotting machine and even one of Napier's own built planing machines! On the first floors were the pattern-making shop, a light erecting shop and two 'Precision Department' special shops, one equipped for light machining, the other for more delicate assembly work and the calibration of balances, etc. To this, and also to his personal small workshop used for proving his inventions and for experimental work, David Napier had arranged for a private entrance leading directly from his substantial adjacent house that fronted on to York Road.

The regular hands-on experience and first hand knowledge James gained of his father's business covered complex machine design and manufacture, high precision machining and assembly work (for its day) and a wide assortment of sub-contract production work for Napier's many discerning customers (see Appendices 1d & 1e). His ten years training had left the young man with great skill and a keen appreciation of the innovative engineering process. It was good, therefore, that father and son, who clearly had mutual understanding and compatible engineering targets for the existing firm, set up a partnership in Lambeth on 1 July 1847. This private family company, having total assets then of £11,664-2s-5d, from that time became entitled 'D. Napier & Son' (DNS), the very same name that was to become world famous in the internal combustion engine field, within a century of that date. For, precisely a century later in the year 1947, a pair of supercharged Napier 'Lion VIID' piston engines were to power John Cobb's car to an unbeatable World Land Speed Record of 394.2mph. But then, only twenty-seven years later, the same historic company's registered name would be changed to 'Napier Turbochargers Ltd' from 1974 when the company was already a subsidiary of Britain's General Electric Company (GEC). How these changes came about will all be revealed later within this Bicentenary record, meanwhile our story must return to the mid-nineteenth century and that initial period of the DNS father and son partnership.

By the year 1847, David Napier was an accomplished and mature engineer aged sixty, having by then seven patents registered in his name, while his second son, James Murdock Napier, then twenty-four years old, was showing promising talent as his partner. He had many new ideas to further develop the existing Napier printing machines, as well as other promising business ventures using hydraulics and steam power, alongside those of his father.

One such venture in which James had been involved since 1842, was the application of hydraulic power to heavy load moving machines for the Great Western Railway (GWR), just north of the Thames at Old Paddington Station. That railway had been engineered as the London and Bristol Railway (opened in 1841) by the highly individualistic Isambard Kingdom Brunel and employed a much larger track gauge, of slightly over 7ft, compared with most other railways set at 4ft 8½in. In time this necessitated the transfer of loads, and of passengers, from his 'broad gauge' tracks on to the lesser gauged rails of other lines meeting under cover at several key interchange stations, and vice versa. Brunel came to Napier for a mechanised rapid means of doing this, for which they devised, by means of hydraulics, powered ground-level rail traversers and various lifting hoists.

It had been from the pioneering engineer Joseph Bramah, that Maudslay had gained his early experience of precision and he went on to manufacture the Bramah Patent Lock of 1784. Maudslay then proceeded to improve and develop a Ram Seal of his own for the Bramah Hydraulic Press of 1795, so gaining also his working knowledge of hydraulic power, which was widely practised within his Soho workshop. Both these advanced techniques at the turn of the nineteenth century, had by then also been absorbed by young David Napier, while he worked there alongside Maudslay from his start in London in 1808. This enabled him to introduce both precision and hydraulic power into his own engineering design solutions.

A view of I.K. Brunel's Bristol Temple Meads station in the 1840s, with a Napier-constructed Rolling Stock Traverser in the foreground. (Courtesy, the BBC Hulton Picture Library)

But it was for the erection of such hydraulic-powered machinery in three GWR Depots that James Napier, while still serving his apprenticeship, was appointed as overseer by his father from *c.* 1844. In that year, the first Napier-built Overhead Hydraulic Travelling Crane at Swindon locomotive works had been installed in their 'C' erecting shop. From much later GWR records, dated 1921, it appears that this 1844 crane had wooden girders with 57ft, 2in. span, which were manually positioned, but its hoist operated via an 8¼in diameter x 8in stroke hydraulic lifting cylinder that could raise a 25-ton load. The girders for this crane had been, eventually, renewed by DNS in 1887, and after this it remained in use until 1914. Three Napier-built hydraulic coach and wagon traverser frames were also built and installed during 1846, these at the Bristol Temple Meads, Cheltenham and Old Paddington Stations of the GWR, all of which then had Brunel's 'mixed gauge' track layouts with rails laid on longitudinal timbers. These traversers permitted the sorting of rolling stock under the station covered roof, vehicles being moved across transversely between the station platforms without the need to shunt vehicles outside it over complex multi-gauge points beyond the station area. Even the station platforms themselves could thus be transversely connected to be all on one level, via these tranversers, so removing the need for station subways and overbridges for passengers, goods and baggage.

Several orders for specially finished hydraulic cylinders were placed directly with DNS by I.K. Brunel himself, the one of 1845 reading: 'Allowance on cast-iron cylinder, bored out of the solid, according to Mr Brunel's order, £20.' Interesting instructions again from the GWR in 1846 were: 'To a 10ton travelling and traversing bridge crane, fixed by the servants of the company, under the direction of one of my men (i.e. James Napier) in the boiler shop, Swindon, £700'. The new 'Goods Shed' at Bristol then provided several works orders for DNS from 1841 onwards. An entry from 1844 reads: 'To the GWR, a stamping-press for making metallic cups necessary for renewing the ends of stoppers of the hydraulic pumps; also a new slide valve, with lever, etc. for the steam engine at the new Bristol goods-shed.'

Against this existing background, with its great variety of output, and coping with even heavier engineering projects, the newly formed partnership was soon to prove itself well able to perform highly specialized precision work during the period leading up to the Great Exhibition of 1851. Clearly, by then, the outstanding Napier in-house product of the 1840s had been the 'Automaton' Coin Weighing Machine for the Bank of England (see Appendix Ic). This small and intricate machine was to be the means whereby DNS entered a new higher precision area, this concerned with full mechanization within the 'world of money' manufacture. The problem was of coins becoming debased during circulation from the 1840s on, causing concern to the banks and mints of the world. At Lambeth this fresh area of work, now being guided by the mind and hand of James, was later to challenge for importance the well established and continuing market for the Napier popular range of printing machines, throughout the whole length of the Victorian era.

The first requirement in 1842, was for the actual construction of a new coin weighing machine built to the basic design of William Cotton, the Deputy Governor of the Bank of England. This perceptive man, having some technical ability of his own, saw that their 'Tellers' who, each day, manually weighed all gold coinage at the Bank using bullion balances, in order to reject the growing number of 'light' coins, were rapidly becoming overwhelmed in their task, suffering eye-strain, fatigue, plus loss of high accuracy due to wear in their balances and to air disturbance. From his idea for a special machine balance, set in an enclosed case, came the basic design for the 'Cotton Coin Weighing Balance', for which he was granted a Patent, No. 9392, in 1842. Realising that this embryonic machine would require exceptional skill in its construction and finished design to be suitable for high quantity production, he was advised by a Peter Ewart (first apprentice of George Rennie) to confidently make an approach to David Napier to undertake this sensitive piece of light engineering. The Napier ledger, dated 22 March 1842, states: 'Bank of England, an experimental model of an improved gold-coin balance, to the design of their Deputy Governor, £170'. Then on 13 August: 'A patent coin weighing machine complete, fitted up so as to work either by hand or power, £213'. Later that year, a paper was read before the Institution of Civil Engineers entitled: 'Cotton's Automaton Coin-Weighing Machine', which stated that this machine could weigh 10,000 sovereigns in six hours and divide coins varying by only $1/50^{th}$ of a grain. By hand weighing, to just $1/25^{th}$ grain accuracy, one person could weigh just 5,000 new sovereigns, or 3,000 sovereigns with worn coin from circulation, in six hours. Also it was noticed that the 'Automaton', after it had been at work for several months, had become 'even more sensitive' in detecting any slight variations between standard and 'light' coins, in fact to within a difference of $1/100^{th}$ of a grain. Napier apprentice A.W. Marshall, himself familiar with the build of these balances has commented: 'By reason of the difficulty of the mechanical problem to be solved, reliability and accuracy of operation required, and fineness of workmanship necessary, the 'Automaton' is conspicuous amongst the engineering productions of David & James Napier. It is a beautiful example of mechanism'. This machine, when it was shown

Early DNS-built 2 group 'Automaton' coin weighing machine as required by the Bank of England in 1842. A bust of the Bank's William Cotton is displayed above it.

at the 1851 Great Exhibition in Hyde Park, attracted much attention. Baron Bunsen, one of the most profound reasoners of the day, said of it: 'It seemed almost to think during the pause which ensued between the reception of the sovereign into the scale and its delivery into its appropriate place, either as a light or full-weight coin'. As well as the Napier firm's own display of a wide range of other exhibits, this new 'semi-automatic' machine was only to be seen and demonstrated in operation by the bank, and received worldwide acclaim, which was to pave the way for its long DNS production run lasting fifty years.

We will now take a closer look inside that 'Great Glasshouse', built in London's Hyde Park for the 'Great Exhibition of the Works of Industry of All Nations' held in 1851, after it had been proposed in 1849 by Prince Albert. The tall and spacious glass and arched iron building, popularly called the 'Crystal Palace', was the work of engineer Sir Charles Fox to the design of Sir Joseph Paxton. Queen Victoria opened the exhibition on 1 May 1851 during a brief time of peace and of growing prosperity within Great Britain. Inside, the display by 'Napier, D., & Son, Lambeth – Inventors and Manufacturers' was not large in size, but contained items of remarkably advanced Victorian technology. It was catalogued in 'Class 6 – Manufacturing Machines and Tools' and, as Stand 158 situated within the North Area. Then, strange to recount, the 'Automaton' machine was not listed with DNS exhibits printed in the exhibition catalogue. This, undoubtedly, was due to the Bank of

Captain's Patent Registering Compass, wound-up by key, as shown by DNS in 1851 at the Crystal Palace exhibition.

England requiring that their special machine be found exclusively on their own stand, where it was shown as the patent 'Cotton Automaton Coin Weighing Machine', this in honour of their former Governor (1843-1845). Also, as this quite recently patented device and its precise mode of operation were in effect still 'secret' to the Bank of England, they had clearly wanted to release its many secrets themselves, rather than via the machine's builder. It is only hoped that acknowledgement of DNS as the machine's final 'perfecter' and manufacturer was stated, although the large brass D.N. & S. nameplate, as fitted to all later 'Automatons', was probably then not attached to its bed. The whole matter of the extent to which the patent rights for the design of the Automaton were shared by Mr Cotton and Mr Napier was never fully resolved, and was actively disputed by James Napier, right up until his Father's death in 1873. James was granted three coin-weighing machine patents between 1866 and 1872, relating to his later innovations within the machines that they had built for the Bank of England and those of a different type for the Royal Mint.

Returning to 1851, the extracts relating to the five main DNS exhibits described in the exhibition's catalogue, which included three printing machines, were stated as follows:

'A Captain's Patent registering compass. This instrument (clockwork powered) registers on paper the exact compass course which a vessel has steered for twenty-four consecutive hours.

Its object is to enable the captain at any time to ascertain if his ship has been steered correctly and, if not, to show immediately the period and amount of the deviation.'

'A Letter-press perfecting and printing machine, worked by a small steam engine; when in operation it is arranged with a combination of tapes and grippers, by which the "flying" of the sheet in laying on, required in tape machines, is rendered unnecessary.'

'Another machine, of the same description, for a larger form.' (Both Patented in 1837 as No. 7343, for Double Ended Platen machines, or Multiple-feed cylinder rotary presses.)

'A single-cylinder letter-press printing machine, suitable chiefly for bookwork.'

'A patent self-feeding and self-discharging centrifugal apparatus suited to the separation of the molasses from the crystal in sugar manufacture, also to other purposes. Exhibited as a novel and useful invention – its very considerable working speed being 1,500rpm'.

Referring, once again, to the 'Automaton' machines, it is important to note that there were two distinctly different machines, both having practically the same external design and appearance. The first, built to Cotton's own patent for use initially by the Bank of

Large DNS-built, steam-engine operated, Double-Ended Platen Printing Press as seen in the 1851 exhibition, based upon an earlier Napier Patent of 1837.

England, separated sovereigns fed down from its hopper rapidly into two lots as 'Standard or Light' to within 1/50th of a grain. However, a similar 'work study' was soon to be carried out elsewhere in London, as records show that:

> In 1851, when the 'Moneyers' were no longer Masters of the Royal Mint, and the new authorities began to regard the process of weighing the coin in detail by hand as a laborious, expensive and inaccurate method, the firm D. Napier & Son, at an interview with Sir John Herschel, the Master, and Captain Harness, the Deputy Master, received an order for five machines to be designed to suit the requirements of the Mint. This involved a complete change in the mechanical arrangements of the machine as used at the Bank, it being necessary to divide the blanks or pieces before they are struck into three classes, 'Too light', 'Too heavy' and 'Medium' between certain given limits. These machines have proved even more accurate and rapid than those made for the Bank; and Professor Graham, the late Master, – has added to the number and dispensed entirely with hand weighing.

Example of the complex Napier 3 group 'Automaton' coin sorting machine, as supplied to the Royal Mint of Great Britain from 1852 onwards. This particular machine was supplied to Spain.

A description of this extremely complex machine's operation, which then followed in A.W. Marshall's book, seems practically impossible to comprehend without a working diagram or sight of the machine itself. Unfortunately neither aid is available to us, either within his record or this one! In 1920, he added that an engineer later working in the Mint of Bombay had informed him that although the 'Automaton' machines were now made within their Mint workshop, all the fine weighing of coin blanks was still done on the old Napier machines! It will be of relevant interest here to note that up until 1960, the telegraphic address of DNS at all six Napier works in the London and Luton areas remained as 'Moneyer London'.

Just how fine were those weighing 'limits' for the Mint machines, that were met by D. Napier & Son after that Mint interview of 1851? From the Coinage Act of 1870, the standard weight of a Mint gold sovereign was 123.27447 grains with 'remedy' limits of plus or minus 0.20 grain. To allow for unavoidable errors this was reduced to plus or minus 0.17 grain by the Mint itself, this being achieved at high speed over very long periods by Automatons from Lambeth works. A particularly vibration-free drive system was needed for both single and groups of machines. That most favoured by DNS was a drive from either an atmospheric (or vacuum) engine for the groups or, for a single one, a small water-operated hydraulic motor with a shaft drive, stood between the four legs of the 'Automaton'. These inherently smooth types of drive motor were then supplied from Lambeth as part of each weighing machine order, this was well before the synchronous motor was invented, and when steam engine power with its attendant heat, vapour and vibration, was still the norm for driving most machinery.

Another high profile project that required prompt attention from DNS, soon after the Great Exhibition, also featured Her Majesty Queen Victoria, but this time she was always seen in 'profile'. This concerned her Royal Mail postage stamps that first came into use in 1840 due to the initiative of Roland Hill, whose Penny Blacks (later Reds) and Twopenny Blues were produced for the Honourable Commissioners of Stamps, at the stamp office of Somerset House, on paper sheets that required cutting into individual stamps manually at Post Office counters. By 1848, a Henry Archer had produced his design for the first stamp perforating machine which, after long development trials came into limited use, but was still unreliable in 1850. Soon the Superintendent of Postage Stamps, Edwin Hill (brother to Roland), was to openly declare that this Archer-built machine was: 'a very bad piece of engineering and its complete remodelling must take place.' This urgent task was therefore presented to DNS in 1853, who, in the space of four months between June and October, redesigned, constructed and installed two new perforating machines, fitted with two sets of perforating dyes (or combs), a table for changing sheets of stamps and four feeding-frames. From the outset, these accurate and more soundly constructed Napier machines proved to be highly productive. Equipped with five of these machines in use on continuous stamp perforation, output rose to 4,000 sheets of stamps per working shift. The sheet forward-feed mechanism, operated by adjustable cams, was of special interest as it could cope with stamps having different hole pitches of either fourteen or sixteen perforations to the inch. From then on, the manufacture of stamp perforating machines and replacement 'comb' dye-sets for use at home and abroad, became 'an appreciable part of the Firm's business.'

A Napier-developed, power-driven Stamp Perforating Machine, *c.* 1866.

Soon after, in 1863, a machine was built for Messrs Thomas de la Rue & Co., to perforate large format Italian stamps, followed in 1866 by an order for several machines and punch boxes for Le Directeur des Timbres Postes, Paris, to perforate most French stamps at the Hotel de Monnaie. By the year 1880, the responsibility for British stamp production had been passed to the De la Rue Company who, having bought the five original Napier machines from Somerset House, continued to use them for several years, this coming after they had perforated, during those previous twenty-seven years, no less than eighty-five million sheets of Queen Victoria's small definitive postage stamps.

The DNS firm had always held to the basic title of simply 'Engineers', right up to the production of high-quality motor cars from Acton works in the twentieth century. The true inference to be taken from this during the Victorian era at Vine Street works, was of a company of General Engineers, able to design and manufacture products from heavy, to medium, to fine instrument weight, and of ensuring precision in all products. To illustrate this versatility, against an earlier background of quite large machine production, the following two lightweight examples are offered. Firstly, reaching back to those early years when David Napier was attached to the Henry Maudslay workshops in 1810, he had spent his spare time devising various fine drawing instruments. Some of these he had submitted to the Royal Society of Arts for their approval and comment, such as his refined 'Universal Perspectigraph', which could produce three-dimensional drawings, and that he had hoped would supersede the common pantograph. Another, and much simpler, product that would remain popular for many years to come were the 'Napier Pocket Compasses', an engraving of which is shown, taken from a supplier's book of 1878.

By that time, this type of folding safety instrument was being made by the famous mathematical instrument company of William Stanley M.R.I. at Great Turnstile, Holborn, whose fine book goes on to describe them in detail as follows:

> The Napier Compasses are, perhaps, the best and most popular kind of pocket compasses, their especial merit being their compact form. The portability of the Napier compasses is obtained by the sides being hollowed out from the inside, so as to admit of the points folding into them. This form also gives the sides (arms) great strength and lightness – The head joint should move smoothly, and the knee and swivel joints should move stiffly.'

Even Stanley then finished his review by admitting that: 'They are a difficult instrument to make perfectly'. We understand that David Napier always carried his prototype compasses with him, safely in a waistcoat pocket'.

Now twenty years on, David Napier, who was nearing retirement from his active role with the company, planned to hand matters over to his son James from 1867. Before that, their strong partnership had enjoyed the satisfaction of tackling some more specialised light products, which quickly scored some apparent successes.

Clock-making has always been a branch of precision engineering in a field of its own, but, when an opportunity arose DNS were ready at Lambeth to seize it and once more to prove their engineering versatility. Thus a small batch of Turret Clocks were designed and built in 1861, eight or more in number, likely for an export order from Spain from where a great deal of business had come during the preceding years, especially via their National Mint.

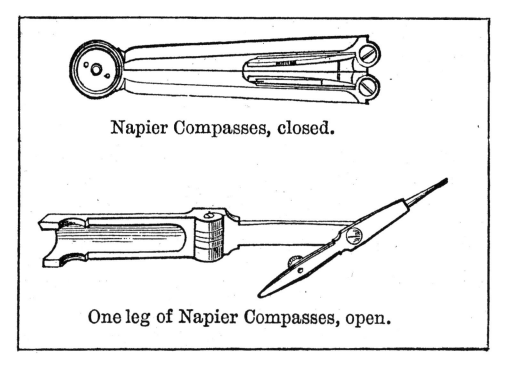

Napier Compasses, closed.

One leg of Napier Compasses, open.

David Napier's compact design for his safe-folding pocket Drawing Compasses.

These large clocks had three faces and a hand-wound movement, the largest one being also fitted with a chime movement. But one clock, although constructed, was then not dispatched, so it was sent instead to be fixed at the 1862 International Exhibition in London. With 'D. Napier & Son. Engineers, London' inscribed on its triple faces, it made a handsome timepiece at the show, where DNS won the 'Foreign Exhibition Medal'.

The tragedies of the Crimean War against Russia (1854-56), form a vivid background to many of the contracts taken on by DNS during the mid-1850s, from the Honourable Board of Ordnance. This growing association of DNS with the supply of ordnance, steam-engine power and machine tools for the main Woolwich Arsenal factory, was to form the beginning of its military associations that were to continue, unbroken, for the next century and a half. The reliability of DNS in completing military work on time and to impeccable standards, led to repeat orders for ordnance at home and from allies overseas. A machining entry in the order book for 1853 was obviously a 'rush job' for: 'Finishing a large number of gun-metal shell sockets, £382-13s-7d … regarding this account, which may appear high …they have been executed subject to all sacrifices contingent where expedition is the pre-eminent object to be attained.' Showing that speed, accuracy and delivery on time in manufacture was then costly: but often worth paying for!

Another 1854 entry reads: 'Henry Bessemer (of steel making fame), – To a cannon, and cutting hole in same, as per instruction.' One can almost 'feel' the hardness of the steel involved, and that complex shape to be held firm during the drilling and boring processes!

It must have been gratifying for ageing David Napier that in 1855, and at the height of the Crimean conflict when DNS had 300-plus employees available, they were approached by busy Messrs Maudslay, Son & Field to undertake manufacture of medium-sized batches of several precision mechanical parts for their Marine Steam Engines. This enabled them to meet Admiralty orders for urgently needed warships. David's early 'service' with them had thus been recognised, while a glimpse of his future DNS Company was given.

D, Napier & Son's export of machinery to the Empire, Russia and to some European countries was to continue at a steady rate for another twenty years. One such importer was the Spanish Government Agent, Zulueta & Co. who, between the years 1856 and 1863, ordered in stages almost a 'complete Ordnance works' from DNS, including a 40hp horizontal steam engine and a 25hp expansive and condensing Beam Engine with shafting and two internal flue boilers with force pump, these to drive the plant. Today, there stands in the grand foyer of the Madrid Technical University, a similar, but even larger preserved beam engine, with a 16ft diameter flywheel which had rotated alongside its massive columns and bed, which carries cast lettering 'D. Napier & Son – London 1859'. The Spanish inscription put by this beam engine, describes it as a: 'Steam Engine, Watt Type, constructed by D. Napier & Son in London in 1859, one of the first steam engines bought by Spain. It was in operation at the National Mint until the end of the nineteenth century.' They add that it was donated and installed in the Superior School of Industrial Engineering in Madrid in 1910. One may question whether such a powerful example of Victorian heavy engineering (seen in a modern photograph) was also within the compass of early DNS projects? Certainly, Lambeth works possessed very large machine tools!

A big D. Napier & Son, London, Watt-type non-condensing Beam Engine as supplied in 1859 to the National Mint of Spain. It is seen here in 2000 on permanent display in the School of Industrial Engineering in Madrid.

So many precision projects passed through those Vine Street workshops in Lambeth, that the records of the orders seem almost endless. Appendix I, at the end of this book, lists and classifies a selection of them, arranged in chronological order, which should be referred to in conjunction with this text. Later chapters, similarly, have Appendices 2 to 5, to which reference can be made for detailed information relating to following chapters, which cover subject matter relating to vehicles, engines, marine craft and aircraft.

Suddenly, in 1873, the death of David Napier occurred at his home in Surbiton, near London, where it is thought he died at the grand old age of eighty-five years. He was laid to rest by James and many of his Napier family in Kingston Cemetery, South West London. He had arrived in England sixty-five years earlier, during 1808, the very same year that the great pianist and composer Ludwig van Beethoven had written his first Choral Symphony, that which includes the chorus – 'See the Conquering Hero come'. It would, perhaps, be difficult to obtain a more fitting tribute to the strength of life and dedication to precision engineering by David Napier, while working in London far away from his native Scotland.

The most outstanding of monuments to the highly skilled work of David and James Napier are surely the great Bullion Balances they built for the Bank and Royal Mint in the second half of the nineteenth century. These large, hydraulically operated balances were to follow the small 'Automatons' into service, which had weighed a single coin in

David Napier, then in
retirement, taken from
a portrait in oils by
S. Tushingham.

James Napier, the son of the
partnership, who assumed
control of DNS in 1867.

hundreds of grains (there being 7,000 to the pound), whereas these named giant balances could weigh gold ingots of up to hundreds of ounces (sixteen to the pound). First of the precise giants was a 4ft beam balance named *The Chancellor* of 1870, supplied to the order of the Royal Mint. This machine, housed in wind-proof glass housing, could weigh bullion bars up to its 1,500 ounce limit, to within two grains accuracy (0.0046 ounce). The last large balance, made for the Bank of England, was supplied in 1888, and named by James Napier *The Chief Clerk.* This could weigh a 2,000 ounce (125lb) mass to within one grain accuracy. Such sensitivity of action demanded from the now ageing, and dwindling, workforce at Lambeth the highest degree of precision, a level seldom equalled, before or since. The present-day Bank of England Museum displays a Napier 'Automaton' coin-weighing machine, but one of the last of the Napier bullion balances named *The Lord High Chancellor*, constructed by DNS in 1879, is now preserved inside the Bank. Testimony to its reliability of operation during eighty-five years of continuous service is that this balance during its working life has given to the Bank the high accuracy weight of well over one million gold bars.

The exceptionally gifted James Murdoch Napier carried on the DNS business on an ever-reducing scale at Lambeth and, it seems, almost single-handed at times. To illustrate this, one prime order he received in 1879 was from the well-known supplier of non-ferrous metals and alloys, Messrs Johnson Matthey & Co. This was to plane down to finished size the cross-section of three long bars, having an 'H section' forged from an alloy of 90% Platinum and 10% Iridium, with both of these features resistant to physical and thermal distortions. The bars, a first of their type, had been ordered by La Commission Internationale du Metre Paris, to precisely establish the 'Standard Metre' as the French unit of length, between lines to be engraved on two gold studs, these to be later secured to the webs of the bars. First of all, James Napier and his smith helped with forging the 'H sections' at Johnson Matthey works. Then he himself, back at Vine Street, set up the job on a selected small planing machine in the precision shop on the first floor, after the men had finished their shift. He then supervised the work, assisted only by a charge hand who, with the door closed, collected the swarf from the skimming of the platinum bars onto sheets of paper. The precious waste metal from this stable alloy was recovered with care, the job itself had been costed at just £315.

At times, James Napier travelled the world widely, sometimes as the representative of the Royal Mint to Empire countries as their expert adviser on money production. James Napier was elected a Member of the Institution of Mechanical Engineers in 1870 and was the only one of his London DNS family to join it. When he died in March 1895, in the house adjoining the works in Lambeth, the Institution were generous in the obituary that the proceedings published on his life and work. The brief opening summary for it stated that:

> James Murdoch Napier was born on 26 April 1823; and was the son of Mr David Napier, the well known inventor and constructor of printing machines. In 1837 he entered his father's works in Lambeth, where he became a skilled workman and draughtsman, and soon displayed considerable capacity for original design.

James Napier's 'The Lord High Chancellor' bullion balance, as supplied to the Bank of England in 1879, where it can be seen today in preservation.

This was then followed by an impressive list giving many of the projects with which he had been concerned. This ends with the sentences:

> In 1853 he devised improvements in letter-press printing machines; and in the following year he designed and constructed a machine for printing Bank of England notes. Amongst his other numerous inventions were registering tide gauges, mariners compasses, barometers, machinery for producing cold the lead bullets for government rifles instead of cast bullets, an apparatus for paying out submarine telegraph cables, machinery for the manufacture of soda, speed indicators and governors, etc.

It now seems almost providential that the company books and many archives collected from the 200 years of engineering by D. Napier & Son Ltd now reside within the very building of the Institution to which James Napier had belonged, and to which he was able to make his personal contribution through its meetings.

James Napier had taken out a total of forty-seven patents, these mostly for complex machine designs as already referred to in this chapter, but also others of a more frivolous and even 'gourmet nature'. Such patents included those four that related to wine glasses and their improved stands, one for a rotary apparatus for cleaning the lower parts (soles) of boots and shoes and then four more that covered various pieces of apparatus for the serving of mustard and dry condiments at table. Perhaps these latter inventions make best sense seen amongst his own Napier domestic household, within the house in York Road.

Sad to recount, when James Napier died, there were left in employment at Vine Street works only seven persons, one being Walter P. Napier, the eldest of his four sons. This experienced engineer, who at that time was still working on the first floor while in charge of the precision shop, then chose not to continue at the Napier works any longer without his father. This action by Walter then left a great opportunity for another, the youngest son Montague, to step in and then own the Vine Street works, which led to its revival. It also led to much new found growth for that 'Napier oak tree', planted by David ninety years earlier, and which now led to the company's steady expansion, once again, into the twentieth century.

3

'THE PROVED BEST' ON ROAD AND WATER 1896–1913

It was Montague Stanley Napier who took tight hold of the DNS reins from June 1895, when he was twenty-five. This exceptional young man was fourth son of James Napier and had been born in the York Road family house in 1870, which fronted the Vine Street works, with the sounds and smells of D. Napier & Son's industry. He had purchased from his father's executors the lease for the York Road premises, including all of its ageing plant, but, most importantly, also the widely felt 'goodwill' towards the then fifty-year-old DNS Company Name in London. Whether or not his older brother Walter had left before Montague's take-over is not clear, but now strong new management was needed.

No doubt the young Montague, as he grew up 'over the shop', had enjoyed those very many opportunities to observe his father's inventiveness and skill, and also his brother's fine precision shop projects, all of these being accomplished at the rear of their house. Then, without any show, Montague rapidly acquired and developed his innate mechanical ability and workshop skills, not through serving an apprenticeship, but from preparing himself well enough to capably continue his family's complex business. The completion of any outstanding orders for 'Automaton' weighing machines, the carrying out of printing press repairs, the supply of cutting tools and replacement parts for machines; all these he continued, with the aid of the very few experienced craftsmen who had faithfully stayed on during this Napier family crisis. Throughout this upheaval, it now seems that Montague's high regard for precision activities within Vine Street works had become aroused, and highly active.

What is known is that Montague Napier maintained a lifelong devotion to the bicycle, and in particular to the 'Ordinary bicycle', that type known today as a 'Penny Farthing'. As an active member of more than one cycling club, including today's well known Bath Road Club, he had competed alongside 'the best', as an above average long distance rider. One top racing cyclist, whom he had known and respected, and often supported in his road races, was the long-distance record-holding Australia- born cyclist, one Selwyn Francis Edge, who was two years his senior. Some time previously, Edge had updated his riding to the new 'Safety' type of bicycle, on which he created London - Brighton - London records for four years between 1890 and 1893, by reducing his times from seven hours to under six. In 1892, he had made a British long-distance record up the Great North Road from London to York,

Mastermind of the twentieth-century DNS power company Montague Stanley Napier, at the time he took control of Lambeth Works.

taking twelve hours forty-nine minutes, the event in which Napier, riding an Ordinary, had achieved fourth place for himself. These two very different men, with cycling in common, were destined through their later co-operation to 'shake the world' of motorised travel over the next two decades. Montague always retained his love of riding an Ordinary high bicycle for exercise, well into his busy later life in the twentieth century, this was primarily to help his own later troubled health, whilst also providing him with much needed relaxation. Not surprisingly his earliest attempts to introduce new enterprises into Vine Street works were mostly items for the then fast expanding safety cycle industry. These products comprised special machinery and tools for cycle builders in the London area, but the irregular demand for these provided insufficient income.

Another DNS contract that he accepted was the manufacture of the new Ritter-Patented, rubber-tyred, Road Skate (this was not unlike the modern 'roller blade' skate in its principle). These spoked, wheel-fabricated skates were given an attractive nickel plated finish and had a neat braking system operated when the skater bent his knees. Such skates were primarily for commercial use in the City of London by messengers and couriers between the banks and offices, where these quick, mobile human-powered foot and leg attachments soon caught on.

However, compared to previous DNS high-value products, they were of only low sales value for their manufacturing company, really needing mass production techniques to which the Napier works was not geared at that time. One DNS employee, nicknamed 'Fish' Smart, gave to the Ritter road skate, and so to Napier, some fame when he became the Road Skating Champion of England. Paired with the next champion named Hutton, he gave demonstrations in the Broad Street area of the City of London, so providing some good publicity for this brave venture into new individual mobility; this was an attractive alternative to the trusty bicycle, walking and the horse-drawn cab and horse omnibus.

From the continent of Europe news of a far more revolutionary road transport system had reached the ears of British engineers – the Motor Carriage, this trend in personal transportation came from France and Germany in particular. Young Montague Napier certainly held the ability and the ambition to invent and perfect engineering innovations of his own using the old, but serviceable, machine tools at Vine Street. As time was to show, he had inherited many of the staunch characteristics of his father and grandfather, along with a natural instinct for orderly precision in manufacture and for sound, practice-based, engineering design. Fortunately, he also had his grandfather's fair but thrifty Scottish attitude towards company finances, those which he was to expand and sustain over the next thirty years, often operating during times of severe industrial depression.

The challenge he rose to, above all others, was to improve upon 'Engine Prime Movers' within road motor carriages and boats he had witnessed operating in the United Kingdom. During 1898 he constructed and ran several two-cylinder internal combustion engines of his own design, one of which he first tried out by powering a light boat on the nearby river Thames. This was, in fact, in embryonic form, the first Napier marine engine of many. Some of his petroleum spirit engines were vertical in-line, while others were horizontally opposed, all being put to the test either on the bench or in his own primitive, wheeled land-vehicle. This 'test car' was then seen at Lambeth by his former cycling associate Selwyn Edge, but Edge was not at all impressed by this 'Napier car' design which was then fitted with a flat, two-cylinder, water-cooled engine. However, he was impressed by a compact two-cylinder vertical engine seen on bench test during his visit to the works. That four-stroke cycle prototype was destined to be the forerunner of thousands of larger petrol engines built by Napier for road vehicles over the next quarter-century. But what were the circumstances that had caused S.F. Edge, quite unexpectedly, to meet up again with Montague Napier?

Selwyn Edge, now approaching thirty, had in the meantime turned his competitive talents to motor tricycle racing, both at home and on the continent. His many successes riding a high geared 6hp De Dion-Bouton tricycle, against riders of the sporting calibre of J.W. Stocks and Charles Jarrott, had once again gratified his racing instincts. These race successes that he had enjoyed during his period as London Manager of the Dunlop Tyre Co., then prompted him to try out some early four-wheeled motor cars, such as a 6hp Panhard-Levassor that was run into second place by a French driver in the 1896 Paris-Marseilles race. That car, known as 'Old Number Eight', he then purchased from the Lawson collection for trial purposes on English roads, from which Edge noticed that several improvements to its specification were essential to suit his tastes as a motorist.

An 1899 aluminium
crankcase 2-cylinder
Napier 2½-litre
petrol engine,
with six overhead
atmospheric inlet
valves and using coil
ignition.

These included replacing the tiller steering by wheel steering gear and its solid rubber road wheels by pneumatic-tyred wheels on which, no doubt, he intended to fit and then demonstrate his own Dunlops. There had been a chance conversation between Edge and another mutual cycling friend, a Walter Munn, who had kept in touch with Montague and seen his progress at Lambeth. So Munn, on hearing about Edge's planned improvements to his 'Old No. 8', was then able to recommended his friend Montague's works, under the name of D. Napier & Son, to Edge as being the most suitable workshop he knew that could carry out the modification of his Panhard car while incorporating Edge's own proposed improvements.

Edge, in his autobiography *My Motoring Reminiscences*, wrote:

Napier undertook to do this, so I ran my car down to his works a few days later and anxiously waited to see what type of steering he would design. I was considerably impressed when, after a short time, he showed me the drawings. The system was on the worm and nut principle. Napier made such a success of this alteration that I saw great possibilities in turning the

engineering gifts which he undoubtedly possessed to good account in the future. Panhard
and Levassor had originally been manufacturers of wood-cutting machinery (in France), and
they had developed into one of the finest motor car manufacturing firms in the world, and I
failed to see any reason why D. Napier & Son should not follow in their footsteps.

The pneumatic tyres when fitted were also a boon to S.F. Edge, and these were followed
by:

> Further experiments on No. 8. For example: a radiator was fitted which had a very marked
> effect on the running and the amount of water used… We (note the use of plural) also
> rearranged the lubricators – and placed those which were most needed within easy reach
> of the driver.

At this early stage of their co-operation over the development of a higher-performance,
British-designed and built motor carriage, S.F. Edge quickly came to recognise and add
in his own words that:

> Napier was a keen lover of workshop discipline; his one thought in life was to have a perfect
> workshop where he could carry out his experiments. Engineering in almost any form greatly
> appealed to him, but there seemed to be some lack of enthusiasm on his part in connection
> with motor cars. I had every hope, however, that his keenness would increase as time went
> on, and this proved to be the case.

Thus it immediately became apparent that such vital Edge-Napier collaboration would
always be a testing time for both men, such was the contrast between their personalities,
outlooks and backgrounds. But it was to be forged on 'mutual trust' and a respect for
each other's individual talents and, as such, lasted fourteen years while not bonded by any
formal company partnership. Now, at last, the reserved M.S. Napier was able to grasp the
very opportunity his ambition had made him hope that he would one day be offered. S.F.
Edge, then went on to describe what resulted when Napier fitted his new engine into
his Panhard:

> Napier realised that we were both on the right track and before long he asked me to let him
> design a new two-cylinder vertical engine for the car (in 1898). This was what I wanted him
> to do, for it would be the first crucial test of his engineering skill – I found this Napier engine
> to be a great improvement on the Panhard one I had previously in the car.

This joint project, initiated by S.F. Edge and carried to a technically sound conclusion
by M.S. Napier, was to cement their relationship in the motor carriage trade of 1899. So
from then on, work labelled 'For Mr Edge' was to assume a high priority in Vine Street
works, where the absorbing task of Otto Cycle four-stroke petrol engine design, then its
manufacture and test, confronted Napier daily. The only issue of greater importance to
Napier was his chief aim to secure a sound future for DNS into the still Victorian, early
twentieth century.

The badly run-down old Lambeth works in 1895, for which Montague had taken over the control from his father James, had previously been built-up by David Napier as a result of the DNS partnership's outstanding success in precision manufacture, despite both men having different outlooks. But Montague, being equipped with a combination of David's perseverance and James's imagination and attention to fine detail, plus being aided by the competitive style and initiative of Selwyn Edge, thus found himself in possession of the winning ingredients for a successful launch into the then new motor industry in Britain.

S.F. Edge was swift to see his opportunity: he left his Harvey Du Cros led Dunlop organisation in London to market Napier Motor Carriages. He would then form a new motor trade company, based on Du Cros' capital, while initially still sharing the Dunlop premises at 14 Regent Street. To further encourage Du Cros into supporting this sales venture, Edge proposed taking agencies for two makes of French '*voiturette*', those of Gladiator and Clement-Panhard, to which Du Cros then agreed, providing a profitable contract could be signed with Napier in Lambeth. This Du Cros/Edge partnership was known as the 'Motor Power Company' (M.P. Co.), with six employees, it was then floated after a sales agreement had been drawn up and signed between D. Napier & Son and the M.P. Co. This was to the effect that the M.P. Co. should market the whole output of Napier cars, as from Autumn 1899, after which date an initial six vehicles should be supplied – three two-cylinder and three four-cylinder cars. Drawings were soon received by the M.P. Co. of the two Napier models as required from Vine Street works. Meanwhile, S.F. Edge had already entered himself for a one hundred-mile trial driving his re-engined Panhard, this to provide prior publicity to the launch of the Napier motor carriages. A certificate Edge then received from the Automobile Club of Great Britain read: 'Panhard carriage and transmission, fitted with an 8hp, two-cylinder petrol motor and steering by 'Napier & Sons' (incorrectly named) of Vine Street, York Road, Lambeth; fitted with pneumatic tyres; owned and driven by Mr S.F. Edge, carrying two passengers'. During the trial the ascents of several long and steep hill climbs were successfully made, including Aston Hill (298ft) at 7mph and: 'The trying Dashwood Hill' (241ft) at 9mph, so its power is unmistakable!' The certificate was signed by Claude Johnson, the ACGB secretary, and Harry J. Swindley, the ACGB Trial Hon. Timekeeper, so making this a reassuring record. As a result, in the ensuing press coverage Edge announced the formation of the M.P. Co., and went on to immediately add that: 'We are ready to receive enquiries for Napier cars'. His endeavours in this trial were to be just the beginning of a long and powerful campaign to publicise British-built Napier cars wherever he competed over the years, so relieving Montague Napier of all direct responsibility for marketing his company's new products. This in turn enabled Napier, after only a very short time, to concentrate entirely on engine development and high-quality rolling chassis design and workmanship, while car bodies remained to each customer's choice, being supplied by some of the finest coach-builders, which were built onto sold chassis at extra cost. It was left to Edge to proclaim, on behalf of his new M.P. Co. and also DNS, their joint aim: 'To build a British car which would not only bear comparison with the best the Continent could produce, but would turn out to be a considerable improvement thereon.' However, the Napier motor carriage was, at this point in time, still far from being 'The Proved Best', as it was to become.

As the new century dawned, the first chassis for the two Napier models due for delivery that spring, for customers now on a short waiting list, were beginning to take shape in Montague Napier's works. Meanwhile, Edge's preparations at 14 Regent Street for the new M.P. Co. were nearing completion, with spaces for the small Clement-Panhard and Gladiator cars now due to arrive any day, to stand alongside a Dunlop tyre display, while still leaving room for the larger Napiers awaited from Lambeth works.

Motor transport enthusiast Edward Kennard headed the list to receive a two-cylinder 'G20' model Napier, but plans for another important trial were to prevent him taking delivery on time. For now the Automobile Club of Great Britain was planning a longer trial, this time over a full 1,000-mile round Britain route and Spring and Selwyn Edge clearly saw that failure to enter the first Napier car for this, when the wider public could experience and see it in action, would be a lost golden opportunity for DNS and his M.P. Co. Edward Kennard was soon approached by Edge, requesting the use of his new 'G20' car for this trial, with Edge himself the driver to ensure it was properly run-in over the trial. This resulted in all available effort at Vine Street works being utilised to ensure the rapid completion of this, the first ever Napier chassis, before 23 April when the trial was due to begin. It was achieved with only five days to spare, just enabling Mulliners to build simple coach work onto the chassis. The engine design was a 2.5-litre, two-cylinder unit of 4ins bore by 6ins stroke, with two circular groups of small triple atmospheric inlet valves set overhead above each combustion chamber, with a single large cam-operated exhaust valve to the side. Its two big cast-iron cylinder liners were pressed into the cast aluminium alloy crankcase. The crankshaft had its two heavy crankpins set in-line (i.e. 360 degree cranks) which were separated by a link supporting only a heavy 'static balance' weight. As one of the two cylinders was fired by spark ignition every 360 degrees of rotation, this engine 'vibrated up and down'.

By that spring day the car had returned to Lambeth and was made ready, just in time for the start of the trial from near London's Hyde Park Corner. An enthusiastic teenager, St John Nixon, was entrusted with the task of 'riding mechanic on the step' throughout the whole of the twenty day event, he being Edge's assistant on the road and in all preparations.

By the finish back in London on 12 May, the Napier had covered a distance of 1,107 miles in total, and although almost untried before the start, Edge reported of the car: 'I was more than satisfied with the excellent performance it put up.' In fact, this brand new Napier, carrying rally No. A10, was placed second overall out of sixty-four starters on the trial and S.F. Edge was awarded the Automobile Club de France Silver Medal for this result. The Gold Medal, for the record, went to the competent Hon. Charles Rolls driving a big 12hp French Panhard car so, once again, giving the Continent the premier award, but this time they were made aware that a strong British-built car challenge was now a reality.

The year 1900 also saw the 16hp 'H70' four-cylinder Napiers enter the motoring arena. In that year one of these 4.9-litre-strong performers was road-tested and approved of by racing driver Charles Jarrott before he purchased it, this with Montague Napier himself as riding mechanic and observer. That had happened because Napier, who seldom drove his cars in public, much preferred to see an experienced racing man put his cars through

A tyre change by S.F. Edge on the first 'G20' Napier car during the Thousand Mile Trial of 1900, watched by a young St John Nixon.

their paces so that they could then provide him with their personal opinions on car performance. Meanwhile, Edge continued to build up his car demonstration and sales company, but he still relied primarily on Napiers for its trade, along with the prestige that they brought. The pre-planned high point of the 1900 car racing season for Edge was to enter and to drive one of the 16hp Napiers in the Paris – Toulouse – Paris race over two days that July. This was the very first occasion when a British-built and prepared Race Car competed on the Continent, and was made even more noteworthy as the Hon. Charles Rolls accompanied Edge as riding mechanic on the H70. A series of problems arose, however, for them both to endure; ignition coil irregularity before and during the event, a broken water circulation pipe and an unfortunate collision, which the Napier survived. But, as the car finally had to be retired after only 80kms; this was a very disappointing ending for Edge and Napier to what could have been a breakthrough event for them. It is regrettable that this event must have left a poor impression with Rolls who, of course, still had four years to wait before his own cars would appear. Napier had pinned his faith on electric ignition right from the start for his cars but, despite this setback with his four-cylinder car, he persevered with it, using better type wound coils and improved tremblers, until he had gained the required reliability from this long-surviving system of petrol engine ignition.

1901 not only saw new order levels maintained for Napier motor carriages and 'Pleasure Cars' for the more wealthy buyer, but it also saw the introduction of other uses for the DNS chassis wherein the model was used for modes of land transport that Montague Napier termed 'Business Vehicles'. This suitably modified group of stronger chassis were

M.S. Napier's first 1901 Business Vehicle was based on his 2-cylinder 8hp 'G20' chassis and is seen here at work in Colchester.

then given utility bodies locally by their purchasers, to permit their use as either public passenger transports or load carriers for goods distribution. Such vehicles have generally become known elsewhere, other than at the DNS works, as 'Commercials'. Hackney Carriages, or popular 'Napier Taxicabs', were not included with these. (See Appendices 2a and 2c.) The first Napier Business Vehicle was, in fact, a two-cylinder light van built on a G20 chassis in 1901, for the delivery of drapery by the Colchester firm Hyam Clothing. That same year a heavier chassis, powered by a larger two-cylinder engine of 5in bore, now with 180 degree crank, was working for Scarborough Motor Vehicle Co., now fitted with a long, tiered 'char-a-banc' body with seating for fourteen passengers. After this, Scarborough purchased a similar Napier chassis for the 1902 season, that carrying an ugly closed omnibus body.

For the 1901 competition scene, Napier had designed and constructed for Edge a real monster of a racing car, very much bigger than the H70, and it was duly entered for the Gordon Bennett Trophy race, to be held that year in France. Following the 'big engine trend' on the Continent, the four-cylinder racer had an engine of 16.3-litres capacity that gave it a speed of 85mph during tests on arrival. According to the rules this Napier had to be British built right down to her tyres, these undoubtedly being from Edge's Dunlop stock in Regent Street. It was those tyres that proved to be this heavy car's Achilles heel when run at speed on rough road surfaces as found on the route of the race, so this big British challenger was withdrawn by Edge and Napier (who himself acted as riding mechanic) at an early stage. The sole finisher was Girardot of France driving a 24hp Panhard, but our Napier-based duo were to be 'third time lucky' the next year, when it

Restored 1902 Gordon Bennett Trophy-winning Napier racing car in 1993. It was driven gaining Britain's first international motor racing award by S.F. Edge.

was again run in France. In 1902, with a newly introduced weight limit of 1,000kg for the Gordon Bennett event, Napier fully complied by designing the lighter 'D50' chassis with an engine of just 6.4 litres. Driving this much improved car with shaft-driven live back axle and a new engine now with four atmospheric inlet valves per cylinder, Edge was successful in winning for Great Britain the famed Gordon Bennett Trophy. The race had been run between Paris and Innsbruck, and while Edge was again running on his British Dunlops, despite some punctures on the way, he was finally the only race finisher. But, at last, the French stranglehold on this top international race had been broken, and also by a Napier from Great Britain, so giving the British some much needed motor car prestige, by way of her first international car racing victory.

Out on Britain's roads, a widening range of Napier chassis was appearing with a power range from the light, two-cylinder 9hp, to the four-cylinder 16hp. 'H70', then on to the heavier 'G100' model which, with its longer wheelbase, could also carry a limousine-style body. The two-cylinder 'G20' cars were rated at 9hp as of 1901, but now with a smoother running engine through having the two cranks set at 180 degrees, despite leaving it with uneven 180 and 540 degree firing intervals. The short-lived H8 Brougham type with an under-floor-mounted horizontal four-cylinder engine was tried in order to minimise engine noise and so compete with the electric cars of the day, but only half a dozen sold. By far the most popular chassis from this period, with a compact 2.5-litre, four-cylinder, 12hp engine and a 7ft 7½in wheel base, was the 'D45' model of 1902-1904, that accepted

Example of the popular 4-cylinder Napier 'D45' chassis of 1902/05 with tonneau coachwork, belonging to S.F. Edge. He and his family had won the 1902 'Battle of Flowers'.

various coachwork, such as either a covered or open tonneau body. During that period, at least 180 of these chassis were produced from Lambeth, some of those orders later being completed at Acton Motor works.

Successful collaboration between Napier and Edge was to scale even greater heights of motoring achievement over the next five years, leading right up to the point when the world's first specially built motorcourse was opened at Brooklands in Surrey. But, before then, significant developments, on and off the road, were to take place at Lambeth works itself, these mostly during the very important year of 1903.

S.F. Edge had become convinced that the way ahead for engine design was to increase the number of pistons thrusting onto the crankshaft to six, arranged with 120 degree cranks giving three overlapping impulses per revolution, and so smoothing out torque to the back axle and its tyres. M.S. Napier was not immediately in favour of this proposal; he perhaps foresaw torsional vibration problems ahead in the longer crankshaft this would require. But he was eventually persuaded to experiment with this design at the start of 1903. During this development, Napier was also planning to move to larger premises, as motor vehicle chassis were more bulky products, albeit mobile, than presses and balances had been when Vine Street works was laid out seventy years earlier by his grandfather. In parallel with these decisions, he had engaged a young, qualified new Chief Draughtsman named Arthur J. Rowledge, who ably dealt with these new engine design requirements under Montague Napier's firm direction, along with S.F. Edge's eager approval.

Meanwhile, S.F. Edge had discovered a fresh outlet for his racing energies, this time on water, within the Automobile Club's Motor Boat Section, formed as a more exclusive group than that which then raced on Continental roads and in English hill-climb events. Owing to Edge's British win in the previous year's Gordon Bennett race, the dilemma of where to hold the next race in 1903 soon arose in view of the government's refusal to allow road-racing in Britain. This was eventually overcome when the Irish Parliament was persuaded to agree to permit the ACGB's race to be run on Irish soil instead. Then, following that, the first International Harmsworth Trophy for motor launches was also to be competed for off the south coast of Ireland in Cork Bay, just a week or two after the G.B. motor race, which was also being organised by the Automobile Club of Great Britain. The shrewd and keen Edge, seeing the opportunity to 'kill two birds with one stone' on land and water, while he could compete with Napier four-cylinder-engined cars and boats in the same country area and during the same year, carefully prepared his 'works entries' for both of these international events which were to be run almost consecutively.

The racing cars that were entered were based on the 'D50' racer chassis of 1902, but now with an enlarged engine of 50hp rating of 7.8-litre capacity. A team of three, all driving Napier cars, was selected, and after eliminating trials had been run in Britain, these were to be driven by Edge, Jarrott and Stocks, Rolls and Mayhew having been eliminated in the trial. In respect to the Irish nation, with its fine green countryside, and to avoid 'scaring the cows', the Napier cars were painted a deep tone of green which, in fact, then became the permanent 'British Racing Green' colour, this lasting for over a century. This green also became the DNS company corporate colour for most purposes until more recent times. The 1903 race, held at 7 a.m. on 10 June out from Ballyshannon was over 350 miles, with the usual strong entries from France, Belgium and Germany. It was won by Jenatzy driving a hastily modified Mercedes after their recent factory fire in Germany. About the race, S.F. Edge paid credit to Genatzy's driving in a modified car, Edge himself finishing in the big 80hp 'K5' Napier some two and a half hours later after tyre trouble! But a better and more positive result lay in store for Napier in Ireland's Queenstown Harbour the next month, when Edge's timely initiative on water now opened up a whole new era.

For the Harmsworth Trophy race a special 40ft all steel-hulled motor launch named *Napier* had been built for his newly titled company, S.F. Edge Ltd, by Tanners Yard, Camden Town to the design of Linton Hope & Co. of London. *The Cork Examiner* reported that DNS had supplied a big four-cylinder engine for the launch giving 80bhp at 800rpm to its two-bladed propeller. 'Napier' was to be piloted in the race by Arthur Evans who had supervised its construction in London to Edge's order. Other motor boats in this British Automobile Club run race for the Harmsworth Cup were the 30ft launch of F. Beadel with an eight-cylinder, 50bhp M.M. Co. engine, and the 30ft J.E. Thorneycroft launch of 20bhp. On 11 July 1903 the final of the 8½-mile race from Queenstown to Cork was run and the Cup was won by S.F. Edge and A.F. Evans in 'Napier' taking 26 minutes 6 seconds, with an average speed against an ebb tide of 19.53mph, their finish being five minutes ahead of the Thorneycroft boat. So early on was this result in power-boating history, that S.F. Edge, and hence also M.S. Napier, were credited with the 1903 World Water Speed Record of 19.53mph, despite running 1.1mph faster in an earlier heat of this Irish event!

On 7 August 1903 the four-cylinder petrol launch *Napier* won the twenty-six-mile handicap at Cowes at 22 knots, before the King and Queen, with Miss Dorothy Levitt at its helm.

From that time on this pioneer Napier-powered launch came to be known as the 'Napier I' in records, a more advanced launch named *Napier* (known as 'Bulb') was built in 1905 and had a bulbous wave-piercing bow and larger engine (see Appendix IVa). It is perhaps worth noting here that this Napier-engined speed record for DNS on water, way back in 1903, preceded the first one they were to make on land by two years, and was the first of many DNS-powered speed records set over the following fifty-five years.

The same year saw some major changes at D. Napier & Son in London. The first was the closure of the old Lambeth plant and a move to The Vale, Acton into a four-acre site with its newly constructed works and grand office block designed by the architect Robert Thomson. It had a fine foyer suitable for car display that was later to be dubbed 'Piccadilly Circus'. The new shops were far better arranged for motor carriage and business vehicle chassis production, and also provided better facilities for internal combustion engine design, manufacture and test. Here at Acton was the opportunity for Montague Napier to at last realise his greatest ambition: to preside over a well organised precision engineering plant with more modern machinery, while he retained some of the most accurate machine tools from Vine Street works. All was now revitalised with new engine, chassis design and development facilities, and, importantly, a well qualified drawing office team, led by Chief Draughtsman A.J. Rowledge, who had moved with Napier from Lambeth, and who was soon after to be promoted to the position of Acton's Chief Designer.

Almost at once, the somewhat random identification codes for vehicle chassis and parts that had grown up at Vine Street was at an end, as Rowledge had the chance to start out afresh with new D.O. ledgers, and introduce a coded motor unit system, starting from unit number one upwards for all main assemblies. The simple code letters used were: Rear Axle – A, Clutch – C, Engine – E, Frame – F, Gearbox – G, Carburettor – K, Steering Assembly – M, and then, quite inexplicably, Front Axle – Y. (Did this start a fashion?) Each unit code letter was then given a numerical suffix, as for example: The 30hp, 1908, 'T26' six-cylinder Car Rear Axle was then coded 'A3', while a much later heavy four-cylinder 'B74' 4-ton Truck Engine of 1916 was coded 'E39'. On arrival at Acton, a fresh start was also made, numbering in sequence all built-up Vehicle Chassis types, these starting from the number '20' onwards, so that over the next two decades this numbering then reached 'No. 79'. To distinguish between Pleasure Motor Carriage chassis and Business Vehicle chassis numbers within the works, they were given different prefix letters; 'T' for each motor car type and 'B' for each business vehicle. A typical example of the full 1903/4 coding could be seen in 1912, when the six-cylinder 'T43' car chassis was built with an 'E29' engine, an 'A12' rear axle, in an 'F27' chassis frame and had a 'G17' gearbox and clutch combined. About a hundred of this go-anywhere, powerful 'Colonial Tourer – T43' model were built and became popular both at home and abroad. This 'orderliness in production' pleased Montague Napier greatly, and helped maintain a regular supply to S.F. Edge of the varied types of Napier vehicle that he aimed to sell from that time.

A third major advance took place in 1903, as the result of S.F. Edge's insistence that the way forward for high-quality Napier motor carriages was to promote a 'Noiseless Napier', which would then be best powered by a well silenced, six-cylinder engine, giving smooth torque to the roadwheels with less need to frequently change gear in town. By the time M.S. Napier had finally agreed to develop a six-cylinder engine for trial, S.F. Edge had already done some advance publicity to the effect that this new car concept would be a world first for Napier and Great Britain. A.J. Rowledge helped prepare this new design, incorporating six mechanically operated overhead inlet valves giving induction into three pairs of 4in bore and stroke cylinders, turning a longer six throw crankshaft now with 120-degree cranks. This very first production six-cylinder car engine design was allotted type code 'E1', this being mounted on chassis frame 'F1', driven by chains via an 'A1' back axle from a gearbox code 'G1'. This 40hp, 4.95-litre Napier six model 'T20' chassis became the sensation of the 1904 Crystal Palace Motor Show. It was for Edge and Napier not only a 'world first' into production, but also showed the new Napier Motor Works at Acton to be the leading British motor carriage and powerboat engine manufacturer at that time, as now they offered a selection of two, four and six-cylinder engines with a widening range of power outputs. The immediate future for 'Napier Motor Works' was then bright, with Edge's continuous promotions raising the profile of Napier sales. All this new demand for the smooth sixes also required Edge to move to larger premises at 14 New Burlington Street, where he then dealt under the changed company name of 'S.F. Edge Ltd'.

Both men were ready for new challenges at any time, leading them to enter Napier's for many motor sporting events with frequent successes on road, hill and water during their rich time of joint endeavour up until the year 1912. Certainly, their early interest in powered aviation and internal combustion railway traction also dated from 1903, when a bold design for a Napier petrol-engined dirigible balloon appeared, this still survives, but without having been tried out in practice. By contrast, two 85hp Napier engine-powered petrol-electric, fifty-two-seat passenger railcars, Nos 3170/3171 were in fact constructed for the North Eastern Railway Company in 1903. These operated with only moderate success during the years 1904 to 1908, running mainly between Scarborough and Filey

Celebrating the successful introduction in 1904 of the 'T20' Napier six-cylinder chassis at then brand
new Acton Works, powered by the 5-litre Type 'E1' engine.

and on branchlines in the Hartlepool area. This was until each railcar's large, vertical four-
cylinder Napier engine driving a DC generator supplying two 55hp axle-hung motors,
was deemed to have insufficient power in that application. The Napier engines were later
regrettably replaced by two more powerful Wolesley 8½in bore x 10in stroke engines
when these attractive, but heavy, 'Electric Autocars' were next rebuilt. One survives to
this day!

   With the prototype six-cylinder 'E1' engine now proven in the medium sized 'T20' car,
larger and more powerful road and marine engine versions were soon put in hand. This
was achieved through Acton producing many variations in bore and stroke for the Sixes,
as had been done earlier with four-cylinder chassis, which were still under development.
These four-cylinder units were particularly suitable for the less costly range of business
vehicles that Edge still marketed, but now with somewhat less enthusiasm. Although the
car hillclimb entries and that for the Gordon Bennett Cup were to continue annually,
Edge required from Napier still bigger-engined cars, such as the 80hp, four-cylinder 'K5'
of 1903 which he had run in Ireland, its engine now also doubling-up as a strong motor
launch power unit. Napier still provided the bulk of the British team racing cars on
behalf of the Automobile Club but, by now, both Edge and Napier had the vision of an
achievement of far greater significance for Great Britain in mind. This culminated during
1904, on completion of a powerful six-cylinder racing car at Acton, this still known by
the Lambeth based code 'L48'. This fast vehicle, and the world's first six-cylinder racing
car, had a 90hp, 15-litre engine with six cylinders of 6¼in x 5in bore and stroke, fed by

six mechanically driven overhead inlet valves, with exposed rockers in pairs above the heads. Exhaust was via large side poppet valves operated from the camshaft below, this layout formed an early 'L-Head' design of cylinder valve gear. Her shaft-driven chassis was finished that year at the Acton works, it had the usual long sided opening bonnet, this came behind a more set-back front radiator still topped by the now familiar Napier 'water tower' filler cap. Edge and Napier awaited her trials that year along the 'Velvet Strand' beach at Portmarnock, Dublin, over which she was driven by their rising star in competition, Arthur Macdonald, who had progressed from an office boy at Vine Street to be the 'crack test driver'. During these smooth sand trials she proved very fast, with much improved performance over the four-cylinder 'K5', but apparently in need of a more efficient cooling system than the flat fronted radiator provided for 'L48's' engine. Gradually their vision was unfolding, the scene was being set for a Napier land car to challenge the world's fastest, following their record held for Britain, by that London-built first racing motor launch *Napier*.

A new business alliance was being forged between DNS at Acton and Yarrow & Co. Ltd, the military steel boat builders on the Thames at Poplar, which over the next few years helped confirm DNS as the major marine internal combustion engine manufacturer, particularly for fast military boats. This was happening at the same time as DNS were testing their four-cylinder engines in the 'Consuta' composition hull motor launches, built for both racing and as pleasure river craft by Sam Saunders of Goring-on-Thames, but later of East Cowes, Isle of Wight, building his sea-going launches. Already a first Saunders 35ft launch, *Napier Minor*, with a single 80hp 'K5' type engine, had shown its 21 knot speed while winning 'The Kaiser Cup' for Great Britain in 1904. But now a new racing boat, this again to a Linton Hope design, was being built by Yarrow, with a 40ft 'skimming hull' in steel, powered by a pair of 45hp Napier marine-type engines and carrying the name *Napier II*. She failed to take the British International (Harmsworth) Cup in 1904, as her light gauge bow plates had buckled before the final, which was then won by the substituted *Napier Minor* instead. That win was contested by the French on technical rule grounds, their protest being finally upheld, much to Edge's disgust.

But the following year *Napier II* came home the winner of the 1905 International Cup race, in style at 24.3 knots, piloted by the Hon. John Scott-Montagu (see Appendix IVa).

Returning to land in January 1905, the Florida Speed Week held in the USA, at Daytona Beach, Florida, presented Napier and Edge with the ideal opportunity to show the potency of their engineering on four wheels, up against the power of Mercedes and Itala, amongst over 200 entries. With the firm intention of encouraging some record breaking attempts, timing equipment had been installed on the sand-beach course, while S.F. Edge and Arthur Macdonald arrived with the six-cylinder 'L48' racer. The modified engine cooling arrangement had radically altered her style, having a partly streamlined front end in place of the flat radiator core, with level rows of fine coolant pipes, offering a larger surface area to the air, adorning the sides and front of her curved 'bonnet', with large top filler now set to the rear. Napier's redesign immediately looked successful as this darkly painted car, carrying racing number '5' was skilfully test driven, on a poor beach surface, before the timed one-mile runs. But it was Macdonald who returned

Streamlined Napier 'L48 Samson' seen in 1907 at the Brooklands track before competing there. It had briefly held the World Speed Record in 1905 at Daytona Beach.

the fastest time that day, averaging 104.65mph over one mile, a first World Land Speed Record for Great Britain and by a Napier-powered land vehicle! For that drive he, Edge and Napier were also to be awarded the 'Bowden Trophy' that January, for also gaining the Ormond Daytona Kilometre Speed Record. In addition, the magnificent 'Thomas Trophy' was won by Macdonald while driving 'L48', that time for the twenty-mile Auto Championship of the Daytona Speed Week. These fine silver-gilt 'L48' trophies remained with DNS for a century, along with Gold Medals and the gilded winged-wheel 'Hotel Ormond Trophy', that was awarded to Edge the following year in 1906, for the fastest five-mile circuit in Florida.

Back in England the fame of Napier Sixes in several power ratings spread, despite the high cost of each chassis that Napier passed to Edge to sell-on to the aristocracy, politicians and celebrities in Great Britain. That is not to mention the growing export market for the Napier marque to wealthy leaders of Empire in India and the Middle East, where agencies were rapidly established. The first design for the 5-litre Sixes had originated from the old Lambeth Drawing Office during 1903, carrying the old-style type code 'L49', and later the 'L76'; these two then became the Acton production cars type coded 'T20 and T20A'. Some 'T20A' big Sixes were to be assembled in Italy under license and using the 'San Georgio' name. The famed 'T21 and T23' large capacity Six chassis, of which 300 were built between 1905 and 1912, were Acton designed and manufactured, both had simpler side valve engines and used alternating bore and stroke sizes. Napier cylinder proportions were chosen invariably in round figures of inches, the 'T21' having 5in x 4in cylinders that gave it a 7.7-litre capacity, while the cylinders of the 'T23' were longer stroke at 4in x 5in and having just a 6.1-litre capacity.

This 3ft-high 'Thomas Trophy' had been one of the cups awarded to Arthur McDonald when he drove 'L48' at the Daytona Speed Week in 1905.

It may be worth observing here the general point that D. Napier & Son engine designs were always carried out in Imperial Units of inches, from 1898 up until British industrial metrication was introduced during 1972, by which time DNS prime mover engine design was virtually over and Acton works had been closed for four years. This applied equally well to gas turbine and rocket engine designs from the late 1950s, for which all screw threads remained in the American style Unified National Fine and Course inch series. It seems that the only exception to DNS designers' 'British unit' loyalty were the long established tapped Metric threads made to accept world standard sparking plug bodies set in mm sizes. These holes were probably the only dimensions ever given in these 'foreign units', that appeared regularly on DNS cylinder head drawings. But it was their inch, cylinder, bore and stroke sizes that Napier had maintained in isolation throughout the years, so notably differing from other engine manufacturers, most of whom designed their cylinder sizes in millimetres, which gave the cubic capacity directly in cubic centimetres or litres. All the cubic capacities of engines, originally expressed by DNS in cubic inches, have been converted in the appendices at the rear of this volume into litres, after having been calculated afresh from basic data in inches, this for comparison with engines of other manufacturers. The simplified formula used for piston engines was as follows:

Cubic Capacity in litres = 0.01287 x (Bore inches)^2 x Stroke inches x Number of Cylinders.

At DNS the full range of inch scale fractions were often employed in fine detail design, where the 'sixty-fourth' (1/64in. = 0.015 in.) remained commonplace. Also in DNS the 'tenth of a thou an inch' unit (0.0001 in.) was commonly used for stating dimensional upper and lower 'limits of size' on all higher precision detail component drawings.

By 1905, the ever expanding and varied range of pleasure car and business vehicle chassis from Acton Motor Works demanded larger workshops and drawing offices, so that an increase in acreage to 6½ was constructed that year within new buildings, then including a large in-house smithy and foundry. To safely operate an internal low speed test circuit around the tightly packed new works, more land bringing the total to eight acres was bought by 1908, so that less routine road evening-time testing would be needed.

Since moving to the Acton site, Montague Stanley Napier had continued as the head and principal directing force in the family business. But from 29 August 1906 the old established firm D. Napier & Son Ltd was incorporated as a Private Limited Company, Mr Napier taking the whole of the shares and holding the position of sole Governing Director. Soon after, and in order to better balance the existing working agreement and the relationship between them, Selwyn Edge then incorporated his Napier sales agency firm, now known as 'S.F. Edge (1907) Ltd'.

In order to carry out unlimited testing of motor carriages in Britain, Edge had been a leading exponent of the plan to build an off-road motorcourse at least three miles long. This was achieved by Summer 1907 on the private estate of Hugh Locke-King at Weybridge, Surrey, to be known from then on simply as 'Brooklands'. This was conveniently placed for Napier Motors at Acton which were, through Edge's determination, to be the first to set foot on the new concrete high banked track and then sample its fine club atmosphere. This applied also to the Napier works team of testers and drivers who were employed by DNS, but operated at Brooklands under the team management of S.F. Edge himself. The thoughtful, reserved and non-driving M.S. Napier had also been anxious to see this track development, and supported the early races on the fast motorcourse, supplying a variety of stripped down and tuned road cars for Edge's team of budding racing drivers to test and demonstrate in this latest of public places. As usual, being so ready to 'lead from the front', Edge immediately promoted the Napier marque by publicly accepting a 500 guinea wager that he (driving a Napier) could maintain an average speed of 60mph over twenty-four hours on the new Brooklands outer circuit. This spectacle, that has been so often recounted and of which paintings were made, took place before the first competitive race in July 1907, very soon after the official opening in June. This wager was handsomely won by Edge, who drove on his own using a green 'T21 Special' model with six 5in x 5in cylinders giving it a 9.6-litre swept volume, a total of 1,581 miles in the twenty-four hours at a high average speed of 65.9mph. His caring riding mechanic was his personal chauffeur Joe Blackburn, who sustained Edge with bananas and grapes at speed, while two pairs of Acton works car testers followed in two more nearer standard 'T21s'. One of these cars was in red and driven in turn by Frank Newton and Fred Draper, the other was in white and driven by both A.F. Browning and Henry C. Tryon,

Typical racing group at Brooklands in 1908, with Frank Newton having driven a big 'T24' Napier six-cylinder chassis. Beside him is S.F. Edge, Blackburn is third from the right.

all of whom also beat the 60mph speed barrier that day and, in time, held senior company posts so becoming four famous Napierians over the next fifty years. After this great feat of endurance by Edge, comparable for stamina with his earlier bicycle triumphs and his Gordon Bennett victory five years before, it may have been easy to overlook the reliability of these three Napier cars during that great twenty-four-hour achievement. This inherent asset of reliability had certainly come about from their meticulous preparation in Napier's Acton works.

The first official races run at Brooklands were on 6 July, when a Napier team of lightweight cars and their drivers entered for all the main events. This could have seemed almost an anticlimax for DNS, except that six-cylinder Napiers from Acton started, and then went on regularly winning races during those first two seasons. In fact, on that first day of competition H.C. Tryon, driving a racing six-cylinder Napier, won the very first event, which was a heat for the Marcel Renault Plate. The full opposition that day comprised Daimler, Minerva, Mercedes, Darracq and De Dietrich cars, all prepared for racing from Europe, with drivers like Charles Jarrott, Dario Resta, E.M.C. Instone and J.T.C. Moore-Brabazon, all these competing for the large prizes. Edge's Napiers carried off two of the prizes that day; one the ten-mile Byfleet Plate won by Newton after a dead heat with Jarrott driving a large four-cylinder De Dietrich, plus the Marcel Renault Plate final, easily won by Tryon over the eleven-mile distance. Further successes then continued against continental marques such as Fiat and Metallurgique, the eventual 'ace' driver for the Napier works team emerging as Frank Newton of Acton, as Henry Tryon had narrowly escaped with his life one day in January 1908 and then retired from racing. He was attempting that day to break three records: the one hour, the fifty and the hundred-mile using a 60hp 'T21' car, and getting well over the fifty-mile target, but then a second burst rear tyre locked the offside wheel causing the car, still travelling at 80mph, to spin three times and crash off the track over the entrance bridge and right across its roadway. He was thrown clear of the car onto the road sustaining only minor injuries, but greatly shocked, and recovered in a few days. This great Napierian of later years had thus been spared to become the long serving and brilliant Head of DNS Research before and during the Second World War, and also became a changed and a prominent Christian personality, both in and out of the Acton works.

After a further near tragedy between Napier ace Newton and Dario Resta, who was driving his Mercedes at the Easter 1908 meeting, plus two actual fatalities during 1908 (neither driving Napiers), these results soon convinced S.F. Edge that the danger to life for his works drivers, of such 'flat-out' motor racing as practised at Brooklands, far outweighed the initial technical and prestige benefits to manufacturers such as D. Napier & Son Ltd or his own company. Regrettably for M.S. Napier, the now forty-year-old Edge withdrew his works team at the end of that racing season, primarily on safety grounds. He had promoted Napiers as never before, so much so that 1908 saw the construction of an all-Napier-built Grand Prix Team race car, ready to take on the motoring might of Europe and the world. The four cars had a lightened chassis for racing, carrying minimal two-seater bodies, and being powered by the 80hp, six-cylinder 'E12' L-Head, 11.5-litre engines. This impressive piece of power engineering from the hands of Montague Napier and car designer Thomas Barrington, was due to be demonstrated by volunteers from the pool of experienced Acton drivers for that year's Grand Prix in France. On hearing of these powerful 'lightweights' running on Rudge-Whitworth-spoked and centre-locked wheels, the race organisers, the A.C.F, soon took fright, banning the cars with their quick-change wheels. Edge refused to budge, insisting on using the wheels and resisting replacement by the more usual changeable rim wheels. Sadly for British motor sport and DNS, this objection by A.C.F. led to the whole Napier team entry being withdrawn by Edge from that 1908 Grand Prix, which had, by then, taken over the international motor racing role formerly occupied by the Gordon Bennett race up until 1905. The four Napier cars, however, survived all these arguments well, later successfully competing both at sprint meetings and at Brooklands. Many future activities there, during the 1920 & 30s, were to further enhance the reputation of DNS, but by then through some different events.

All this happened while a new bond to marine engineering was being forged, this by Edge, between the London boat builder Alfred Yarrow and Montague Napier, now with a growing range of marine engines, as shown in Appendices 4a, 4b & 4c. But confusingly, the 40ft racing power boat named *Yarrow Napier* had, in fact, been built in Sam Saunders' yard, utilising his trusted Consuta construction hull during 1906, and was powered by a six-cylinder Napier 144bhp marine engine. She was supplied to the order of the, by then, Lord Montagu of Beaulieu, who retained the 1906 Harmsworth International Trophy with her, for Great Britain. The name, which had been applied after her launch, was clearly designed for publicity purposes, and for the eyes of the British public and traditionalist Royal Naval engineers at the Admiralty.

A 66hp Napier Marine Engine of 1908, with its controls, clutch and gearbox.

The DNS marine engine catalogue for 1906 showed the fullest range of petrol fuel units for both cruising and racing boats, all backed-up by the water racing records set by both river and sea cruisers that had been powered by them. These units fell into two distinct classes of engine; lightweight race tuned units for launches and then more durable cast iron crankcase cruiser boat units. The overall power outputs ranged from 35bhp to 72bhp (the K5), the former light racing class having inlet valves operated from overhead for their four cylinders. The latter class gave either 15, 20 or 66bhp from four cylinders, still with atmospheric inlet valves, plus just one larger six-cylinder engine of 150bhp. All were supplied with Napier reversing gear and a clutch to install directly into boat hulls, with a propeller and drive shaft supplied if it was required. Now, at that time, the most notable boat for endurance and reliability was a 45ft, 9-ton motor yacht, built by F. Miller of Lowestoft, and named *Napier Major*. She was fitted with just the standard 20bhp marine motor and was frequently handled by S.F. Edge himself, who won many club events in it, and dozens of trophies for DNS, from his and the boats' performances around the British Isles. By and large, Montague Napier and his family had kept on dry land, and close to the Acton works, but Mrs Napier was once photographed steering a fast cruiser herself out in open water, no doubt encouraged by Selwyn Edge and Miss Dorothy Levitt, the then celebrated Edge-trained lady motor-racing and launch-racing prodigy, who was earlier an employee.

Some of the earliest DNS contracts with the British Admiralty had involved prototype Yarrow-Napier high-speed, steel-hulled Motor Torpedo Boats. One such example was a 60ft steel-hulled MTB built by the Yarrow yard in Poplar in 1905, powered by no less than five Napier engines of 72bhp driving just three screws. The centre engine drove one screw which, after it had been run up, was used to 'drag start' both pairs of similar sized engines coupled to the wing screws, so increasing total power to 360bhp. She was found

Pair of numerous 'T31' Napier taxicabs, ready with London drivers in 1910.

to be capable of 26 knots, the Navy finally buying this fast and manoeuvrable MTB boat which they renamed *Mercury II*, and which they then used for fleet communication duty off Spithead. There she was inspected and tried out by King Edward VII during his Fleet Review. Two others of a similar class, with five motors, were sold by Yarrow to the Austro-Hungarian Navy. Larger petrol engine-driven MTBs were later to be sought by the Navy, in place of the heavier steam engine-driven MTBs of the time. These were then built by Yarrow in 1908, its yard by then sited at Scotstoun on the Clyde. The 90ft prototype, known as '1225', had a beam of 13ft 6in, and was powered by four big Napier designed, but Yarrow built, six-cylinder marine engines of 200bhp, these driving four screws. Although fast, she was never commissioned by the Royal Navy, but some of these Yarrow MTB types were then sold to the Australian and Brazilian Navies.

Meanwhile, back at the motor works, the Napier vehicle chassis variety still grew; it now ranged from a 10hp two-cylinder 'T29' type, on to which were built the big fleet of white-tyred London taxicabs of 1908/9 operated by the Du Cros Company, to the 60hp 'T24 Six' luxury chassis with an 'E5' L-Head engine with upwards of a 9-litre capacity. Upon these were coach built individual bodies for buyers, as Limousines or Sportsmans Grand Tourers. Nearer the middle of the range was the 15hp, four-cylinder 'T28' chassis for in-town lightweight saloon duties, and then the 30hp, six-cylinder 'T36 Noiseless' chassis for finer Landaulette or Drophead Tourer bodies; both these types by now had sturdy side valve engines. By far the largest chassis sales were made for the Edwardian Landaulette bodied, larger variant of London taxicab, that went into service from 1910, providing an 'age of elegance' mode of transport through the Capital on a summer's evening, with its rear hood lowered. Almost 500 of these were built upon the 'T31B' chassis, powered by the rugged four-cylinder 15hp side valve 'E14' engine, which could double for light saloons.

Delightful 15hp, four-cylinder Napier 'T38' Tourer of 1912, as preserved in 1958 by Lord Bruce and shown at the DNS 150th Anniversary car rally in Regents Park.

Nearby West End London stores found 'B34' 8cwt Napier vans like this to be ideal for deliveries.

S.F. Edge had, by 1911, discovered a large market for his 'go-anywhere' convertible car, which was given its high ground clearance to be suitable for off-road country areas and abroad throughout the British Empire. This led to a strengthened four-cylinder 'T38' chassis design known as the 'Napier Colonial' 15hp car, which provided the world with almost a preview of the British Land Rover series forty years later. Given a new found popularity, the 30hp six-cylinder 'T43' chassis was similarly designed and used for either faster road, or off-road use by 1912, it forming the basis for a 'Convertible Colonial' or a Landaulette.

Meanwhile, Napier and Edge, between them, had not neglected the home and overseas markets for strong, reliable four-cylinder business vehicles to augment the high cost, high quality, usual pleasure cars from off the busy production line at Acton. By 1912, the 'B34' 8cwt and 'B52' 1-ton delivery van chassis were in demand, particularly from London's West End, to whose stores and businesses hundreds were supplied before 1914. The close by Borough of Kensington also purchased these chassis, mounted by a low body with covers to permit the emptying of dustbins, so bringing 'style' into their refuse collection fleet.

But then, out of a fall in the demand for these reliable and quieter Napier business vehicles, while their sales were still being handled through Edge's Burlington Street agency, there arose a disagreement between Manufacturer and Distributor, neither of whom had previously interfered in each other's profits or financial affairs to any great extent. But now, in 1912, one was being accused of some lowering of quality in his business vehicle specifications, while the other was now claimed to be over-pricing his vehicle sales, even profiteering, within the market of the day. Their originally cooperative working relationship, based to a large extent on mutual esteem, then quickly soured into one of suspicion within one of the most successful of all motor businesses. After buying-up the shares of S.F. Edge (1907) Ltd, M.S. Napier pressed on to gain the overall control of vehicle design, manufacture and sales within both firms, so successfully that by mid-1913 he was able to launch a new public company, while he retained the old title of 'D. Napier & Son Ltd'. Napier having, in effect, bought-out the S.F. Edge Co. in 1912, share by share, now completely parted company with Edge, who then moved on into new fields before the First World War broke out. Selwyn F. Edge, himself a lifelong teetotaller and sportsman, had in 1901 been the Founder President of the 'Motor Cycle Club' (MCC), Britain's very earliest motoring club of any type. He was later to be honoured, after the traumatic events of 1912, when he was made the President of 'The Society of Motor Manufacturers and Traders' (SMMT) for 1913-1914. It is therefore sad to recount, that in a fine full history of DNS, written in 1921 specially for Montague Napier by a former Vine Street works, Lambeth apprentice, Alfred Marshall, there was no mention, whatsoever, of Selwyn F. Edge made in connection with the DNS Co.!

As a footnote to this chapter, which traced the start of Napier's internal combustion power engineering and its earliest development, most Members of today's 'Napier Power Heritage Trust' wish to pay tribute to the timely inspiration given to the DNS Company through the enterprise of Selwyn F. Edge. His indomitable spirit, great sportsmanship and keen publicity expertise brought to the fore the engineering genius of Montague S. Napier and for fifteen years inspired many who worked under him within DNS.

Two such contrasting characters in business were, almost inevitably, in time to clash, but the result of their turbulent working relationship had established DNS as the leading British car and launch engine manufacturer up until the First World War. 'SF', as he was known to his friends and family, always saw to it that Napiers were the 'Proved Best', through their achievements on road, track and on water, by his hands. Further to that fact, over the next sixty post-Edge years, the DNS Company's ability to take on almost any engineering challenge for the good of Great Britain, with or without guaranteed great financial gain, was generally maintained in a somewhat similar spirit to that which existed up until 1912. This legacy of 'a flare for innovation' and record making, was to prove invaluable for the company well into the 1960s, despite unwelcome rationalisations. It even exists to the present day.

4

ACTON AIR POWER – A GREAT WAR NEED 1914–1924

D. Napier & Son Ltd (DNS) had always had the tradition of producing fresh ideas when prevailing circumstances demanded new products of their precision engineering business. Following M.S. Napier's buy-out of S.F. Edge's Napier marque-based motor carriage and business vehicle marketing company during 1912, Montague Napier had been swift to revitalise his then enlarged company, by incorporating it as a Public Company on 21 July 1913, with a total share capital holding of £650,000. DNS was now briefly to market its vehicles under the name 'The Napier Motor Company', with premises within Edge's former Napier car showrooms at 14 New Burlington Street, London, covering customer enquiries and car demonstration. These were in addition to DNS's offices and the famed Napier Motor Works on The Vale in Acton. The open offer still stood, for all potential and existing customers to visit the motor works by appointment for a conducted tour and, in particular, to watch the high-quality construction of their vehicle chassis in progress. The wide range of chassis and engine capacities that had been offered up to 1912, was soon reduced to just four by 1914 to suit the majority of buyers in the UK and the Empire, rather than cater for all those 'specials' for exceptionally wealthy clients. Even the Napier models supplied before 1911 to our three Edwardian British Prime Ministers, H.H. Asquith, A.J. Balfour and Lloyd George, had not all been true 'top of the range' cars, of the class that had been supplied to the Duke of Marlborough's fleet at Blenheim Palace for his own use and that of the rising young star, Winston Churchill, MP.

The less expensive four-cylinder side valve 15hp chassis 'T45' was still retained, with its 2.75-litre 'E30' engine, some of which were interestingly fitted with new experimental 'piston valves'. That was then further developed into the 'T46/47' chassis, until in 1913 a new 15hp 'E37' side valve engine was introduced for the redesigned 'T53/54/55' chassis variants. Up until the start of the First World War, late in 1914, over 1,000 of these 15hp chassis were built and sold. The popular pleasure car with a four-cylinder 16/22hp engine in the 'T64' chassis was also continued until over 200 had been sold, before being further developed into the model 'T66', these models all had the 3.2-litre 'E44' engine, now with its 'sloping valves'. Representing the Napier six-cylinder models were just two remaining chassis sizes after 1912; the luxury 45hp 'T51' chassis, had a 6.1-litre, 4in bore x 5in stroke, side valve 'E32' engine, but sales of these 11ft 6in long chassis, intended for limousine

Example of a D. Napier & Son Ltd Capital Share certificate from January 1914.

Winston Churchill observing Army Manoeuvres from his six-cylinder 'T44' Napier Tourer from the number at Blenheim Palace, seated alongside Lord Birkenhead in 1915.

or Grand Tourer coachwork slowed, in fact finding only forty customers. Whereas the smaller, less expensive Napier Sixes, which had provided higher comfort everyday transport for the upper middle classes between business and the countryside, continued to find buyers, until the First World War stopped production. These had the 30/35hp 'T44' chassis powered by a 4.1-litre 'E34' side valve engine, 150 examples of which were built and sold. (Appendix IIa lists Napier Pleasure Cars, from 1900 until 'the last' in 1924.)

With growth in the DNS organisation, by 1913 M.S. Napier, then over forty-three years old, was to experience the first sign of his failing health, no doubt due in part to the stress he suffered during litigation in 1912, when separating from his former wonder salesman S.F. Edge. He was now in need of sound support from his two key long-serving men, H.T. Vane, from Edge's sales company, and experienced engineer A.J. Rowledge of DNS, in order to sustain his leadership as the company's only remaining Napier family member and, by now, its 98% shareholding 'Governing Director'. For the overall management, Napier had appointed Henry Tempest Vane (could his second name be a thirty-year premonition of the future Napier 'Sabre'-engined 1943 Hawker 'Tempest V'?) as a new Director of DNS and his acting Deputy Chairman, just in case he was to be indisposed. Both these men were well acquainted with the origins and work of the company along with each other's ways and capabilities. For his talented assistant on all engineering design matters, Napier had appointed Arthur J. Rowledge as Chief Designer, a very wise choice in the event, as soon became apparent. This well-qualified, energetic younger man, having earlier DNS experience from Lambeth works days, had been Chief Draughtsman and Stress Engineer during the whole of the previous, history-making, motor decade at Acton. He complemented precisely Napier's own inherited designing ability, so they were to form a world beating design team over the next decade. Both of these appointments permitted the inherent 'Engineer' in M.S. Napier to actively preside over, and lead, his well ordered precision engineering workshops and experimental and test facilities, these forming fundamental parts of his natural interests, and stemming from the similar example that his father James had set.

The respite was short lived, however, as in the late summer of 1913 Napier Acton's skilled workforce, by now numbering about a thousand engineers, suddenly saw their opportunity to start an all-out strike for better pay and working conditions. The strike committee were not willing to negotiate over matters to any great extent with H.T. Vane, who represented M.S. Napier. The strike lasted a full two months and hit car and van production at a time of growing trade difficulty, due chiefly to competition in the quality car market from overseas and from their main UK rival, Rolls-Royce of Derby. Fortunately, another key DNS player emerged to finalise the negotiations, the firm but patient and highly respected Works Manager Bruce Ball. At the risk of his own job, he finally agreed terms and made a 'settlement' with the strike committee; this was based on his own authority alone and greatly displeased Napier and Vane who, nevertheless, by then had no alternative but to accept terms. But the DNS board of management had, through this dispute, indirectly gained a powerful ally by retaining Works Manager Ball, which was to their eventual benefit. He oversaw the men's return to work that 20 October, basically satisfied over several improvements they had won from DNS. The imposing tall figure of this same gentleman, still the Works Manager, was to be seen in the press with bare head walking alongside H.T. Vane, wearing his top hat, two years later when proudly conducting King George V through Acton works. This was during a morale-boosting wartime visit, to see high volume aircraft production progressing in London inside the Napier 'New Concrete Building'.

That workforce settlement, although it had increased wages and overheads, was to herald a period of relative calm in preparation for DNS at Acton being declared a 'Government Controlled Establishment' and manufacturer, a situation that was to last throughout the First World War that lay ahead.

In a lighter vein, inspection of all DNS Board Meeting minute books, that M.S. Napier personally signed from that time on, will quickly reveal that the new script style company logo, by then displayed on Napier radiators was, in fact, a stylographic copy of Montague's own hand signature. This simple and effective logo – *'Napier'* – from 1912, replaced the much-loved earlier engraved radiator brass header tank lettering 'D. Napier & Son. Engineers, Acton Vale, London W.', this being the chassis builder's name and profession. This had been clearly stated since 1905, as if to further emphasise the strong, century-old general precision engineering tradition of DNS, into which the motor carriage had taken an important, while only temporary, place. The interim plain block capitals logo – 'NAPIER' – in use during Edge's time, had often been applied to London Taxicab radiators, 'Colonial' models, some smaller sixes and also to some of the lighter business vehicles. The heavier types, such as the 4.9-litre 'B59' 2-ton chassis, had large raised plain cast upper-case letters set into their aluminium alloy cast radiator header tanks. Finally, following the end of the First World War in 1918, all Napier car radiators were pressed to a slightly convex curve and finished in nickel plate over brass or copper, with the bold *'Napier'* logo embossed into them and filled black. This attractive logo was placed centrally within the header tank curved face and below that distinctive, and still curiously very tall, 'water tower' filler cap. This same logo was still briefly to be seen in use up to forty years later, and after the Second World War, decorating covers of 'Deltic' marine diesel manuals.

All too soon the First World War started in earnest during 1914, and the DNS management felt the duty to supply the Army with trucks, rather than finish the 500 car chassis that they had planned to build that year. The War Office immediately placed orders for the supply of 200 heavy truck chassis to carry four-ton loads, these based on the 'B65' type and powered by the big 50hp 'E45' engine. A further order for 250 'B62' covered trucks to carry 1½-tons, using the 24hp 3.2-litre 'E37' engine, was also completed in 1914, whereas only 300 of the planned car chassis were manufactured, with those being the last for years.

The works were busier than ever as the 'controlled establishment' order came into effect on 2 August 1915. DNS was by that time producing chassis and bodies for almost 200 ambulances, 100 box vans, plus 400 assorted business vehicles for the armed forces. Some of these were fitted out as mobile field kitchens, machine tool workshops, mobile searchlights and machine gun tenders, plus a wide range of troop and personnel carriers. Nearly 2,000 business vehicles in all were built and supplied from Acton Motor Works throughout the first two years of the war. But a revolutionary form of mechanised warfare was by then being employed over the battlefields of Europe – the armed warplane.

A pair of 3½-ton 'B65' Napier trucks produced in 1914 for the War Department and destined for the British Expeditionary Force.

DNS, having had long and renowned success in developing and producing reliable motor boat and motor land transport engines of the highest quality and performance, became an obvious choice for the War Office to be manufacturers and testers of engines for the Army's newly formed Royal Flying Corps (RFC). This followed a brief flirtation with three 200bhp, V12 aero engines of type 'E53', implemented by Vane during 1914, whereby, following their successful testing, DNS became the target for further wartime aircraft contracts. These were not only for aero engines, but for R.A.F. airframes as well, notably the RE7 and RE8, and even Sopwith 'Snipes'. This, being another diversification in disciplines, called for government investment by providing and rapidly constructing a four floor steel-reinforced building. This had strange rhombus shaped floor areas and big large lift wells, it fronting right on to The Vale roadway. Here, in comparatively quiet and clean surroundings, biplane airframes and wings for the RFC, built to the designs of the Royal Aircraft Factory, Farnborough, could then be safely 'doped' after assembly. Meanwhile, down in Napier works, within the foundry, smithy and machine shops, assorted engine components to power them were being produced to satisfy new aircraft standards for weight, accuracy, and early A.I.D. inspection requirements.

The two military aero engines produced at Acton were the V8 Sunbeam 'Arab' and the V12 RAF 3A, both medium power water cooled types much in demand by the RFC at, and over, the frontlines. Napier and Rowledge had studied available drawings closely and critically, deciding that if these two engines were to be made successfully at Acton, then a partial redesign and a redraw was essential before their DNS works were set in motion. This was how it came about that the RAF 3A engine design drawings were to carry a Napier engine type No.- 'E56' of 1916. This was also why they were finally approved and signed by A.J. Rowledge himself, and also why this engine, that had originated as an RAF design, now carried a bold 'Napier' name cast on to every propeller shaft housing. Similarly, by 1917 the Sunbeam 'Arab' engine-design drawings also carried a DNS-type number – 'E63' – but these still retained the bore and stroke sizes as 120mm x 130mm.

The 1916-built Napier new concrete building in The Vale at Acton's 'controlled establishment' for aircraft construction, this in addition to vehicles and aero engines.

This is now thought to be the only occasion when the Acton works were ever required on a drawing to manufacture and inspect cylinder sizes in metric units, throughout its entire life! During the RAF 3A engine production run of 260, the twelve thin, rolled steel, cylinder water-cooling jackets for each of that engines twelve cylinders, were photographed being welded and water-tight-tested by a row of apron-wearing young ladies sat in a sparsely equipped Acton workshop. At the same time, many of the lightweight components for both engine types were being machined by women operatives employed at Acton works to assist in the war effort. Many, trained by DNS craftsmen, made good, reliable machine operators.

Sub-contract manufacture of other firms' engines, some of doubtful sound design, in the opinions of M.S. Napier and his Chief Designer, was technically a risky business that could 'backfire' badly for the sub-contractor, and through no original failure of their own. These two very experienced designers were soon attracted to another fresh idea for DNS; the company was now heavily involved in routine war work with much labour expended on the supply of business vehicle chassis to the Army and the Red Cross. This service was rendered at the expense of the virtual loss of all private Napier pleasure car manufacture. Now; the fresh challenging idea was to originate a design of their own for a powerful aero engine for RFC use, this in head-on competition with the existing military engine makers of the day, some of whose power units had already been found wanting by Acton's engineers. The year was now 1916, and DNS were about to build 450 'Arab IIs' and complete in full the earlier order for 260 'RAF 3A' engines, when news was broken in August of an experimental DNS engine design in which the space between the 'V' of the usual two-cylinder rows had been filled by a central third-cylinder row. This 'W' cross-section, to be termed as Broad-arrow configuration by some, was at first envisaged as an eighteen-cylinder 'W' engine, of type number 'E59'. But after thirteen long years of experience with whippy and twisting six throw crankshafts behind them, Napier and Rowledge decided instead on a stiff, slab forged four throw crankshaft at the heart of their new design. The experimental twelve-cylinder 'E62' unit that first emerged had 4⅞in diameter bores and a stroke of 5¹/₈in, giving a cubic capacity of just 18.8-litres. On test, the power output and torque from this unit was quickly seen to be insufficient for the purpose, causing an immediate redesign with much increased bore size, now giving the standard 'Triple Four' 23.94-litre swept volume capacity, from twelve 'over-square' cylinders of 5½in diameter bore x 5¹/₈in stroke. This, the most historically important DNS engine design, was allocated type No. 'E64' by the year 1918 lasting not only during that year, for this became the Series II type number of the 'Napier Triple Four' engine – alias the 'Lion'. This innovative power unit was a 48 poppet valve engine, these being operated in three equal banks of four cylinders by three pairs of bevel gear-driven double overhead camshafts. The drives to the DOHC's came from the rear end of the crankshaft, from where three telescopic drive shafts each turned a pair of camshafts above their cylinder head, the one opening two inlets, the other two exhaust valves in each 2-litre cylinder. Reference to the engine cross-sections reveals the same valve gear design that was perpetuated for all 'Lion' variants over the full twelve years of its development, and for the thirty-eight years of its manufacture in the Acton, Park Royal and Liverpool works of DNS. With only a moderate compression ratio of 5.3:1, this compact engine produced initially 450bhp at 2,000rpm, and clearly from the start had great development potential at higher revs and compression ratios. This work the now ailing M.S. Napier was to see through to fruition, but only from his distant viewpoint in France.

After major surgery in 1915 and a partial recovery during 1916, Montague Napier's condition had again worsened during 1917, this while the detail design work for the 'Triple Four' was being completed by Rowledge. So, reluctantly, Napier had to permanently withdraw from the busy Acton design office scene from 1918 and then worked, as best he could with poor health, in the more beneficial (from a health point of view) French town of Cannes. From there he continued to govern DNS in conjunction with the Acting Chairman and DNS Director H.T. Vane in London but, more importantly, now ran his own private design office working in parallel with Acton's D.O. There, from 1919, free from the shackles imposed upon him during the 'controlled' period of the war, and from the constant prompts and demands of S.F. Edge during peacetime before it, Napier was, at last, able to express his own mechanical genius throughout the development period of his great 'Masterpiece' – the 'Lion' aero-engine. That is not to deny Rowledge full credit for all his vital assistance and his real input to this design, born of his drive, mathematical knowledge and meticulous attention to detail.

M.S. Napier's bold design for DOHC valve-gear exposed for his twelve-cylinder 'E62' Triple Four 'W' layout aero engine of 1917.

Rear of the 1918 'E64 Lion Series I' aero engine of 24-litre cubic capacity, with the magnetos and the three bevel gear-driven shafts rising to the cylinder heads.

Both the type testing in an Acton test house, and the flight testing of the 'Triple Four' engine at R.A.F. Farnborough, progressed well. Flying in an Aircraft Manufacturing Co. 'Airco DH9' biplane test bed from 16 February 1918, the 'Lion' made its first flight in DH9, No. C6078, the actual engine being No. 1/13080/WD23259. Being winter, it was flown fitted with hot air pipes and winter carburettor muffs, until moving to Martlesham Heath aerodrome, by then fitted with an enlarged radiator. By the time the Armistice had been signed on 11 November, some operational aircraft of the newly constituted Royal Air Force had been fitted with these more powerful E64 'Napier Aeromotors', as they were to become known at Acton for several years, particularly when used by civil airline operators. It was only as news of the power and reliability of this compact and advanced twelve-cylinder 'W' layout engine quickly spread through the RAF, that their pilots and Air Staff adopted the emotive name 'Lion' for the new power unit from 1920 onwards. Could that name have been coined from its more aggressive power in the air with the exhaust's low growl, via twenty-four exhaust valves exiting into three exhaust manifolds, these opening out to four stubs for each cylinder bank? Or, perhaps, to pilots in their single-engine aircraft cockpits the high centre cylinder bank's rounded DOHC cover and stub exhausts could, at times, resemble the 'long hairy mane' of a lion's head and shoulders, as it dominated their forward view? This adverse feature of the engine's installation was found to be partly offset by the very low position of the two side cylinder banks, each set wide at 60 degrees to the vertical, so giving 120 degrees between them. As was to be discovered later, in some of the closely faired fighter and Schneider floatplane engine installations, the recessed side channels so formed, permitted better forward vision when the pilot leaned over to one side of his cockpit. This, no doubt, was much easier said than done, particularly while at speed in the air and when banking!

DNS had served their country well during the 1914-18 war, with supplies of aircraft, a mixed bag of Acton's improved aero engines, heavy transport for the Army and a wide variety of purpose-built tenders, troop carriers and reliable tough chassis for ambulances.

Apart from many Staff cars built upon the well proven 'B70' Extra Strong 'Colonial' chassis, driven by a rugged 20hp four-cylinder side valve 'E50' engine via a four-speed 'G31' gearbox, fewer than 200 pleasure car chassis were built between 1915 and 1919.

At about that time there was the suggestion that the company was to change the main thrust of its productivity to that of precision built, higher performance engines for the growing military and civil aircraft markets. Napier, Vane and Rowledge had all been more than willing to explore these more specialised, high value, prime-mover products, and so move away from the traditional DNS general precision engineering type of business during the hostilities. But now in peacetime again, the choices were more 'open' and their personal tastes could now be gratified, as long as these converged to give a unified way forward. Henry T. Vane, from his background with Edge, much preferred the Napier road vehicle type of business that had been a great success for DNS over one and a half decades. Montague S Napier, observing the stronger competition then affecting the quality car market, and also the lowering of prices in the popular car trade, through its widespread use of mass production techniques, wished to enter the growing, higher precision aero-engine field. Arthur J. Rowledge, purely as a design engineer, could tackle either type of product with equal ease and enthusiasm, which, in fact, he did until 1921. That year, after a technical dispute, he left Acton for the Derby works of Rolls-Royce, becoming a highly successful designer there.

The DNS Board, including Napier, Vane, Cooke and White, could not accept Napier's view that car production would be uneconomical in the climate of the day, and that a shift to aero engines should be made instead. This aim was particularly close to Napier's heart, with his triple four designed, its prototypes built and tested, and already an interest shown from the RAF and civil firms. Vane, plus his other two fellow directors, voted for DNS to continue in their known road vehicle business, leaving the ailing Napier to consider his more isolated position as their wealthy Governing Director. After a short interval, Vane and Rowledge were again summoned to Cannes for a planning meeting in January 1919, when Napier announced his decision to steadily pull out of the car-making trade before, as he said: 'It will be the motor-car trade giving us up'.

On designing a new Napier car model for 1921, he wrote to the Board:

> In order to produce a good design we need to bring all the best brains to focus upon it, which would mean our neglecting aero engine work, which I consider to be far more important.

His new great enthusiasm for 'Air Power' had now to be matched by his willingness to 'risk' personal capital, in order to fund his production of 300 'Lion' engines at Acton, while from these he would receive large royalties at the point of sale. To satisfy the other directors' views, Napier somewhat reluctantly agreed in January 1919 that Rowledge's existing design for the new 40/50hp 'T75' car chassis, could have just six prototypes built for evaluation, as long as these did not slow the manufacture of the batch of his 'Lions'. Naturally, neither of these new products had any firm buyers at that point in time.

This classic 'T75' chassis had a large curved radiator core now set deep into a more rounded radiator surround – every bit as imposing as a Bentley – standing up in front of its new S.O.H.C. tall polished aluminium alloy engine and raked steering wheel column. Otherwise, the chassis looked almost conventional, as Rowledge had relied mainly upon the good riding and stability of its 'T71A' predecessor's frame and suspension, retaining half elliptical front axle springs, while introducing strong cantilever springing at the rear. The live back axle was now driven through a new bevel gear differential in place of the former's robust, higher frictional loss, worm gear back axle. By far the strongest point in favour of Rowledge's chassis design which, eventually, turned out to be the very last Napier car chassis, was the completely new type 'E52' engine. This 'shining beauty', unmistakably related through their common designer to the aero 'Lion' from the same period at Acton, had an all-aluminium alloy head, crankcase, and cylinder block, which housed the six cylinders within steel liners of 4in diameter bore. Fitted with aluminium pistons with a 5in stroke, these modest proportions gave it a swept volume of 6.18 litres which produced a power output of 85bhp at 2,500rpm. Also in common with the 'Lion', was its use of light tubular connecting rods, which undoubtedly had saved weight in the aero-engine, but were purely a novelty in such a big car engine application. An overdue and welcome change was the entirely overhead operated valve gear, driven off a bevel wheel from the front of the crankshaft, via a tall drive shaft and bevel gears onto the long single

Napier 'T75' chassis of 1920, clearly showing the front SOHC drive to the overhead valves of the 6.2-litre 'E62' engine and the rear-only brakes.

overhead camshaft. From this its twelve cams drove downwards, close to the valve stem contact end of the six inlet and six exhaust patent 'Napier swinging tappets', which were pivoted at the opposite ends. It had the added luxury of aero engine-style dual ignition, the two parallel, or individual, systems were by a magneto and a battery fed ignition coil. Carburation was provided by the Acton developed, single Napier-SU, dashpot and needle carburettor with choke control. The deep 'T75' chassis was strongly built and supplied on Rudge-Whitworth centre lock wheels, giving it a low unsprung weight, but was still not fitted with front wheel brake drums as standard. These were supplied for later models of the 'T75' with power assistance if required, by 1923, when the braking performance of many cars was improving, with most of DNS's rivals setting the pace. Till then, a Napier had only rear axle drum brakes plus the Napier long-favoured and powerful transmission shaft brake, but that again gave its braking action to the same rear wheels. It appears that weight transference forward on reduction of speed was, then, not too well appreciated at Acton in the design of their vehicles, quite unlike some other makers. This final range of chassis could be supplied with frames of various length, depending on the type and size of coachwork customers preferred. The standard 'T75' had a wheel base of 11ft 5ins, but when it was enlarged to 12ft, the chassis number was changed to type 'T79'. Most bodies, from a wide range of styles, were built onto 'T75' chassis at the nearby Cunard Motor Carriage Company, in which DNS had a controlling interest at that time. Body designs for this, the Napier 'Swan-song', ranged from a Limousine-Landaulette, to a Cabriolet, to a Sedanca de Ville, or a Sedan, all these for those formal chauffeur-driven occasions. Alternative styles ranged from a Touring body, to a Coupe, to a Torpedo, or a three-seater Clover Leaf, these being more attractive for those with an open air life-style. Sadly, these elegant variants, with their highly priced chassis, were not attracting too many customers by 1924, when Napier agreed to halt chassis production at Acton. He had initially sanctioned 500 chassis to be built, in fact, less than 200 were completed up to 1924, after which time the hitherto lucrative Napier motor carriage business was deemed to be almost 'dead' on the worldwide, high-quality car market.

Outside No.10 Downing Street, three Cunard-bodied 'T75' Napiers await their VIP passengers.

Montague Napier's own silvered 'Clover Leaf Coupe' always made a splendid sight as he was being chauffeured around London, with a Silver Lion radiator mascot emblem mounted above the tall filler cap.

An endearing 'T75' feature resulted from the intuitive action taken by Henry Tryon, who by 1920 had risen from tester and race driver to Senior Development Engineer at Acton. A 'drumming vibration' was experienced by chauffeurs at a certain engine speed; this was clearly due to a periodic torsional vibration in the six throw crankshaft, and was felt at the engines back end. This was similar to that met with in some much earlier sixes, and which S.F. Edge had confidently described as being a 'Power Rattle'! Now in 1921, Tryon took matters into his own hands, and specified 'A concave crown piston, giving a lower compression, to be fitted to number 6 cylinder'. As he predicted, this stopped that vibration, and without significantly losing power on the road! So it now appears that both engine and chassis were somewhat 'flawed' in those majestic 'T75/79' models, while this supports still further Napier's unpopular decision to concentrate instead all the resources of his company into his aero-engines. Rowledge, offended by these disclosures was soon to leave DNS at Acton for Derby, taking along with him to Rolls-Royce design experience in both these areas. That left Montague Napier carrying full responsibility for developing the 'Lion' engine himself until he was, eventually, to be ably supported long term by a newly appointed DNS Chief Designer, Captain George Wilkinson.

Right from the word go, in 1919, while flight trials of the 'Lion' series II continued at Farnborough and Martlesham, the engine was also strenuously put through its paces by the aeronautical sporting world. The first post-war 1919 Aerial Derby, flown from RAF Hendon, was keenly contested and won by Captain G.W. Gathergood in a hastily prepared Airco DH4R racer installed experimentally with a 'Lion I', the plane averaged 129.3mph over the 189-mile-long course. Such an installation was perfected soon after in his DH9R biplane, when he flew another 'Lion' over Napier Acton works, while his navigator took the famous aerial photograph of the works, seen in 1919. Another notable record that had been made the previous year, on 2 January 1918 from Martlesham, this just fifty-six minutes from take-off of a DH9, was a then World Altitude Record of 30,500ft. Its two RAF test pilots, Captain Andrew Lang and his observer Lieutenant Blowes, both using oxygen, had taken off in that very first Airco DH9, powered by a normally aspirated 'Lion I' engine, with a take-off rating of just 450bhp. As the result of flight testing, this type was then to be developed as the services RAF Airco DH9A, fighter two-seater. We should note that a similar routine test Napier rocket engine altitude record was to be made, this some forty years later.

Clearly the excellent performance and reliability of the 'E64' engine was then thought exceptional, so much so that the civil airline operators became immediately interested in 'trying the Lion' in their single- and twin-engine passenger aircraft. Instone Airlines Ltd and Air Transport and Travel Ltd were two firms, which between them had pioneered regular flights from London Croydon to Paris, Brussels, Berlin and Amsterdam, using a variety of aircraft and engine combinations. Some of these highly successful pairings powered by the 'Lion II' were the DH16, DH18A, DH23 and DH25, all flying by 1921 on internal and European journeys. Other aircraft, such as the advanced Vickers 'Vulcan' ('Flying Pig')

A 450bhp 'Lion II'-powered De Havilland 18A passenger aircraft of Instone Airline Ltd undergoing engine runs at Croydon aerodrome in 1922.

and Twin 'Vimy Commercial', the Bristol Type 62 'Ten-Seater' and the Westland 'Limousine III' all used early 450bhp 'Lions' from 1920. At the same period, some twin-engined large Handley Page W8, O400 and W10 airliners were either built or re-engined with 'Lions', these culminated in the experimental HP 'V1500' four 'Lion'-engined airliner, also in 1920. The biggest 'Lion II' project of all was the six-engined prototype of the Tarrant 'Tabor' transport/bomber aircraft for the Air Ministry. This giant triplane, built at Farnborough, crashed due to either instability or a controls failure, on take-off for its maiden flight in 1922, killing the two crew members in its nose, while some ministry officials and others on board survived.

The merger of ATTL and IAL forming Britain's 'Imperial Airways Ltd' in 1923 meant that airline services were soon to intensify out of Croydon Aerodrome. One contemporary reference by them stated: 'Imperial Airways Ltd – the only British Air Service to and from the Continent'. Of that service in 1924, using 'Lion'-powered DH 34s, another reported – 'The DH 34 airliner has for a long time enjoyed an excellent reputation for reliable service. Machines of this type have been flown five hours a day for months on end over our European routes. Fitted with the 450bhp Napier 'Lion' engine, it has shown a remarkable degree of efficiency in the manner in which it has maintained schedule time.' (Refer to Appendix Va for more details of these aircraft.)

From 1921 the RAF took delivery of 'Lion II' engines for its big twin-engined heavy Vickers 'Vernon' transports and even heavier 'Virginia' bombers, the latter to remain 'standard' machines up to almost the Second World War. These large RAF biplanes that saw long service at home and overseas appeared partly owing to the outcome of a strange failed experiment made by the Air Ministry starting in 1920 when they wanted a single large engine for their heavy bombers. DNS was awarded a contract for this,

The large-winged RAF Vickers Virginia bomber with twin 'Lion VAs' in 1928.

By 1920 this big 'X' layout sixteen-cylinder 'E66 Cub' of 1,050bhp had been developed for new single-engined RAF bombers.

the world's first 1,000bhp aero-engine, that M.S. Napier then misleadingly named the lion's 'Cub'. This sixteen-cylinder four-row engine with a huge 60-litre capacity, design type 'E66' of 1920, had 6¼in diameter pistons with a 7½in stroke. The sixteen cylinders were in the configuration of a 'squashed X', with top and bottom including angles of 52½ degrees and 127½ degrees respectively, leading to a right angle at each side of this water cooled, quadruple SOHC 64 valve engine, which once again had four valves per cylinder. The expected performance was soon forthcoming during 1920, when a full 1,055bhp was indicated at 1,900rpm on testing the first prototype, with flight trials following in the big Blackburn 'Cubaroo' single-engine bomber. DNS built six engines for evaluation, before 'the penny dropped' at the Air Ministry in 1925, when the whole idea was abandoned in favour of developing some safer, mainly multi-engine heavy bombers for the RAF. This big 'Cub' was briefly resurrected by Napier and DNS in 1926, as design type 'E73' before its end. For its final 1,000bhp demonstration at the Hendon Show, powering a sturdy Avro 'Aldershot', a reporter was heard to say, and then publish, that the great power of the 'Cub' seemed to 'throw its aircraft about the sky'.

The originally laid down 300 'Lions' had been rapidly taken-up by military and civil operators alike, so that Acton works then found the constant demand for this new engine hard to satisfy. In total, 130 distinct aircraft types worldwide had the 'Lion' engine specified as their power unit, this over the fifteen-year period since the prototype ran during 1917. Its development under Napier and Wilkinson was rapid and purposeful, so much so that the power output from the 24-litre engine was trebled in ten years to 1,350bhp. That story is told in the next chapter from 1925 onwards, development being continuously spurred on by the demands of two great British racing aircraft constructors, namely Gloster Aircraft Company and Supermarine Aviation Works Ltd, who were both consistent British contenders for the international Schneider Trophy floatplane air races between 1919 and 1931. In the meanwhile, the 'Lion' power unit was in demand from 1920 for air races in the UK, such as the Kings Cup race and the Aerial Derby, which was won twice more, by Gloster 'Bamel' racers, with specially tuned, higher compression 'Lion' engines in 1921 and 1923. Perhaps of greater significance was the victory for Great Britain in 1922 in the Schneider Trophy race held in Naples, when Captain Henri Baird flew a 'Lion II'-engined Supermarine *Sealion II* pusher-propelled biplane flying boat, giving to Britain our first Schneider Trophy win at 145.6mph. The team behind this triumph was led by the then Supermarine boss Hubert Scott-Paine, whose young flying boat designer was a Reginald Mitchell who was supplied with a 'well tweaked' Napier 'Lion II' by Acton's George Wilkinson. Success like this breeds strong friendships: these two engineers then continued their teamwork for future races; they scored a third place with *Sealion III* at 151.6mph in the 1923 Schneider race run-off at Cowes. In this race they followed home two Curtiss CR-3's from the USA powered by V12 Curtiss D-12 engines, that being a well-known model to Napier.

This Gloster 'Mars I' of 1921 was a highly successful racing biplane, equipped with a well-tuned 'E64 Lion II' power unit.

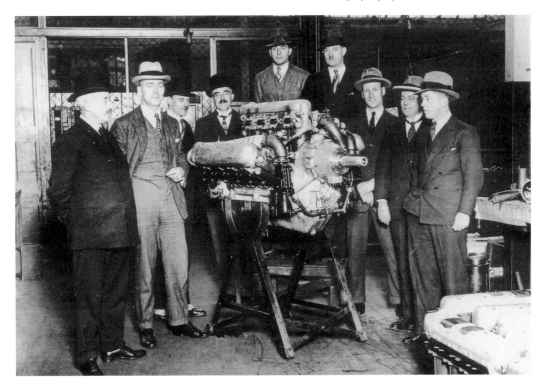

An Acton photograph of 1922 showing a 'Lion' engine ready for its Schneider Cup-winning Supermarine *Sealion II* amphibian. Viewed from the left: second is Hubert Scott-Paine, fourth is Henry Vane, seventh is Reginald Mitchell and eighth George Wilkinson.

The second British contender Gloster had the experienced Henry Folland as the Chief Designer, who had already relied on Napier powering his 'Lion-hearted Mars' racing biplane aircraft. Now, in 1925, using the earliest 700bhp 'Racing Lion VII', this 'E74' direct drive engine supplied by DNS via Napier and Wilkinson was earmarked for Folland's biplane 'Gloster-Napier IIIA'. She was then flown by Captain Hubert Broad into second place in Baltimore USA at 199.2mph behind the winning Curtiss RC3-2, but also well ahead of the Italian Macchi M-33, whose team were to have their greatest successes during 1926.

From 1922, more powerful military versions of the 'Lion' were being developed by DNS for the RAF. These were also being sold crated-up in batches overseas, or in British designed fast fighter planes sold to foreign air forces. The Vickers 'Vixen I' fighter of 1923 was originally intended for the RAF, or for the Fleet Air Arm in a 'Vixen I' float plane version, both powered by a 'Lion VA' of 550bhp at 2,350rpm. This 'E75' Series VA engine had its compression ratio raised to 5.8:1 and was fitted with forged H-section master and slave connecting rods, while separate starboard single and port duplex Napier Claudel-Hobson carburettors still remained at the front drive end, close to the air intake. In the event, some overseas air forces, such as those of Chile and Portugal, were mainly to benefit from the fast Vixen fighter while, apart from six 'Vixen II's' in 1924, the RAF still remained loyal to their air-cooled rotary and radial-engined fighters.

The 'Lion VA' appeared again and again in several of the advanced, all-metal constructed, fast fighters of the mid-twenties, but these sleek, water-cooled machines were not adopted. These were; the Avro 'Avenger', the Gloster 'Gorcock' and the Vickers-Napier 'Vivid', all airworthy by 1925 but ignored, other than for test at Martlesham. But events of the next few years, in the hands of the RAF High Speed Flights were to change RAF reliance on radial power.

Meanwhile, flying out to sea, the Royal Navy had once again found the powerful products of DNS to be reliable and desirable for the dangerous task of torpedo bombing. Blackburn Aircraft and the Fairey Aviation Company had both built specialised carrier borne, single 'Lion'-engine aircraft for the FAA from 1920, and in good numbers too for the financial profit of DNS, and M.S. Napier in particular. Fairey 'Pintail' and 'III D' floatplanes of 1921 were the first over the sea, these two being steam-catapult launched from the earliest naval aircraft carriers, for defence and reconnaissance. The torpedo bomber role was left to the Blackburn-Napier combination for its early success, with such blunt nosed aircraft as Blackburn's Lion II-powered 'Swift' of 1920 and their 'Dart' of 1922. Both these, and 'Lion'-engined 'Blackburn Trainers', saw long service until being replaced in 1929 by a further Napier-powered torpedo bomber, the much sleeker Blackburn 'Ripon'.

The Napier 'Lion' aero engine had, by 1924, become so deeply entrenched in the international aircraft market that Heinkel and Dornier of Germany, Fokker of Holland and Mitsubishi of Japan had all become regular customers at Acton. Also, in the home market, DNS's main rival in-line aero-engine builder, Rolls-Royce in Derby, were now definitely 'feeling the pinch'. Montague Napier's switch to specialise in airborne power units had certainly proved to be a winning formula, leaving high-quality car building to 'them up the road' in Derby, plus several others on the continent of Europe and the USA. DNS Company profits had peaked in the year 1924-25 at almost a quarter of a million pounds, permitting some raised dividends for shareholders, but Napier also saw this as providing cash for investment in government Gilt Edge stocks, which DNS 'put away against a rainy day'. Such a 'rainy day' was eventually to arrive during the depression of the 1930s, just a year or two after Montague Napier's unexpected and untimely death early in 1931.

In 1924, Napier, and also Wilkinson, became interested in an alternative power unit to the all-conquering 'Lion'. This centred on no ordinary 'V' engine, but on an air-cooled, inverted in-line, turbocharged 'V' engine of moderate capacity and power to challenge existing radial engines. A start was made with design type 'E77', having eight cylinders of 5in bore and 4¾in stroke to produce up to 350bhp. Napier persisted with these inverted 'V' engines up to 1926, by increasing the number of cylinders to twelve in two new turbo-blown designs 'E80/81'. But all these were to no avail, as by then the Air Ministry admired the American water-cooled Curtiss D-12 so much that a contract for a similar V12 engine development was offered to Rolls-Royce, with Rowledge firmly set in their design team.

'Lion' type engine development at Acton now took three main routes during the mid-1920s, all focusing on using the basic Napier 'Triple Four' design, for new aircraft. In taking the first route, that being to improve pilot forward vision, the W12 'Lion' was inverted, which gave it, in effect, the 'M' configuration of engine type 'E68' of 1923. This type became known as the 'Lioness' engine, which, after several modifications to its carburetion system, produced a similar output to its 'male' counterpart. Although clearly improvement to pilot vision resulted (from his peering over its now dry sump), its inferior lubrication and some reduced reliability meant applications were few for these 1925 'E71 Lioness' versions, which were then further developed as Turbo-blown test engines.

Pursuing the second route, it was thought that the inevitable loss in power due to the rarefied air at higher altitudes could be dealt with by applying Turbo-supercharging. In order to remove an engine-driven compressor drive-shaft power loss 'penalty', inherent in mechanically blown supercharging, this was replaced by turbine-driven power instead, which was gained from heat energy wasted in the hot exhaust gases. From the start, this development programme was hampered by restrictions imposed by the effects of high

Turbo-blown 'E75 Lion VS' of 1925, showing its low-slung integral blower with upper charge-cooling units leading to three induction manifolds.

temperature on the then known steels that were strong enough for hot turbine impellers. These turbine wheels were prone to frequently break up on test and in flight, so reducing the engine to one of 'normal aspiration' only and now with choked induction passages, if not actual engine damage and loss. The early engine turbo-blower installations tried were bulky, and soon were to include inter-cooler heat exchangers as well, which all ended up being detrimental to the size of the engine's frontal area. The power output of these turbo-blown engines at 30,000ft was shown, through repeated tests at the Royal Aircraft Establishment in Farnborough, to be equivalent to a normally aspirated one flown at much lower altitude. The E79 'Lion VS' was the last of the type to be built, it was flight-tested in 1925 at Farnborough, by which time its carrying DH9A aircraft's ceiling had been progressively raised to 32,000ft. With the 'Lion' engine revs limited to 2,100rpm under 13.7lb/sq.in boost, the exhaust turbine and its centrifugal compressor were then turning at 30,000rpm. The high failure rate in these one-piece turbines, and their closely supporting and overheated single row ball-bearings brought an end to these experimental 'blown' engine tests in 1926. By that time mechanical drive superchargers were being seriously considered at Acton in connection with both standard Series VIII engines and, more especially, for future high-powered racing versions. Two additional flying test beds for the turbo-blown engines had been a Gloster 'Guan' and Fairey 'Fawn', the latter having been 'Lion VA'-powered in regular service, so making test installations easier. The 'E76' Racing Lion design of 1925 was a high-revving direct-drive engine with a redesigned lightweight valve gear; and was not fitted with hand-starting gear. It was the sole representative out of six DNS racing engine types to be turbo-blown as designed.

5

A LION'S SHARE OF WORLD RECORDS: 1925–1932

The 'Racing Lion' Series VII engines had been the subject of the third route taken by DNS engine development during the 1920s, and were starting to perform well by 1925. For these, a more radical redesign of the 'Lion VA' had been needed in order to reduce the engine frontal area and weight, while at the same time greatly increasing its power output. George Wilkinson, with this task in Acton's Design Office, meanwhile maintained full communication with Montague Napier working from Cannes. Their very bold move in order to achieve a reduced external size was to cut down the length of the Lion's twelve connecting rods by exactly one inch! That move eventually proved to be the correct one, both in its objective and in the amount, so reducing the overall height of each 'Lion' cylinder bank by about 1½ins. Both bore and stroke remained constant during this redesign, so leaving the engine cubic capacity untouched at 24 litres and its well-tried crankshaft and main bearings almost unaltered. With increased engine rpm, and 'angularity' of the side slave-rods, the shortened conrods were upgraded in material strength for delivering over twice the power. Similarly, the reliable three sets of DOHC valve gear were refined and strengthened for 50% higher running speed, using new higher lift cam profiles with more closely fitting, plain and flush camshaft covers over them. The triple up-draught carburettors were re-positioned at the rear of the engine, while a higher performance pair of Watford magnetos and their distributors were placed forward and low down at both sides of the propeller shaft casing. This had been extended forward in the direct drive units that drove metal Fairey-Reed propellers, as they were necessarily longer in the geared engines that now had double reduction gears. The unit weight savings so achieved were, in fact, negligible in 1927, when compared with the initial 900lb 'Lion' design of ten years earlier. But when comparing the 450bhp output of a reduction gear fitted 'E64' Series II engine having a high weight/power ratio of 2.0 lb /bhp, with that of a geared racing 'E90' Series VIIB, which by 1927 had a 1.06 lb /bhp ratio, the extent of DNS power development becomes apparent. The eventual lowest peak of the 'Lion' engine's weight/power ratio was to be reached in 1929, by the then supercharged 'E91 Series VIID' racing engine, a unit which by necessity weighed 240lb more, but in delivering its high 1,360bhp output had the very low 0.86lb /bhp weight/power ratio for that time.

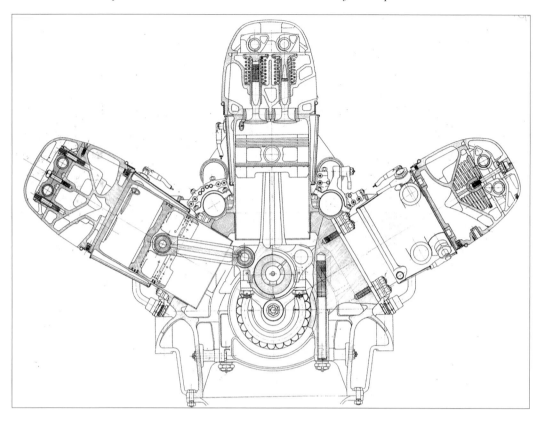

Cross-section of the 1927 Series VII 'Racing Lion' engines, embodying 1in-shorter connecting rods and higher compression heads.

A.V. Roe 'Avenger I' fast fighter Type 566 of 1927, with a partly faired 580bhp direct drive 'Lion VIII', giving it an air speed in excess of 200mph

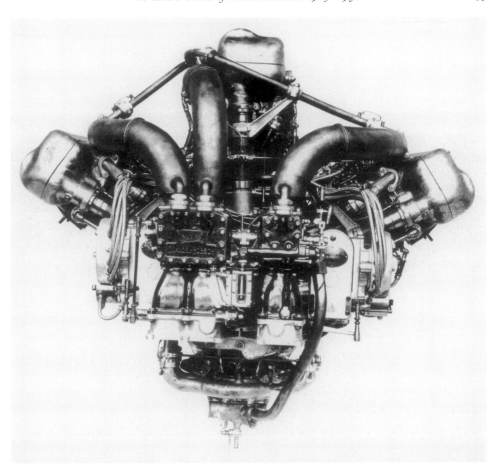

Rear end layout of the standard build 'Lion VIII' of 1926, showing the revised grouping of the three carburettors and two magnetos.

Returning to the earlier, normally aspirated standard 'Lion' engines of Series VIII onwards, a similar redesign of the carburettor positions took place under Wilkinson as they had done earlier in his Series VII racing engines, this time by placing both a duplex and a single carburettor unit at the rear end of the engine. But, in these aero engines, to Series XV, the dual magnetos and distributors remained at the rear, beside the three carburettors. In 1928, an 'E83' Lion VIII, with a 6.25:1 compression ratio and direct drive, powered an A.V. Roe & Co. 'Avenger' all-metal fighter plane to win the long circuit Kings Cup Air Race, at an average speed of 161mph. By contrast, this followed the use of two 'Lions' installed in a re-engined Dornier 'Wal' flying boat, in which Commandante Franco made the first air crossing of the South Atlantic Ocean in 1926, from Madrid to Buenos Aires.

British-built flying boats were popular 'from the word go', constructed on shore usually as amphibians by Vickers at Brooklands and Supermarines at Hamble, both companies relying on the pusher propeller fitted 'Lion II' engine. In 1920, a Vickers 'Viking III' won the Air Ministry Amphibian Competition held at Martlesham Heath and Felixstowe, where its pilot Captain S. Cockerell carried off the first prize of £10,000.

This win was followed by its purchase by the Air Council, who carried out flight trials on the river Thames, when Captain Cockerell taxied it ashore at the House of Commons early in 1921!

Napier was obviously pleased and surprised to learn of this free publicity in high places for his 'Lion' engine, which continued to power most variants of these aircraft, several of which with 'Lion' power were then exported to the Canadian forces. Supermarine on the Solent, not to be outdone, had R.J. Mitchell design the fine 'Sealion' series of single Lion engine flying boats with pusher propellers; these boats were soon entered in full racing trim and colours for the Schneider Trophy races of 1922/23. The win for Great Britain in 1922, referred to earlier, fully vindicated the airframe and its designer, as well as the versatility of the Napier 'Lion II' in pusher installations, high up underneath the upper mainplane.

A twin-engined endurance record was achieved by Lion-powered British Supermarine 'Southampton' flying boats for the RAF, when flying from the coastal stations both at Felixstowe and Calshot.

DNS publicity continued to report records and special achievements made by their own engines as in the days of S.F. Edge, and long after his sudden removal from the company scene back in 1912. The following extract, from a 1928 advertisement, illustrates this: 'The greatest formation flight ever carried out was made with four Supermarine-Napier 'Southampton' flying boats, each fitted with two Napier engines. The machines flew from England to Australia and back to Singapore, covering 180,800 engine miles without mechanical trouble'. This RAF aircraft, with a crew of five, became a reliability legend in its own time, and lasted in service around the world until 1937. Its 'Lion' power units were versions of the 'E70' Series VA of 525bhp, with that type remaining installed throughout the life of the airframe, which in later versions was entirely aluminium alloy,

An RAF/ RNAS Fairey 'IIIF' biplane, powered by a fully faired 'Lion XIA'.

in place of the earlier type's wooden hulls. These big aircraft travelled widely and could be found 'flying the flag' near water, from which it would be beached on a mobile chassis.

By far the most profitable Air Ministry contract of the later 1920s was shared between DNS and Sir Richard Fairey's nearby Fairey Aviation Ltd at Harmondsworth Airfield. Following on from the 200 Lion-engined Fairey IIIDs of 1920 onwards, a more versatile development had come by 1927, with seating for three aircrew and powered by the now rearranged 'E92', 'Lion XIA' engine, which delivered 560bhp at 2,350rpm. The maiden flight of the prototype took place from Northolt on 19 March 1926 when, after successful flight testing, it was flown to Hamble for conversion to a floatplane, to be then further tested on the Hamble River. From later that year, these aircraft were being delivered either as floatplanes to the FAA and RAF, or as landplanes for light bomber duties, mainly to the RAF. By 1930, some 600 Fairey IIIFs were in service and were to continue on in their various roles until 1940. Their record achievements, during that time of relative peace, were made chiefly during 'flag flying excursions' throughout the British Empire, all stemming from trouble-free completion of long RAF reliability formation flights.

Supermarine's Chief Designer, Reg Mitchell, working at Hamble, was thus already well acquainted with Napier engine reliability, as well as the Racing Lion developments going ahead at Acton. These were still being led there by Mitchell's friend and associate of Napier's, George Wilkinson, who was now his 'opposite number' at DNS Acton. He had started in 1912 under Rowledge then served with the RFC during the war, gaining the rank of Captain, before returning to DNS in 1921 to replace A.J. Rowledge as Chief Designer in charge of the then small DNS design team. Wilkinson had, so it now appears, the ideal placid personality to work in tandem with the brilliant and demanding, but also isolated, Montague Napier. By Wilkinson regularly travelling by air to and from Cannes, and the private design office there, he was able to gain the necessary inspiration to transform fresh ideas into reality on return to Acton, working alongside his able staff in the main D.O. The DNS Company Chairman H.T. Vane went along with this arrangement for the next ten years, Wilkinson reporting to him at Acton, while he coordinated most of the 'Lion' development testing along with H.C. Tryon, in addition to new design work.

Down at Hamble, Mitchell's bold Schneider Trophy floatplane design for the 1925 race was revolutionary in the extreme, but gave a clear indication of his thinking on the subject of high-speed flight for the future. This beautiful cantilever monoplane aircraft, the Supermarine 'S4' floatplane, was of all-wood construction, but without any visible stays to the wings or to the tall struts reaching up from the two floats. Its 'Racing Lion' Series VII, short duration 'E74' engine gave 700bhp at 3,250rpm, being cooled by under-wing Lamblin radiators, while it was closely faired-in to the wing and the front cockpit.

Shortly after the preliminary trials in Baltimore, USA, when it was piloted once more by Captain Henri Baird, the 'S4' crashed at sea due to wing 'flutter' leading to his loss of control. The pilot was rescued from the water, but its race entry was over for that year. It was Folland's similarly Napier-engined biplane, the Gloster III floatplane, that entered the race at Baltimore, and scored a creditable second place to James Doolittle's Curtiss R3C. An important consolation prize for all concerned in the 'S4' Schneider Cup failure, was when this rebuilt aircraft took both the World Air Speed Record for Marine Aircraft and the British Air Speed Record at 226.7mph on 13 September 1925 off Woolston.

A 'Racing Lion VIIB' engine for the Schneider Trophy of 1927, with Watford magnetos placed either side of its double-reduction gearbox delivering 875bhp.

The British firms and their RAF High Speed Flight pilots, took a 'year out' in 1926, when the Italian Macchi's again won the trophy in Hampton Roads in the USA. But for the 1927 Schneider Cup event to be held in Venice, a strengthened and more powerful pair of British aircraft designs emerged from Gloster Aircraft and Supermarine, and both were certainly in with a chance. During the two intervening years in the Acton works, DNS staff and development engineers, then working to a new Air Ministry order, had been pressing ahead while perfecting an alternative pair of 'Racing Lion' engine designs, to suit the varying needs of both Folland and Mitchell within their airframes. The resulting two similar types of new engine were more powerful than ever before from using a 10:1 higher compression ratio. The two types were the 'E86' direct drive 'Lion VIIA' with 900bhp at 3,300rpm driving the propeller, and the 'E90 Lion VIIB' that gave 875bhp at 3,300rpm, which had a compact compound train 'double'-reduction gear, with its low output shaft in line with the crankshaft, as an alternative type for driving larger diameter propellers. Folland had retained the familiar biplane construction for his new Gloster '4B', in which he had installed a geared 'Lion VIIB' engine. Whereas Mitchell with Supermarines took no chances this time with his new and startling 'S5' aircraft entries, installing in one the 'Lion VIIB' engine, while its sister plane sported the direct drive 'Lion VIIA'. With trials and practice in the UK completed, the RAF pilots with their British floatplanes proceeded to the 1927 competition on the Italians' home ground in Venice. It was run over seven laps of a 50km inshore course, and all was to start well for Britain. But the Gloster '4B', being flown by Flt Lt Sam Kinkead, developed propeller spinner trouble after he had completed the fastest lap at 277mph, when he was lying second to the Supermarine 'S5' N220, both these aircraft running with the 'Lion VIIB' geared engine. For this reason Kinkead was forced to then 'ditch' safely in N223, but its 'Racing Lion' engine has been kept since that time, and more recently preserved by

In Venice 1927, showing (left) the Supermarine 'S5' 219 floatplane (placed second), with a 900bhp 'Racing Lion VIIA' engine, riding alongside a Macchi M67.

the Napier Power Heritage Trust. The three Italian entrants, all flying Macchi M52 planes with big 1,000bhp Fiat AS3 engines, had a bad time, two suffering engine failure and the other having fuel leakage, which eventually forced it to 'ditch' and retire. That left the race to Great Britain's Flt Lt S.N. Webster flying the N220 Supermarine 'S5' with 'Lion VIIB' engine, coming home as the Trophy winner at 281.5mph. Flt Lt O.E. Worsley took second place at 272.9mph, flying the N219 'S5', with the Fairey-Reed propeller 'Lion VIIA'.

Further to this race win, a British Air Speed Record of 319.57mph was later made on 4 November 1928 in an 'S5', by Flt Lt D. D'Arcy Greig when flying 'N220', off Calshot. Tragically, the unfortunate Sam Kinkead had been killed earlier that autumn, when he also was trying for that British record in 'S5' N221, after he failed to pull out of a dive.

Certainly during 1927 the Supermarine-Napier joint name had become world famous, not only to aviators, but to the British sporting public who so 'loved a winner'. The much needed good publicity for aircraft, and their Napier engines, was widespread. The elation at DNS Acton was genuinely heartfelt, at both boardroom and shop-floor levels, for now the old company of DNS had proved itself able, once again, after twenty-two years, to produce 'Serious Power' for international events! The effects of this turning point for British speed and reliability were to last for a further twenty years, when the achievement was built upon by a pair of these same 'Lion' masterpieces, then producing 2,800bhp in a land car which travelled at over 400mph!

The seed of an idea had been sown in the minds of speed-loving racing men and women: viz. would they now, at last, be able to acquire from Napier a 'Lion' power unit for land and water records? First in the queue was Captain Malcolm Campbell, the already well-known Brooklands racing driver and speed record contender with Major Henry Segrave. Until then, both had relied mainly on Sunbeam engines in their record cars, but now with the possibility of a 24-litre Napier 'Lion' under the bonnet, they saw that new British and World Speed Records might be within their grasp.

Moment of triumph in Venice, as Supermarine 'S5' 220 wins the Trophy for Great Britain, piloted by Flt Lt Webster and powered by a 'Racing Lion VIIB'.

Campbell had achieved 150mph by 1925, in his first *Bluebird* with an 18.3-litre Sunbeam engine, but in 1926 Segrave beat that record, by 2mph only, driving a Louis Coatalen tuned 4-litre racing car at Southport sands. That was soon surpassed in 1926 by Parry Thomas in his Higham Special 'Babs' record car, in which he reached 171mph on Pendine sands, powered by a 27-litre, V12 Liberty aero engine. A day or so later, Thomas was to die at Pendine while trying again. Meanwhile, it was Campbell who had wrested a direct drive 'Lion VI' engine of 500bhp from H.T.Vane at Acton, to power his newly constructed Napier-Campbell *Bluebird* record car, built at Brooklands by Thomson and Taylor to the design of Joseph Maina. With this car Campbell went for the British and World Land Speed Records at Pendine, where he succeeded at almost 175mph early in 1927. That same year, when a W12 Napier 'Lion'-engined 'S5' floatplane had won the Schneider Trophy, Segrave made his attempt for the land record in a very big Sunbeam car, with 1,000bhp gained from a pair of 22.4-litre 'Matabele' aero engines. He again beat Campbell's record, becoming the first man to travel at over 200mph on land at Daytona Beach, setting the next target for his British rival to beat at over 204mph. Campbell and Leo Villa, his lifelong mechanic, arranged for modifications to his existing *Bluebird* car, now enclosing its chassis and streamlining the front end by adding a pair of high slab surface coolers placed either side of a short tail fin to maintain line. But the most significant change was their gaining the power of a 900bhp 'Racing Lion VIIA' engine from Acton works where, after enlisting the able assistance of George Wilkinson and Henry Tryon, the record car was assembled.

The car was fast and well-behaved for Campbell at Daytona in 1928: he took back the record at just on 207mph. The American R. Keech overtook that on his home ground, but by only ½mph, he drew on the 1,500bhp produced from 81 litres of three Liberty engines in his crude looking, huge chassis car 'White Triplex', and that was still only in 1928.

The next year was to herald several world records on land, water and in the air for Great Britain, and in all but one case, their power units were from DNS works in Acton.

The 1929 Schneider Trophy race was hosted in Southern England, over a pylon marked course off Ryde Pier, Isle of Wight. The two types of British aircraft were once again entirely new, both being powered by new engines of much greater power. Supermarine's Reg Mitchell had been persuaded to rely now on an engine from Derby, the big 36.5-litre supercharged 1,900bhp at 2,900rpm Rolls-Royce 'R' engine, for his Supermarine 'S6' floatplane design for this 1929 race. That left Henry Folland at Glosters as the sole user of the newly developed and powerful Napier 'E91' supercharged 'Racing Lion VIID', delivering 1,350bhp at 3,600rpm via a double reduction gear train. The new star of supercharger design, a young Alfred J. Penn, had been engaged by Wilkinson at DNS two years earlier, expressly to handle work involved in creating a matched supercharger for the 'Racing Lion' engine that could, as they predicted, deliver three times the power of Rowledge's original standard design. Folland's all new 'Gloster VI' airframe, awaiting the 'VIID' engine, was this time a beautiful low wing monoplane, strikingly sleek in appearance, one having been painted and named for the race *Golden Arrow*. Disaster for DNS, and so for Glosters, then struck, as both the 'secret' and ready-tested engines were, on arrival, found to have been damaged in transit between Acton and Calshot. After a hard race-against-time, when one was finally installed for flight test just a few days before the race day, a fuel starvation problem then occurred during the banked pylon turns with loss of power. This proved not to be correctable in time for the event itself, so, very reluctantly, the engineers and RAF crews had to retire this aircraft. That left the two 'S6's' and, as reserve, one old 'Lion VIIB'-powered 'S5' to represent Great Britain against the Italian team of three new Macchi M67 floatplanes, powered by broad-arrow W18 cylinder, 1,800bhp Issota Fraschini 'Asso'engines. One of these crashed in practice, killing its pilot, and all of them suffered from engine fumes entering the cockpit. Hence an earlier Macchi M52R float plane replaced the lost aircraft for the great race on 7 September, between these two now well matched teams. The race pace was set, and won, by Fg Off. H.R.D. Waghorn in the 'S6' N247 at 328.6mph, while the other 'S6', N248, was disqualified due to pilot error. Both the Macchi M67 pilots retired during the race, leaving the older and much slower Macchi M52R to finish in second place piloted by Dal Molin. Just behind him the third spot was taken by Flt Lt David D'Arcy Greig in the Napier-powered 'S5' at 282.1mph, slightly faster than Webster's speed in Venice.

Ultimate 'Racing Lion VIID' of 1929, having a rear supercharger supplying its three-cylinder banks, the engine delivering 1,350bhp at 3,600rpm.

Major Henry Segrave in the cockpit of the *Golden Arrow*, fitted with a 'Lion VIIA' engine and gunsight, before his WLSR on 11 March 1929 at Daytona Beach.

The problems surrounding the British defence of the Trophy in 1931 are well known and well recorded, when a rebuilt and Rolls-Royce 'R'-powered 'S6B' was the only entrant at Spithead, it flew well and took the Schneider Trophy outright and unopposed for Great Britain at the improved speed of 340mph. The two Gloster VI aircraft, numbers N249 and N250, with Napier 'Lion VIID' engines were still available and used for RAF HSF practice in 1931 but, apart from a briefly held World Air Speed Record of 336mph in 1929, they were not flown 'in anger' although, as reported, capable of speeds of 350mph. A re-run of the 1929 event, with *Golden Arrow* behaving well, would have been close!

Across the Atlantic at Daytona Beach, Florida, a different type of British contest was heating up between the two English land speed record drivers, Segrave and Campbell.

With Campbell and Keech neck-and–neck during 1928, at around 207mph, Henry Segrave took a major step forward for 1929, ordering a spectacular new car designed by the same Captain J.S. Irving who had designed his big 1,000bhp Sunbeam of 1927. But this time, it was schemed for low air resistance and compact power from a single 900bhp Napier direct drive 'Lion VIIA', an ex-1927 Schneider Trophy engine. The chassis was built at Kenelm Lee Guinness's KLG sparking plug factory in Putney close to Acton. KLG had once held the speed record himself at 133.7mph in 1922 at Brooklands, driving the same 18-litre Sunbeam that he passed on to Campbell in 1924. Now in 1929, in Irving's latest design, the closely faired in 'Lion' was forward of a gunsight cockpit, and had side-cooling radiators mounted between the front and rear driving wheels, external to the flat body sides. This, possibly the most lovely of all speed record cars, was officially known as the 'Irving-Napier Special'. But then, strangely in the year 1929, it was invariably also called the *Golden Arrow*, although frequently seen in non-reflecting black paint, as well as gold, this name has often been confused with the 1929 Gloster VI floatplane coloured red and gold. Driving the car with its 930bhp at 3,500rpm engine not fully extended, Segrave set a new world record at 231.4mph by a clear margin, this with the engine turning over at just 3,250rpm. The fatal accident of American Lee Bible, so very soon after at Daytona Beach, then curtailed any further attempts there at record breaking. Major Segrave returned with *Golden Arrow* to the UK, to a true hero's welcome and was knighted for his success in this, his third World Land Speed Record for Great Britain.

Now even more determined, Captain Campbell grasped the Napier nettle firmly. He requested that the Air Ministry power his rebuilt *Bluebird* chassis, now designed by Reid-Railton, with one of the spare 1,350bhp supercharged 'Lion VIID' engines from the RAF's disbanded HSF. Under due secrecy, except to Tryon and Wilkinson at DNS, this was adapted and then quietly supplied to Thomson and Taylor at their Brooklands workshops and installed into the lowered chassis. In this, the propeller shaft was now alongside the driver and the radiator was a quite separate, front-mounted unit, fully in the airstream. With the extra 450bhp now at his command, Campbell gently demonstrated the car on the Brooklands banking making short bursts along the straights, but the bonnet was never seen lifted in public at the request of the Air Ministry. Returning to the USA and Daytona in 1930, after several 'scares' with the high revving engine and KLG built gearbox, Campbell then achieved a record speed of 246.1mph.

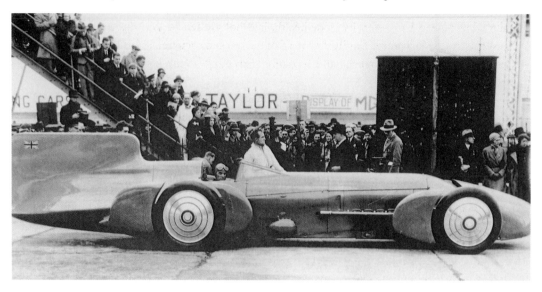

Captain Malcolm Campbell demonstrating his fourth Napier-Campbell *Bluebird*, with the supercharged 'Lion VIID' under the bonnet, at Brooklands in 1931.

Meanwhile, on the other side of the world, from Sydney, Australia, rumours of a new world speed record car named *Enterprise* reached England, also that it was powered by a Napier 'Lion VIID' engine. This was being built for racing driver Norman 'Wizard' Smith, and according to its designer Don Harkness, a 300mph record attempt would be made in New Zealand on Ninety-Mile Beach, in, or around, 1932. To this news Campbell responded at once by again modifying his *Bluebird*, to give more power at the driving wheels and less front air resistance. *Enterprise* was finished and under test at the end of 1931, and went on to break the World ten-mile speed record in 1932, setting it now at 164mph. The 300mph threat from 'down under' eventually came to nothing owing to bad beach conditions, but Malcolm Campbell, who by then wanted the success of being the first man through the '250mph barrier', went ahead with a further *Bluebird* record attempt later in 1932 at Daytona. In this he was only marginally successful, but did pass through his own target 'barrier' by making a significant new world record at 254.0mph.

A larger new *Bluebird* with big Rolls-Royce 'R' power was soon to follow, enabling him to bring his later records up to 300mph. But Sir Malcolm Campbell had, already, received his knighthood for the six earlier world records, when in the last four cases he had depended upon lightweight, reliable Napier 'Lion' engines, chosen with Air Ministry and DNS help, from out of its three main stages of power development over just five years.

All other matters occupying Acton works, and the business of the DNS Board, paled into insignificance when hearing the news of the sudden death of Montague S. Napier in France at Ville de Cistes, Cannes on 22 January 1931. There was a deep sense of shock felt within the whole company, who were left for the very first time in 123 years without a direct line Napier family member at the helm. But M.S. Napier had seen the successful development of his concept completed, the world beating 'Triple-Four' engine, which brought many tributes from far and wide. This private, self-motivated man, who had lived abroad and been hampered by poor health, had not chosen to join the activities of the Institution of Mechanical Engineers, or of other learned societies, as his father James had done before him, whose work had been fully appreciated in the Institution's Proceedings with a detailed obituary.

However, the major newspapers and the *Autocar* magazine that February were pleased to publish 'Montague S. Napier – an Appreciation', written by Sir Harry Brittain, KBE, a trusted friend and member of the Board of D. Napier & Son Ltd. It read as follows:

Those of us who enjoy the incomparable gift of perfect health often fail to realise the heavy handicap which weighs on others who, in spite of physical disability, so frequently achieve outstanding aims. Montague Napier, who died at Cannes on Friday last, was an illuminating instance of mental brilliancy surmounting bodily pain. For years past, under doctor's orders, he had been forbidden the climate of his native land, and as an invalid passed his days on the shores of France; but never for a moment did his active mind relax, and his keen, inventive brain was concentrated upon the solutions to engineering problems, the subject of all others to which he devoted his life.

He was Chairman of D. Napier & Son, the old British firm founded by his grandfather, David Napier, in 1808. To the leadership of this firm his own father, James Murdock Napier, in due course succeeded, and in Victorian days the firm was well known as a manufacturing unit of various types of exact and delicate machinery. Towards the end of that century the internal-combustion engine was developed, and a revolution in road transport followed. Napier's were early in the field, and the genius of the then young Montague Napier brought into being the first six-cylinder engine, which gave a lead to this country, and was adopted by motor manufacturing concerns throughout the world. Many a record was won for this country by cars bearing the name of Napier.

Then came development in the air, and here again Montague Napier evinced a flair for the future, eventually deciding to specialise solely in this new method of transport. Working steadily at his retreat on the hills of Cannes, in close consultation with his colleagues at home, he was responsible for the Napier 'Lion' engine, which has had a wondrous series of records to its credit, including the winning for England, on two occasions, of the blue ribbon of the air – the famous Schneider Trophy.

As one of his old colleagues, I lament the passing of an outstanding engineer, of a thoughtful, forceful genius of his age. I still more lament the passing of the man. This handsome, great-hearted Briton possessed also a genius for friendship. It was a joy and an education to be with him. A great lover of books, he was a deep thinker, sure of himself and his conclusions, and so obviously a master of the subjects that interested him. As long as health was granted to Napier, he revelled in all physical exercise, and was the keenest of yachtsmen. He had the mind of a philosopher, enjoying most the simple things of life. When illness struck him down he accepted it with fortitude – and worked on quietly. At the age of sixty he comes back once again to rest in his native land.' - H. B.

Following Montague Napier's funeral, he was laid to rest in Kensal Green Cemetery, London, alongside his mother, Fanny J. Napier. Then, almost immediately, back at Acton the Chairmanship of the Board of Directors of DNS was assumed by Henry T. Vane. His revised board still included Henry Cooke as its secretary, along with F.A. Davies and Sir Harry Brittain. But soon it was George Wilkinson, newly appointed Chief Engineer, who spoke up and addressed the Board on the topic of 'healthy competition amongst engineering businesses', a subject that had not featured in board meetings at Acton much before then, when they were usually 'chaired' by M.S. Napier. Because of the very strong sales of 'Lion' engines, Napier had till then always looked out for government orders and to the military markets of the world for the bulk of his contracts, which was just as his predecessors had done down the years. Without the traditional Napier family view on competition there, a new company outlook now seemed likely to present itself.

Montague Napier was survived by his wife, Alice Napier, his two daughters, Margaret and Phylis, and two sons, Selwyn Montague Napier and Carill Stanley Napier, born in 1907. This younger son, Carill, had undoubtedly inherited from his father the feel and love for things mechanical and, in particular, for aircraft and flight. Following his apprenticeship with Westland Aircraft Ltd at Yeovil, Somerset, this young man returned to the DNS Acton engine works in 1928, clearly as the Napier family 'heir apparent', working under the watchful eye of Managing Director H. T. Vane. Their two personalities soon clashed, the only solution being that Carill Napier moved on. This he did to civil light aero engine design and manufacture at the Cirrus Engine Section of Blackburn Aircraft Ltd, Brough, Yorks. He became a flyer and held a pilot's license; he owned the aircraft that had been presented to him by his supportive and wealthy father, Montague Napier. With his keen expertise in the air and having become the Chief Engineer at Brough works before 1938, Carill's future and, in the light of his father's premature death, possibly that of DNS itself, then seemed assured in the aircraft power industry. But then, the outbreak of the Second World War changed everything! Not content to reside in this passive leading technical position with Cirrus engines, Carill soon volunteered as a ferry pilot for the RAF with the Air Traffic Auxiliary. Flying with them on active service up to 1942, he became the First Technical Officer for the ATA, and their 'Pilots Reminder Book', published in 1943, was dedicated to his memory. The late Captain Carill S. Napier died in the RAF Halton Hospital during 1942, subsequent to his crashing on take-off in a Blenheim bomber. His grave can be found today in Halton Churchyard, often visited in November by family members and those in the Trust. One may well question in retrospect whether, without his tragic loss during the war, much of the latter-day history of DNS could have turned out quite differently. But here and now is not the place for such conjecture, as the next sixty years of the Napier Company await re-discovery within this volume, and one's eager comprehension.

Another key figure in the convoluted story of DNS around this period was Major Frank B. Halford, who, after an agreement reached with M.S. Napier in 1927, had started in his role as a forward looking Consultant Designer for future DNS aero engines. This arrangement, without that special link Wilkinson had held with Napier in France, would now undermine Wilkinson's position from then on as the DNS Head of Engine Development. He had been awarded the Royal Aeronautical Society's Silver Medal for his part in the Schneider Trophy victory in Venice of 1927, the very same year that Frank

Tiny frontal area of a sixteen-cylinder Napier 'Rapier' air-cooled 350bhp engine of 1930.

Halford had set to work. Halford's choice as a paid consultant for DNS, was not so surprising in view of Napier's then determination to enter the technology of air-cooled engines, Halford also being a firm believer in that method of cooling cylinders, leading to reduced weight. The joint agreement reached specified that capacities of any new DNS-built engines, designed by Halford, should lie within the range between 404 cubic ins (6.6 litres) and 718 cubic ins (11.8 litres). During Napier's lifetime, Halford's first two DNS designs appeared: both were air-cooled, had push-rod-operated overhead valves and their sizes fell between these two capacity limits, but after that his twenty-four-cylinder engine designs fell well outside those limits.

The first design was quite similar to the Cirrus 'Hermes' and the de Havilland 'Gypsy' types, being the 'E97' inverted six-cylinder 8.2-litre engine named 'Javelin'. Giving 160bhp at 2,000rpm it was only a marginal success, powering several Percival light aircraft, such as the 'Gull Four' and a racing 'Mew Gull', these being in direct competition with similar aircraft using 'Gypsy' and 'Hermes' engines. During the 1930s this power unit had earned an unenviable reputation for 'cutting-out' on take-off, a problem that remained unsolved!

Napier had referred to the second new and much more radical design as his 'H-Engine', this was the 'E93' sixteen-cylinder 'Rapier I' of 1929, which could produce 300bhp at 3,500rpm from its supercharged 8.83 litres. Its development then continued at Acton up to an 'E100 Rapier Series VI', which then gave 395bhp at 4,000rpm with 2½lb boost at 6,000ft.

A second line of new development triggered by Napier in 1929 from his Cannes design office involved compression ignition aero-engines, like those then being developed in Germany. Napier had spotted that the opposed-piston uniflow type being developed by Dr Hugo Junkers was most promising, so they went ahead to arrange for its manufacture under license at Acton. This was in fact done after his death in 1931 under Wilkinson's direction, he becoming Chief Engineer, following George Pate's resignation in 1929.

Thus, type No. 'E102', named 'Culverin', was built, and successfully test-flown in a three engine installation, mounted high up in a Blackburn 'Iris' biplane flying boat. The 'Culverin' diesel of 4¾in bore, was internally a copy of an in-line, six-cylinder opposed-piston, pressure charged Junkers 'Jumo 204' aero engine, giving an output of 720bhp at 1,700rpm when the prototype first ran on load at Acton on 24 September 1934. But, externally this 67in tall, 23in wide upright diesel had DNS features visible all over its two light alloy crankcases, its cylinder block, blower and tall phasing gear case with high propeller shaft. Despite the then lack of interest from the RAF and Air Ministry, with no production orders being received by 1936, this exercise was far from wasted, because ten years later a similar opposed-piston design of compression-ignition engine would then form one third of an eighteen-cylinder Deltic. So M.S. Napier's action was to prove the 'opening of a door' into a greater future for DNS after the Second World War and beyond, even into the twenty-first century.

Yet another compression ignition initiative springing from the late M.S. Napier's work, was the astonishing type 'E101'. This design was for a twenty-four-cylinder, diesel aero engine in the 'H' configuration, having cylinder dimensions of 5in bore x 4¾in stroke, these being identical to those of the 'Sabre' petrol engine to be created five years on! It now seems certain that it also employed single sleeve valves, this according to a sleeve worm-drive patent taken out by DNS in 1931, and that it operated on the four-stroke diesel injection, compression ignition cycle. Test units with two and six cylinders ('E101T/6T') were built and run at Acton from 1932 onwards, as clear photographic evidence from the period shows. This work, initially set in motion by Napier himself, was clearly well within the province of that special Acton-based trio of Henry Tryon, Sir Harry Ricardo and Frank Halford. These greatly gifted men were to continue meeting for discussions on all technical development and research at Acton for well over a decade, on into the Second World War. Then, in 1933, the London Midland & Scottish Railway was operating a 165bhp 0-6-0 diesel shunting locomotive No. 7403, on trial from the builders in Hunslet near Leeds. Its in-line six-cylinder engine as installed was a Brotherhood-Ricardo High Speed, Sleeve Valve unit, practically a smaller version of one quarter of the Napier 'E101' diesel 'H' aero engine. The design work for 'E101T' test units was undertaken in a small 'advanced project' design office, similar to Napier's former one in Cannes, staffed by some elite design specialists, such as Bill Nowlan, who had actually worked in the DO over in France. Clearly all these hush-hush activities were happening in order to herald the

In 1935 a tall C.I. Napier-Junkers 'Culverin', opposed-piston engine of 720bhp.

coming within DNS of the 2,000bhp 'Sabre H' engine design – the 'E107' of 1936 – this was to have nearly identical water-cooled cylinders on a lightened design of crankcase, and burning petrol instead of diesel fuel-oil.

Returning to the RAF around 1930, not only flying speed was a prime consideration at the time, but the importance of greater endurance flying for their pilots and crews was increasing, as was navigation and load carrying. Once more, whole-hearted co-operation between DNS and Fairey Aviation was forthcoming in the design and construction of the large Fairey Long Range Monoplane project, using a single 'Lion XIA' 520bhp engine.

This two-seater 'Postal' aircraft, with a high cantilever wingspan of 82ft and a large chord wing containing big fuel tanks carrying over 1,100 gallons of aviation spirit, was first built in 1928. Endurance flights made in 1929 included an April non-stop flight to India in fifty hours, thirty-seven minutes, while covering a distance of 4,130 miles. But, a long distance record attempt that December ended in tragedy when 'J9479' struck high ground near Tunis, killing the RAF crew. The replacement 'Postal' was planned by the Air Ministry to capture the 'Distance record for powered aircraft' in 1930, and first flew in June 1931 fitted with faired undercarriage wheels.

With a latest type, specially tuned 'Lion XIA', lean-burn engine developing 530bhp at 2,350rpm, that gave the 'Postal' a possible range of 5,500 miles in a straight line, given favourable winds and precise navigation. The experienced crew chosen were pilots Sqn Ldr O.R. Gayford DFC and Flt Lt G.E. Nicholetts AFC, who flew from RAF Cranwell on 6 February 1933 at 07.15 hrs. Lifting off at a weight of 17,500lb after 58 seconds over a run of 4,500ft, a course was set to the Mediterranean at a steady speed of 110mph. On board was 'George', a secret early automatic-pilot system designed at RAF Farnborough to relieve the pilots of some routine tasks, but that system gave up on the second night beyond Nigeria as dust clouds were forming. Angola was reached amidst some positional confusion and strong head winds so they turned west to the coast and landed near Walvis Bay at 16.40 hrs on 8 February. They had flown a total of 5,410 miles in fifty-seven hours and twenty-five minutes at an average speed of 94mph overall.

The agreed approved Air Distance Record now belonged securely to Great Britain and was set at 5,309 miles point to point, with typical jubilation back in our British aero industry.

Somewhat earlier, following the loss of M.S. Napier, a 'crossroads' point had been reached in the affairs of DNS. Their dilemma was whether to continue solely in aero-engine manufacture, or to diversify again into building high performance cars, or some other related product. This time, Edge's old colleague, now DNS Chairman, Henry Vane, took the opposite view to what he had held ten years earlier in 1921, now saying that cars

1933 saw a 'Lion XIA' marathon in the Fairey 'Postal 2' long-range monoplane, flown 5,309 miles non-stop to South Africa by Sqn Ldr Gayford, seen on the right.

would 'never make profit' for the company, in view of the new competition within that market and the shortage of money in the country. The other directors all wanted to go ahead with a new car venture, but were also keen on maintaining production of the 'Lion' engine and Halford's new aircraft engine designs, possibly as insurance against partial failure in the car market. In the ensuing vote on 18 February 1932, Vane was overruled so had to resign from the DNS Board. The Chairmanship passed temporarily to Sir Harry Brittain, then shortly after to a City Banker, Sir Harold Snagge KBE, JP who became the new Chairman. So who, it was asked, would design this new Napier car?

This situation followed that second great disappointment of 1931, when DNS had been beaten to the purchase of W.O. Bentley's company, and also to his personal services with his outstanding flair as a designer of high performance sports cars. In the then prevailing circumstances at Acton, it was noticed too late that W. O. Bentley's car building business in nearby Cricklewood had recently failed, and been placed in the hands of a receiver so could be available for purchase. Almost casually, the Board decided to put in a six-figure bid for that famous marque of sporting and racing cars, while Bentley himself was to be invited to come to Acton to design a new, superb 'Napier-Bentley' car. This he did for a time while several unsold Bentley chassis were held in store at the Acton works. The often recounted sad outcome of this potential Bentley deal is now well known, when surreptitiously a somewhat higher bid was put in by Rolls-Royce, then in the guise of the British Central Equitable Trust, their legal representatives. In court they won the day, in October 1931, Bentley with his former company assets being bought out for slightly over £125,000. So that 6½-litre Napier-Bentley design was never to see the light of day!

Now moving on, from the 'sublime to the ridiculous', later in 1931 the DNS General Manager F.A. Davies put to the Board his proposal for a new business vehicle that would require minimal design work in its construction, and would 'sell itself' to the big four national railway companies. This was for a solidly built, light, three-wheel, forward drive tractor to haul delivery drays, so replacing carthorses then still in use almost everywhere. A small two-cylinder, Jowett-engined 7hp 'Colt' tractor, by the Karrier Company, was already in prototype service with the LNER, as there was still much scope for a larger tractor, both for them and the other three railways. This commercially based work was quickly put in hand, practically alongside the Napier-Bentley project, but Acton soon came to name it 'The Mountain Goat'. Its power unit was simply a 10hp four-cylinder side valve one designed as 'E99', with a 2½in bore x 3½in stroke, this based upon the current reliable 'Morris Ten' engine. The tractor steered via a single front wheel giving 90 degree of turn, its two rear load carrying and driving wheels having drum brakes. This 'Mechanical-horse' had a swivel mounted, self-locking coupling on top of a short rear chassis, which completed the 'hitch-up' arrangement to a dray-type trailer when this stood level on two jockey wheels. DNS claimed that the combination of tractor and standard trailer could 'turn round within its own length', and so was somewhat better at this manoeuvre than a horse-drawn dray. Despite the forecast annual sales to railways of up to 5,000 tractors, the Board eventually decided to sell off the design and prototype to Scammell of Watford for just £4,000. That company went on to make a great success of the mechanical-horse in the railway market.

There had, indeed, been varied 'traffic through those Napier crossroads' in the five years from 1927, both before and after the loss of the DNS Governing Director in 1931. More traffic was to come in the next decade too, with more new records set on land, on sea and in the air. Two DNS amalgamations, one with the Bristol Company, the other with Gloster Aircraft Company, had trial negotiations set up, but both were abandoned.

With hindsight, it seems extraordinarily forgetful, even short-sighted, of the DNS Board, and Vane in particular, during the early 1930s not to have recalled the words of S.F. Edge written in 1906 regarding the new potential marine transport market for DNS. They clearly had, at that time, failed to see a strong future for Napier in marine engines. That statement by S.F. Edge, then obviously shared with M.S. Napier, had been published in their joint names after 1904, when the fast launch 'Napier Minor' was first adopted by the Admiralty for 'scouting experiments' in Naval manoeuvres. It went as follows:

> Napier has thus, for the first time brought before the public the possibilities of the high-speed motor launch for warlike as well as pacific purposes, and has established a new industry likely to develop into even greater importance than motoring on land.

During the next fifty years, DNS came to appreciate its truth while excelling with marine power. Meanwhile, several British record breakers from 1929 had taken to the water in highly powered hydroplane launches, with the aim of either winning back the International Harmsworth Trophy from speedboat racer Gar Wood of the USA, or gaining a World Water Speed Record for Great Britain. These wealthy, intrepid, sporting boatmen and women had invariably used Napier 'Lion' power for their attempts, simply adding more engines in order to increase the total power output for their bigger fast-boats. This same principle was then to be employed, well in advance of the Second World War, by most light coastal craft of the Army, Navy and Air Force, when in these vehicles the 'marinised Lion XIA' engine used in multiple provided a versatile, reliable and compact power unit, it becoming the 'Power-Napier Sea Lion' petrol engine. The story of its successful British development in the hands of some world-beating racing marine engineers will be featured in Chapter Six, where some refreshing aero-engine designs will also be revealed.

6

HERALDING THE HIGH-REVVING
REVOLUTION 1933–1945

Without Montague Napier in person at the helm, a definite future direction for DNS was not going to be settled for at least five years after 1931. Also, because of the larger than hitherto DNS Board of seven members, in residence from 1933 onwards, decisions made by consensus were arrived at more slowly under the Chairmanship of Sir Harold Snagge.

Other Board members at that time were: Managing Director Sir Harry Brittain, General Manager Frederick A. Davies, Secretary Reginald C. Johnson, Chief Engineer George Wilkinson, Leonard Williams and Air Vice-Marshall Amyas E. Borton CB, DSO, AFC. Within the company the accent was now on revolutionary new designs for petrol fuelled aero engines under the bold leadership of Frank Halford, each of which had, by its 'H' configuration of cylinders, the 'initial' of its overall designer. Within two years, Halford had somewhat reluctantly accepted a DNS Directorship in 1935, and saw to it that W. H. Arscott was installed as his Senior Design Assistant in the Acton Design Office, Arscott having moved from Halford's private design offices in Golden Square, Piccadilly.

Halford's small-capacity sixteen-cylinder Rapier I engine for DNS, first flew on 11 July 1929 in the prototype DH77 experimental light interceptor monoplane fighter, which was an attempt on the part of de Havilland, with encouragement from Halford, to enter the RAF military aircraft field. This small fighter had a good climb rate for interception, a top speed of 200mph with light armament, all generated from the 315bhp of its small 'Rapier' engine. Still, with no RAF interest after the Hendon Air show of 1930, this DH77 was used to flight test 'Rapier II' engines at Farnborough until its disposal in 1934. But, by 1936 the further developed 'Rapier' engine met with greater military regard scoring 'a winner' within a lightweight seaplane, the biplane Fairey Seafox. These were soon delivered to both the RAF and the Fleet Air Arm and were powered by the 'E100 Rapier VI' of max 395bhp at 4,000rpm, and 3lb/ sq.in of supercharger boost when catapult launched as 'fleet spotters'. They saw much service well into the Second World War, one 'Seafox' in particular, flown-off daily by Lt Lewin, from HMS *Ajax*, spotted targets for the guns of Royal Navy cruiser ships, and became instrumental in the final scuttling of the German pocket battleship *Graf Spree* off the river Plate. Truly a butterfly, stinging the big bee!

It had remained for Wilkinson to soldier on into the 1930s with the development of the last of the standard 'Lions', the 'E92' Series XV, which gave 555bhp at 2,350rpm, but this from an increased weight to 1,000lb. But also, the more exciting and little known type 'E94', a 'Racing Lion VIIC' of 975bhp at 3,750rpm, a normally aspirated engine with 11:1 compression ratio. This burnt a 'fuel cocktail' of 60% light petrol and 40% benzole during its secluded life powering a 'Top Secret Project', the one-man MTB code-named *Empire Day* later in 1936. This small hydroplane, with 80mph capability, was to the design of the Spurr Company who provided the test pilots for both its 'slow stealth' and rapid approach (and exit) to targets to deliver its single torpedo. Notably, this very high compression Lion VIIC engine had almost as high a compression ratio as the current Napier diesel 'Culverin' design, which also started its test programme in 1934!

But from out at sea, a charismatic 'tidal wave' was then to sweep in and invade those aero-bound shores of DNS Acton. This was in the person of wealthy Hubert Scott-Paine, owner of the British Power Boat Company at Hythe, near Southampton on the west bank of the Solent, a person of great mental and physical stature much akin to DNS's former mentor S.F. Edge. It was Scott-Paine, or 'Scotty' to his friends and employees, who had earlier in 1920 employed Reginald Mitchell at his then Supermarine Aviation works at Woolston on the Solent, so leading to the design and development of the 'Lion'-powered *Sealion II* flying boat, the first Schneider Trophy winning aircraft for Great Britain in 1922. That occurred after 'Scotty' had approached the cautious H.T. Vane, who then 'lent' to him a suitably tuned 'Lion II' engine to power it. Much earlier, back in 1913, the same Scott-Paine had built a racing car which had a big 180bhp Napier engine, this for his partner Pemberton-Billing, and for their Brooklands racing events before the First World War. Now, and much more importantly in 1928, it was 'Scotty' who had accepted a very fast boat-building challenge given to him by Major Henry Segrave, this to be his water record hydroplane *Miss England*. With the same confidence Scotty again requested from Vane an ex-Schneider 'Racing Lion VIIA' for the boat, and once again Vane, now Managing Director of DNS, who had once worked for S.F. Edge during his great days in Napier motor racing, rose to this new challenge and so supplied one to the British Power Boat Company, almost as if to acknowledge those 'clearly prophetic' words from S.F. Edge that were stated earlier. The outcome from the successes achieved by the courageous Segrave in *Miss England* was to convince Scotty of his own supreme capability to build 'Power Boats', powered by Napier engines wherever possible, that should be world beaters! Later derivatives of such boats became vital to the nation before, during and after the Second World War.

Miss England sailed to New York on 31 January 1929 on board RMS *Majestic* and reached Florida soon after Segrave's World Land Speed Record had been struck at 231.4mph, using a similar direct-drive Racing Lion VIIA. On first trial, off Daytona Beach, this hydroplane performed so well that Segrave cabled home: 'Mile today at 78 on ¾ throttle. Boat ran dead horizontal, handles beautifully, no wash. Hull simply wonderful. Motor wonderful. Congratulations – Segrave.' Segrave then raced against Gar Wood in the larger *Miss America* over two legs of the speed championship; Segrave won the first while averaging 60mph. The British boat lost the second leg, but reached 87.2mph, and was then offered the World Championship Trophy by the American team.

In 1929, racing in the 'Lion VIIA'-powered hydroplane *Miss England* built by Hubert Scott-Paine, Sir Henry Segrave took the single-engine water speed record at 92mph.

There followed attempts at breaking the World Speed Record, but the single Napier 'Lion'-engined *Miss England* averaged just 91.91mph, as against the American's twin-engine-powered record of 92.8mph. Scott-Paine's boat design had now been well proven, the 'Lion' had again been utterly reliable and Britain once more held the International Championship. On returning, King George V conferred a knighthood on the heroic Sir Henry Segrave for this pair of records, shortly before he was tragically killed the following year, by hitting a submerged timber log on Lake Windermere when piloting the much more powerful twin Rolls-Royce 'R'-engined *Miss England II*. Lord Wakefield had by then donated his own *Miss England* boat to the Science Museum collection where, to this day, she can be seen restored, intact and on display on the ground floor 'History of Transport Gallery' at South Kensington.

At much the same time, the flamboyant Miss Marion B. Carstairs ('Betty or Joe' to her friends) entered the seriously fast powerboat arena in the UK, with a range of powerful craft, the first three of which were designed by S.E. Saunders at Cowes. They were all named *Estelle*, after her mother, and their performance indicated they were to be challengers for the 'International Championship' that was usually held by Gar Wood of the USA. Her five hydroplanes had all been 'Lion'-powered, with power outputs varying from the single 875bhp 'Racing Lion' in *Estelle I* and *II*, up to the three supercharged Racing Lions installed in *Estelle IV*, these produced almost 4,000bhp when on full song!

Scott Paine's British Power Boat Co. adapted the 'Lion XIA' engine for marine use, it becoming the 500bhp Power-Napier 'Sea Lion' engine.

So competitive were she and her racing mechanic Joe Harris, that her own 'Sylvia Yard' was put in hand at East Cowes to build her final two larger hydroplanes, as Sam Saunders had declined to assist any further from his boatyard. Carstairs was often to be seen in Acton's test houses, seeing her beloved 'Lions' on test before despatch to her Isle of Wight yard. Right from *Estelle I* of 1928 to the *Estelle V* of 1930 capable of 95mph, her sea racing career had met with an unusually big patch of bad luck, ranging from an engine fuel fire to a broken propeller shaft, plus collisions with flotsam and buoys. Saddened by the loss of her friend Henry Segrave at Lake Windermere, Carstairs gave up powerboat racing in 1930 saying: 'I tried for the Harmsworth Trophy three times without success, I cannot afford another attempt.' However, a year later she was delighted when Kaye Don succeeded in *Miss England II*, using twin Rolls-Royce engines giving 4,000-plus bhp.

 Scotty, being in the mould of S.F. Edge, not only saw to it that he was producing the 'top' machinery, but he needed to prove it himself in competition, and for the world to see them in action. The 1933 International Harmsworth Trophy was now Scotty's target, following his recent hydroplane design success for British Power Boats during 1932, when a tender just 27ft 6in long for Baron Empian's yacht 'Heliopolis' was required, which could travel on water at a minimum of 60mph. This powerboat was built using one of twelve 500bhp 'Lion XIA' engines that he had purchased second-hand from the Air Ministry, and then marinised at Hythe to become the prototype 'Power-Napier Sealion' marine engine. These, now with direct drive, were mounted on a strong bed plate and close-coupled via a clutch into a Meadows reversing gearbox. That fast tender on trials reached 63mph, so Scotty reasoned that a supercharged 'Lion VIID' of 1,350bhp at 3,600rpm, put in a shorter and lighter multi-step hydroplane should be capable of a speed well in excess of 100mph, and be very competitive in America, maybe even to the extent of bringing back the Trophy.

Without delay, an Alclad covered, 24ft light-alloy multi-step hydroplane was designed and built in great secrecy, powered at the rear by a 'Lion VIID' engine, coupled directly via two step-up ratio vee-drive gear boxes to a fine mid-propeller rotating at 9,000rpm. When unveiled at Hythe she was named *Miss Britain III* and caught everyone's breath, for she weighed in at just 2.5lb/bhp and appeared just like a 'silver fish upon a platter'.

When shipped to the St Clair River, forty-five miles from Detroit, *Miss Britain III* passed her test runs, ready for competition against Gar Wood's *Miss America X* with her four 1,600bhp Packard engines. This was to be a classic 'David versus Goliath' speed event, where a 1,350bhp single-engine boat was to race against 6,400bhp from four engines! At the end of the really close second heat, Gar Wood had averaged 86.9mph against Scotty and Tommy Quelch's 85.8mph, with the small British boat was catching up fast! On return home to a typically warm reception, Scotty ran *Miss Britain III* at 102.1mph on Southampton Water, using the spare 'VIID' engine and then averaged 100.132mph in setting a single-engine British salt water record that stood unbeaten for over fifty years. More was in store for 1934 in Europe, when *Miss Britain III* raced for the Count Volpi Cup for sheer straight line speed at Venice and Scotty won at the very high average water speed of 111.1mph, the first British boat to win this event since Sir Henry Segrave did so with *Miss England* back in 1929. *Miss Britain III*, that fine silver hydroplane, can be seen today beside her Lion VIID engine in the National Maritime Museum, Greenwich.

Scott-Paine himself raced internationally in his 'Lion VIID'-powered aluminium hydroplane *Miss Britain III*, reaching speeds in excess of 110mph.

There was favourable publicity for Hubert Scott-Paine and for his British Power Boat Co. in the wake of these feats of water speed in this country, but not so wholeheartedly from amongst officials at the Admiralty. It also took a while for Chief Engineer George Wilkinson at DNS to appreciate the practicability and soundness of all the modifications that Hythe had engineered into the Sea Lion marine engine. When he was satisfied, and tests with alternative Amal carburettors were completed, running on a loaned DNS test bench, he reported back to the Board at Acton. They then readily accepted an agreement for the production by DNS of a newly named 'Power-Napier Sea Lion' marine unit, this being in conjunction with the B.P.B. Co., in which Acton would provide the direct drive 'Lions' to a former Series 'XIA', modified build standard. Being a long-standing DNS product, this highly developed Lion XIA engine was then nearing obsolescence as an aircraft engine, so this new lease-of-life for what was basically the old E89A aero engine, that had then been in production for over six years, made very good commercial sense and was not expected to affect the development work-load then being devoted to Halford's air-cooled engines. This agreement also specified that Sea-Lion units be fitted with three single-amal carburettors and heavy cooling heat-exchangers as specified at Hythe, plus that their differing manifold arrangements for the centre and wing (both starboard & port) engine positions within the wide triple-engine rooms anticipated in new sixty foot Naval and RAF launches be taken into account. Thus, in the end, Acton's engine test bench arrangements did, in fact, require considerable modifications to run-in this variety of marine engine build types. By 1938, more than 200 Sea Lions had been fitted new at Hythe, but over the next twenty years 2,000 were needed, plus spares, for the fighting services of the Army, Navy and Air Force who used British Power Boat High Speed Launches (HSL), Fast Patrol Boats (FPB) and the MTBs. During the Second World War variously built Tank Landing Craft (LTC) were also powered by two Sea Lions,

Twenty-four-cylinder air-cooled Napier-Halford 'Dagger' engines were developed to 1,000bhp.

then, finally, in 1956, a new Air-Sea Rescue Target Towing Launch (RTTL Mk.1A) built by Vosper, had 3 Sea Lions fitted in each, while awaiting a Rolls-Royce alternative. So the Napier Lion engine spanned a forty-year period from its design to the end of its production run, mainly caused by a lack of demand for its use in military service.

The only aero-engine from the Halford stable that could 'replace' the rugged 'Lion' was by 1935 under test and about to go into production, but was larger in capacity than M.S. Napier's signed agreement permitted. This high-revving machine was the E98, twenty-four-cylinder air-cooled 'Dagger I' with a cubic capacity of 16.85 litres, a 7:1 compression ratio and an output of 630bhp at 4,000rpm. Two slim crankshafts running side by side, took drive from its left- and right-hand side vertically opposed cylinders, transferring it to a central reduction gear output shaft, set on the cross line of its 'H' configuration. The frontal area was small, despite the need to channel cooling air backwards to the four rearmost air-cooled cylinders, that done via a DNS designed, duralumin close cowling.

Flight testing was done by Fairey's test pilot, Chris Staniland, in a Fairey 'Battle' flying test bed, to optimise engine cowling designs for following higher compression versions. One was the 'E105 Dagger III' giving 800bhp, with double entry blower, as fitted to the Army Co-operation Hawker 'Hector' aircraft. This was the very last biplane ordered in any quantity by the RAF, with them being subsequently used for making reconnaissance and light bombing missions early in the Second World War. With cooling under control, Halford now schemed a 'E108 Dagger VIII' with 1,000bhp delivered from its twenty-four cylinders of $3\frac{13}{16}$in diameter x $3\frac{3}{4}$in stroke, with 7.75:1 C.Ratio at max 4,200rpm. Some 500 'Dagger' engines of Series III and VIII were ordered by the Air Ministry from Acton works where their experienced Machine Shop Superintendent from 1922, Henry Baume, had just replaced bowler-hatted Mr Allen as Works Manager in 1936. This was prior to the great increase in shop loading at Acton that accompanied those big re-armament orders of 1938. Soon these air-smoothed 'Dagger VIIIs' became the 'whining' twin-power units of the Handley Page 'Hereford' bomber, 150 of which were to be built by Short Bros & Harland in Belfast, to where 175 of these Series VIII engines were promptly despatched for the first batch of airframes. Early in the Second World War these RAF Squadron bombers saw active service in Europe and the North Atlantic area, when icing conditions allowed. But all 'Herefords' were later relegated to the secondary role of Bomber Crew training, in preparation for flying more modern types of bomber aircraft.

Only on the 'Napier-Halford Dagger' was a bold joint nameplate such as this displayed twice on every engine, this because its 16.85-litre capacity was well above their agreed maximum limit of engine size set back in 1927. This nameplate indicated the joint design work and patents of both D. Napier & Son and F.B. Halford contained within this larger Acton-built engine. The DNS-built 'Dagger', which held Halford design features such as his Patented 'Hydraulic Tappets' operated from its four sets of single overhead camshaft gear, clearly needed acknowledgement on this fine, but noisy-to-live-with, high-revving engine, in which the inherent installation problems of in-line air-cooled engines had been finally overcome. From 1935 a return to water cooling would be made, this for a big twenty-four-cylinder unit from Acton, the powerful Napier 'E107 Sabre' of 36-litre capacity, based jointly on Napier and Halford design work and which was shortly to be needed by the RAF.

Returning briefly to terra-firma, and going back to 1933, one discovers the greatest 'Lion' engine impresario of all time, John Rhodes Cobb, that unassuming 'gentle giant' amongst the ranks of extroverted track racers and record breakers using Napier power that had hitherto graced the British motor sport scene from year 1900. John Cobb was an accomplished Brooklands racing driver when, in 1933, he approached Reid A. Railton, Chief Designer at Thomson and Taylor Ltd, Brooklands, requesting that he design for him a car which could produce superior acceleration, 190mph top speed and greater endurance running on the high banked and, by then, undulating Brooklands Motorcourse. Cobb remained convinced that a long-life, 6:1 compression ratio, 'bog-standard' Napier 'Lion XIA' aero engine could produce all of this projected performance for his racing car, having an adequate 530bhp output at a moderate 2,350rpm, more effectively than the more powerful, but also more temperamental, short-life 'Racing Lion'. So an inexpensive, 'low hours', RAF surplus 'Lion XIA' was obtained, and Wilkinson at DNS Acton then obliged by having the engine converted for Cobb's project, fitting a long Sea Lion-type direct drive crankshaft, removing the aero propeller shaft reduction gearbox and adding a blanking-off plate to top the drive end crankcase. In the massive, finely fashioned, Railton car chassis, a Moss three speed and reverse gearbox was there to receive the great engine torque via a Borg and Beck single plate clutch. But surprisingly, despite the finesse in the design of the rugged front axle and steering mechanism, the remainder of the chassis was virtually a suitably 'beefed-up' copy of the Napier 'T75' design of 1920! This Railton design also had semi-elliptical front suspension, *no front brakes*, a double cantilever leaf spring rear suspension for its drum braked, fully floating, rear axle with E.N.V final drive and differential, a transmission brake, and even its set of Rudge-Whitworth wire wheels!

John Cobb raced his Reid-Railton designed 'Napier-Railton' at Brooklands from 1933, using reliable power from a modified 'Lion XIA' engine.

When the finely fashioned, deep-framed Railton chassis had been assembled, the 24-litre 'Lion' – the very heart of this car – was then installed at the Thomson and Taylor works, ready for Cobb's preliminary running trials. This done, a polished silver, light aluminium alloy 1930s-style racing body was added by Gurney Nutting, to complete the legendary 'Napier-Railton', this racing car was tailor-made for big John Cobb's exclusive use for record breaking at Brooklands, and also widely abroad during the next four years.

Such a high profile racing car project was an inspirational one for Napier staff and the craftsmen in the works, many of whom recall their visits to Brooklands and their admiration at the time for the purposeful Cobb and his unique Napier-powered track racing car, which carried the large sign-written black letters 'Napier-Railton' along its aluminium side cylinder fairings. 'Their' first racing appearance was at the 1933 Brooklands August Bank Holiday meeting when, from the handicap 'scratch mark' in the first event, John Cobb broke the outer circuit standing-start lap record at 120.6mph and, after gradually extending the car, won his first race against Kaye Don in a Bugatti. In that day's next race around the outer circuit of 2.7 miles, he was pleased when 'they' set a new lap record of 137.2mph, that beingfor 'Class A' vehicles of over 8,000cc. With more power in reserve, and that used only when other competitors and the curved and steeply banked track permitted, John Cobb pursued the Brooklands lap record year after year. In October 1935 he drove the 'Napier-Railton' on a wet day after the year's closing race meeting, using a fresh set of tyres and with great determination, raising the outer circuit lap record to 143.44mph – that for all time! Final climax at Brooklands Motorcourse was in 1937, when John Cobb won the British Racing Drivers Club 500km race there and averaged 127.05mph.

At 140mph, Cobb flies over the Brooklands Weybridge bump whilst setting the outer circuit record at 143.44mph in 1935.

Record breaking on the Bonneville Salt Flats in Utah, USA, gave a completely different driving challenge to Cobb and his support team when, without the curves and bumps of Brooklands, speeds rose dramatically. For example the twenty-four-hour endurance record there was set in 1936, with the same car and engine, at a 150.6mph average speed, in contrast to S.F. Edge's twenty-four-hour endurance record at Brooklands of 65.6mph back in 1907.

This fast 'Napier-Railton', at the same Bonneville record making visit, once again driven by Cobb, averaged 167.69mph for the one-hour record, and 168.59mph over the 100 mile distance!

While in the Utah Desert, John Cobb clearly then decided to go all-out for the World Land Speed Record on Bonneville Salt Flats, but with a brand new speed record car with a far greater power output available. Again it was Reid Railton that designed the new car, which had 2,800bhp of Lion power and was made ready for action back at Utah in 1938. From that time, 1937, Cobb's speed records would then be set in direct competition with another British racing driver, George Eyston, running his big car *Thunderbolt* powered by a pair of highly supercharged Rolls-Royce 'Merlin' V12 engines producing 5,000bhp. This series of records therefore triggered a 'head-to head' WLSR confrontation between Napier and Rolls-Royce machinery, which was to continue between these two British car and aero engine rivals, and between their respective drivers, right until the Second World War stepped in.

It was the threat of another war with Germany that, by 1935, had caused F.B. Halford, the Air Ministry and influential Napier engineers, to propose the development of an aero engine of twice the 1,000bhp power capability of the medium-sized, air-cooled 'Dagger'. That complex engine had maintained the Acton design team and workforce in active new development work during the mid-1930s Depression, and in fact beyond it until 1938. But, in 1935 possibly the greatest technological challenge of all time faced the management of DNS. Although Sir Harold Snagge himself was 'no engineer', he now had two energetic and experienced Technical Directors on his board, in the persons of Chief Engineer George Wilkinson and a new director, the still part-time Chief Designer of the 'Dagger', Frank Halford. On the ground at DNS too, were designers of the high calibre of George Murray and Bill Nowlan, plus those with engine development expertise such as Ernest Chatterton (piston engines), Alfred Penn (superchargers and turbines), and last but not least Henry Tryon (leading new research). These men, who had seen those earlier days following 1931, when DNS had lacked clear engineering direction, now seemed poised in mid-1935 to tackle the huge task set by the latest Air Ministry directive, this in competition with the other three members within 'The Big Four'; the task being to engineer a petrol fuel, aero piston engine of 2,000 plus bhp. Almost immediately a pair of new 'E107/2T' two-cylinder test units were ordered by the Air Ministry, and soon six prototype, twenty-four-cylinder 'E107' engines were ordered 'straight off the drawing board'. It was soon revealed within DNS under a veil of complete 'Official Secrecy', that the new DNS engine would be largely based upon their earlier two and six-cylinder Burt-McCollum sleeve-valve diesel-test units. These models had undergone long-term testing for Montague Napier's 'E 96 & E101' C.I. projects, that had earlier arisen from his own twenty-four-cylinder 'H'-configured diesel aero engine designs.

A highly effective worm and wormwheel sleeve drive system for their single sleeves had been patented for DNS by G. Wilkinson back in 1931, soon after Napier's death. Even the 5in bore and 4¾in stroke of the twenty-four compression ignition cylinders of 'E101' were to be retained, but it was necessary that the 'E107' compression ratio be much lowered down to a moderate 7:1. This was done by moving the junk heads further away from the sleeve ports, as with the high supercharger boost this was essential to offset detonation with the available petrols. A similar single sleeve valve design had been adopted, also with difficulty in manufacture, for all the new air-cooled Bristol engines since 1932, but they employed spur gears to drive the sleeves.

Former freelance consultant designer Frank Halford, soon to operate from DNS Board level, coordinated the efforts of this growing new design team at Acton, feeding in any ideas and improvements he thought wise through his Senior Design Assistant, W.H. Arscott, who was resident in the design office and invariably took much responsibility during Halford's frequent absence due to his work alongside other companies. A six-cylinder sleeve-valve test-unit was finally tested by the Research Department in 1936/7, before the first twenty-four-cylinder build was available to run in 1938, on a former 'Dagger' test bed. This lengthy test programme was supervised by George Wilkinson and results were compiled by Eric Carlisle at Acton works, where brief visits to test houses were made frequently by Frank Halford, accompanied by his close adviser and colleague from Golden Square, Dr E.S. Moult. This highly compact twenty-four-cylinder engine with a 36.65-litre capacity was soon to become known as the 'E107 Sabre'. It had a two-speed, double-sided supercharger that supplied fuel/air mixture from a four choke, updraft Napier-SU carburettor mounted to the rear of the central split crankcase. Although the 'E101' diesel had been of a vertical 'H' layout, it was then realised by designer Ben Barlow that a 'Flat H' layout would not only assist in servicing, and pilots' forward vision in single-engine fighter installations, but would also give better accessibility to all auxiliary units that could then be mounted either on top of, or below, the engine crankcase. This new layout, in effect, had made the 'Sabre' power unit a pair of twelve-cylinder, horizontally opposed water cooled engines, one above the other, with their two crankshafts combining their drive into a single propeller shaft output, through a helical gear-driven, torque-beam equalised reduction gearbox. With this G.A. layout then settled and Air Ministry 'rubber-stamped', engine detail design could now be begun in earnest.

1936 was a turbulent year for the British Nation, the 'Year of the Three Kings' historians have called it, but the death of George V after twenty-six years on the throne was only the start of the country's turmoil. This popular King's successor was due to be Edward VIII when crowned, but his sudden abdication then brought his diffident younger brother George to the throne in his stead. Thus, that same year, the new King, George VI, found himself at the head of a then proud colonial nation, once again preparing to defend itself against the 'old' enemy that they had fought against a mere eighteen years before. The Royal Air Force was equipping itself with whatever aircraft were available at the time, but faster and bigger planes would soon be needed to oppose the growing Luftwaffe. The recent secret developments started at DNS Acton works were typical of those elsewhere in the UK, but even in those often perilous times Napier engineers were still to be found patriotically involved in record bids.

For DNS, that same year, 1936, had established itself as the 'year of the three engines' a new situation that was to last for the next five years under the pressure of rapid re-armament. One, the 'Lion XIA', was now an old product but, in its revised form as a marine engine for Scott-Paine's high-speed launches, still gave a few new development and production problems. He, acting for his British Power Boat Company, had finally been successful in gaining orders for his high-speed motor launches (HSL) from a pair of fighting services, using the trusted and more readily available 'Sea Lion' engine installed now in triplicate. First was the Royal Navy who, in 1934, ordered six trial MTBs, Nos 01 to 06, for evaluation of its torpedo-launching capability by the Admiralty. These 60ft HSL-type craft, with a speed of 40 knots from triple 'Sea Lion' engine power, performed so admirably that repeat orders were soon placed for a further twelve similar MTBs, so forming three flotillas of six fast, highly manoeuvrable offensive craft for use in British Coastal Waters. It was further realised by the Admiralty that in coastal waters similar HSLs equipped with submarine hunting and destroying weapons could search out and catch in-shore U-Boats. These lesser-known wartime secret-applications of the heavier 63ft BPB Co. HSL, were fitted with just two reliable Power-Napier 'Sea Lion' engines which enabled a water speed of 30 knots when armed, were, in 1937, ordered in repeat batches, so comprising some sixty Motor Anti-Submarine Boats (MASBs or 'The little ships') for RN service around the UK and into the waters of the ports of later occupied Europe.

Two great Napierians at Acton, both of whom had received special recognition from Montague Napier himself, in the form of a 'job for life' with the firm (should they wish), were still holding responsible works positions, but were now nearing retirement. One was Mr W. (Billy) Mangan, the site works engineer who occupied the Napier Cottage beside the main works entrance. From there he wrote a valuable short history of DNS products. The other was Mr Fred Draper who, as the Second World War approached, was Superintendent of Engine Test at Acton. In addition he tested the shale oil-fuelled

A flotilla of Royal Navy MTBs in 1936 off the Isle of Wight en route to Malta, each powered by three 'Sea Lions' giving them 40 knots speed.

'To the rescue' in the Second World War, No.156, a British Power Boat Co. 64ft 'Whaleback' ASR launch powers through the sea in 1941, on the 1,500bhp from her three 'Sea Lions'.

'Torpedo Motors' that DNS built and supplied to the Admiralty, driving the torpedo rounds fired by those three new MTB Flotillas.

It follows that the RAF would soon recognise their need for larger, sea-going launches for air-sea rescue duties around the UK coast, in preference to adapted seaplane tenders. The 1935-built prototype for the 'RAF 100 Class', a 64ft HSL capable of 35 knots with a range of 500 miles, was a resounding success in sea trials, leading to the 1936 RAF order for numbers 101 to 114. In the engine room the two outer 'Sea Lions' faced rearwards for fast travel using 1,500bhp, while the centre engine faced forward and alone drove a central propeller via a Napier vee-drive gearbox for cruising, economy and for manoeuvrability. Later orders in 1939 for Nos.117 to 132 were to be merged, after No. 121, with those for the improved 1940 BPB Co. design of 63ft, RAF Type 2 'Whaleback' HSL, of which sixty-eight were constructed during the early years of the Second World War, each requiring three 'Sea Lions'.

A second engine, and in stark contrast, was Halford's 'Dagger III & H6' then entering full production alongside 'Sea Lions', so these provided rival priority claims for Works Manager, Henry Baume. While, thirdly, the design and unit testing of the highly secret 'Sabre' engine continued to absorb most DNS brains and their concentration, as directed by the Air Ministry.

All this while on the Board of the Napier Company more changes took place in 1937 as the result of the resignation of Sales Director Sir Harry Brittain; his place was taken at the start of the following year by The Hon. Thomas H. Brand. Also strengthening the DNS Board during 1938 was C. W. Reeve CBE, who became an Executive Director in May and DNS Joint Managing Director. A surprise 'family' appointment to the Board late in 1937 had also taken place, that of a younger cousin of Montague Napier, named Ian P.R. Napier M.C. He had hailed from that same, main Napier and Clydeside-based engineering family, and was in fact the great grandson of Robert Napier of Shandon.

Against the hectic background of growing re-armament orders within D. Napier & Son, there still survived the 'will to compete' for world records and world 'firsts', when the opportunity presented itself. This DNS did on three separate occasions during 1938-39, with performances from three different Napier engines, both old and new. Two were speed record attempts, but the first was more of an 'endurance record' by its nature.

The problem had been, how to take off and cross the North Atlantic from the UK to the USA, carrying a heavy payload of Royal Mail, plus the fuel load required for such a long flight? A strategy had been formulated by a Major RH Mayo using a short 'Empire' flying boat mother ship, *Maia*, to carry the very heavily laden trans-atlantic aircraft into the air, both climbing on four engines, then separating. This solution gave rise to the ingenious 'Short-Mayo Composite' pair of flying boats, both of these designed and built by Short Brothers of Rochester. The upper, payload-carrying flying boat was named *Mercury*, it was powered by four Napier 'Rapier VI' engines giving it a total power of over 1,500bhp, with built-in four-engine reliability. This 'semi-official' project, with Royal Mail and Fleet Air Arm flying involvement, was powered by four 'Rapier' engines gained from surplus Fairey 'Seafox' production engines at Acton and supplied to Shorts late in 1937. Both of these unique aircraft passed their trials and the first combined flight took place on 4 January. 1938. Finally, a first air-to-air separation took place on 6 February. in a shallow dive well out to sea. It was 21 July when an enormous Postal payload carried by *Mercury* made an Atlantic crossing from Foynes in Ireland to pass Montreal, flying 2,930 miles non-stop in twenty hours and twenty minutes, the first of many deliveries.

Four 385bhp 'Rapier' engines powered the transatlantic 'Mercury' floatplane upper component of the Short-Mayo 'pig-a-back' launch system of 1939.

Realising the potential of the 'Composite' for long distance records, starting on 14 December. 1938, Captain D. Bennett piloted *Mercury*, carrying a massive fuel load for her four small air-cooled 'Rapier VI' engines, 6,045 miles non-stop between the Firth of Tay and the Orange River Estuary in South Africa. From the time of the separation and launch from *Maia*, to touch down forty-two hours later, *Mercury* itself had set a new 'Long distance record for seaplanes'.

During the same period, speed on land was once again making the headlines in the UK, as John Cobb and George Eyston engaged in WLSR bids and records, just as Sir Henry Segrave and Sir Malcolm Campbell had done ten years previously, much to the credit of Great Britain in the technological and motor-racing world. But it was the first time on land that the two major water-cooled aero engine manufacturers, D. Napier & Son Ltd and Rolls-Royce Ltd had both been chasing the same World Land Speed Record at the same time in the same area of the United States – on the smooth Bonneville Salt-Flats. George E.T. Eyston was the first to make his attempt on 19 November 1937, cracking Campbell's record with Rolls-Royce power at 312.0mph. This he bettered on 27 August 1938 with an average on two runs of 345.5mph, still without a reply from John R. Cobb!

Cobb's new low, finely streamlined WLSR car had, once again, been designed almost to perfection by Reid Railton at Brooklands, but its two supercharged 'Racing Lion VIID' engines were only the used, and Acton reconditioned, engines out of Marion Carstairs' powerboat *Estelle V* of 1930 vintage, giving a combined 2,600bhp to its four wheel drive.

Railton had cleverly arranged both engines diagonally behind the driver, the forward one driving the rear axle, the rear one the front axle, with iced-water cooling during the runs. John Cobb took to this car, known initially as the 'Railton-Napier Special', and on his first serious attempt on 15 September 1938 clocked up 350.2mph – twice the top speed of his 'Napier Railton'! The game Eyston, with Rolls-Royce, responded with a 357.5mph average run later that year, but it was Cobb who returned again to Bonneville in 1939 to raise the WLSR to a new 'wartime figure' of 369.7mph. John was not content even with that result, believing he could be the first man to drive on land at over 400mph. This he did in fact achieve, after the Second World War: the barrier was broken when Napier Acton squeezed a little more power from those old 'Lions' to provide in the region of 2,900bhp output. John Cobb in 1947 made his first measured-mile run at 403mph, but a disappointing return run lowered his WLSR average for Great Britain and D. Napier & Son to 394.2mph. This world record stood virtually unchallenged for sixteen years, a suitable memorial to Cobb who died on the water in 1952. His brave world land speed record was eventually overtaken in 1963 by a 'Proteus' gas turbine-powered car, driven by Donald Campbell averaging just 403mph!

An amazingly bold, third Napier-powered record bid for the World Air Speed Record started in 1935, but was inextricably bound-up with the crucial testing of one of Great Britain's top secret defence preparations against the real threat posed by Nazi Germany in Europe. By 1937 it had been disclosed that an Ultimate World Air Speed Record bid was planned by a new 'Napier-Heston Racer' aircraft, while its cost of construction was to be underwritten by Morris Motor's Lord Nuffield. Perhaps rather surprisingly,

Before being enclosed by teardrop body, John Cobb is seen at Brooklands during trials of his 'Railton-Napier Mobil Special' WLSR car in 1938. She enjoyed 2,800bhp of 'Lion VIID' power, giving John the WLSR three times, the last being 394.2mph in 1947.

German 'intelligence' sources in the UK were soon to confuse this project with the development of a new fighter aircraft powered by a similar type of 'Sabre' engine! So, no wonder Napier Acton works had become well known to the Luftwaffe, well in advance of war, and so became a prime target during the blitz! The unusual background to this British air challenge, planned to be staged before 1939, was stimulated by the aim for dominance in air speed by both German and Italian aircraft and engine design companies. A similar ploy by Adolf Hitler had also been used to intimidate engineers working in European countries on racing car development, they often found themselves up against superior performance German Auto-Union and Mercedes-Benz cars, largely due to state funding. Great Britain had long dominated the World Land Speed Record scene, exemplified by John Cobb and his 'Railton-Napier Special' in 1938-39, as recounted above. But the additional prize of national air speed superiority was then far more indicative of military air-power superiority and a morale booster in case of an armed conflict or, worse still, a threatened invasion. For Great Britain to regain the W.A.S.R by 1939, would demonstrate alike to friendly and hostile world powers the potential strength of the RAF in resisting the large German Luftwaffe, or any similar world threat. The Board of DNS, very aware of that rationale decided, with the Air Ministry's support, that the Napier Company and the nearby Heston Aircraft Company should make a joint effort to regain our British national pride in the air. This was to be done using the latest DNS engine technology during its development programme, with the project costs backed by Lord Nuffield's generosity.

But what world target speed was to be aimed for by these joint ventures?, and what new technological advances would be harnessed to provide enough single-engine power when installed in such an advanced, light, yet very strong airframe? Answers to these questions had been prepared by Sir Harold Snagge of DNS and their Senior Installation Designer Arthur E. Hagg, then shared with both Major George P. Bulman, the Deputy Director of Engine Development at the Air Ministry, R.A. Clare, the Chief Technician and Aerodynamicist of Heston Aircraft and with Lord Nuffield, who had by then assured Bulman that he would provided the bulk of the money for the complete aircraft and its actual engine. The answer to the British 'target speed' question was emphatically given as '480mph plus!'. This figure was arrived at because, following the record speed by the Supermarine 'S6B' seaplane of 407.5mph in 1931 with a Rolls-Royce 'R' engine, the Italians had continued to develop their tandem type, twin Fiat-engined Macchi-Costoldi seaplanes with up to 3,000bhp, and so had made an Absolute World Air Speed Record of 440.7mph in October 1934 at Lake Garda. But Germany, on the other hand, without Schneider Trophy experience in high-speed flight, were now being encouraged by Hitler 'to catch up, or else'; their efforts amounted to just 380mph in 1937 by a Messerschmitt, and 394mph in June 1938 by a Heinkel. But, later in 1938 a new Messerschmitt Bf 109R was developed with a much boosted Daimler-Benz 601A engine; this prototype aircraft achieved a W.A.S.R of 468.9mph. The Germans had finally overtaken their Italian friends! The task that D. Napier & Son engineers had set themselves was immense as, coupled with Air Ministry requirements that the revolutionary 'Sabre' engine be partially test flown in the Nuffield-Napier-Heston Racer itself, the aircraft was being rapidly built and checked at Heston, before preparation for the 480mph plus world record speed attempt.

The DNS Board could see that the 'Sabre' would be needed in large quantities by the Air Ministry, but by December 1937 still only six engines had been ordered, apart from the already provisioned two and six-cylinder test units and the first four twenty-four-cylinder prototypes. Before the end of 1937, the first full scale engine had been run at Acton during November, on a new higher power dynamometer. By March 1938, the first fifty-hour test had been successfully completed, this included a steady power output performance of 2,050bhp. Sir Harold Snagge, Chairman of the Board then became anxious to obtain a firm production order for the 'Sabre', so in May 1938 he approached the Air Ministry for a substantial order for Acton works. By the end of 1938 the six prototype twenty-four-cylinder engines had been built, and by February 1939 these were all running to provide development test results. In March DNS were finally advised that a large order was about to be drafted for the engine and, further, that greatly enlarged DNS facilities were also going to be provided, outside of Acton. The first substantial order was placed in July 1939 for 100 'Sabres', plus material for 100 sets of parts to be manufactured in readiness, this before the engine had cleared any Type Test, let alone any 'Sabre' engine had been flown! Both these climacteric events did, however, take place marginally before 'A state of war with Germany' was declared by Tory Prime Minister Neville Chamberlain in September 1939. The Air Ministry's first type test of a prototype 'Sabre', with a hydraulic clutch change two-speed supercharger, had now been completed at Acton in August; rated at just 1,800bhp, this was indeed a cautious and modest start for what was, within just five years, to become the most powerful aero-engine to see service during the Second World War.

Powerful front end of the 'E107 Sabre' engine, which was first seen in 1939.

From RAF Northolt aerodrome, the maiden flight of the big Fairey 'Battle' flying test bed with its 'Sabre I' installation had been made on 31 May 1939, again with Fairey's Chris Staniland as Test Pilot. This was a challenging job he relished until Napier's own Flight Test Aerodrome, with its own flight staff, was opened at Luton in March 1940. RAF Northolt had entertained the DNS Experimental Installation Department since November 1938, mainly for 'Dagger' installation flight testing but, in the meantime, it had became a busy Home Defence station and training unit for the ATA. So DNS, with full Air Ministry approval and backing, then chose the high location of Luton Municipal Airport for its flight test airfield on grass, under the management of Cecil L. Cowdrey, the Chief Installation Engineer. Equipped then with just a basic hanger and huts, while sharing the airfield with Percival Aircraft, seventeen Napier engineers had just arrived by the time that Staniland flew in the Sabre-Battle from Northolt for continued flight testing. Road transport to and from Acton was needed to carry engines and personnel, which then included Chief Installation Designer C. V. Vickers and his D.O. staff. Soon, a second 'Battle' was delivered, which was to receive Luton's first 'Sabre' installation carried out in their own hanger. These two original test aircraft eventually accumulated some 700 Sabre flying hours between them, both before and after 'reinforcements' had arrived in the form of three specially designed and built, larger single-engine flying test beds during 1941. These heavy Folland 43/37s, with a wide, non-retracting undercarriage, could better withstand the great torque being produced by the 2,200bhp of the later 'Sabre III' engines at take-off. That engine was being developed for the carrier-borne Blackburn 'Firebrand' Naval strike fighter, which was partly constructed and then test flown from Luton. The compact 'Sabre' then weighed-in at a ton apiece when dry before their installation in the Follands, with this strenuous work being done at DNS Luton under the guidance of their Chief

Flying test beds at Luton for the 'Sabre II' onward were the big Folland 43/37s.

Ground Engineer H. Ball. Those three Folland test aircraft served DNS well during the war, covering much later prototype 'Sabre' flying, which amounted to well over 500 hours from the now aptly named Napier Luton Flight Development Establishment (FDE).

The London Acton main works of DNS also needed to expand and eventually they took new premises acquired at nearby Park Royal, where almost out-of-town prolonged test house running of high revving 'Sabre' engines could be better tolerated than in The Vale, by Acton High Street. Further open air 'propeller stand' type engine test facilities were later to be set up near the former London Undergound train sheds at Aldenham, on the abandoned extension from Edgware to Watford. Several in-town sites were also requisitioned for the purpose of engine overhaul and rebuilding, such as the use of parts of Earls Court Arena.

The DNS Board, still working from the vulnerable West London area, was faced with the need to expand the company workshops dramatically in order to fulfil the expectation of the mass production of their powerful 'Sabre' engine, so essential to the Ministry of Aircraft Production's war effort in support of the services, soon about to engage in battle.

By the end of October 1939, the choice had been made of a vast site at East Lancashire Road in Liverpool, where there was a pool of labour 10,000 strong from which, it was hoped, enough could be trained for precision engineering work in a new DNS production factory. In July 1940 some essential engineering staff were moved from Acton works to Liverpool in order to oversee the building of new Napier machine shops, assembly areas and test facilities, all told covering a floor area of over a million square feet, and all of which were to be ready for operation by the end of 1941, employing a freshly trained precision-engineering capable labour force. The first fully tested 'Sabre II' engine to emerge from Liverpool works was delivered in February 1942, that being just thirteen months after Acton's own first production 'Sabre II' unit. By 1942 the total DNS workforce exceeded 10,000.

World air speed record contender in waiting; at Heston in 1940 the 'Sabre I' of the 'Napier-Heston Racer' is ready for ground running.

The outbreak of war, with its effects on time and talent at DNS Acton, had inevitably blurred somewhat the earlier resolve of the company to 'take on the world' yet again in making a high profile air speed record bid to unseat the enemy owned Messerschmitt. A pair of 'Napier-Heston Racer' airframes were being expertly fashioned in the Heston Aircraft works, showing a 'stocky' but streamlined fuselage with short tapered wings, all constructed from timber for speed of manufacture of this beautifully designed and purposeful looking aircraft. By December 1939 one airframe was ready for the 'Sabre I' engine installation into its steel bearers. This was a special, highly boosted example from the prototype batch giving an output of 2,450bhp at 3,800rpm for a much shorter service life which was sufficient for an estimated 508mph speed record capability. January and February 1940 saw tethered engine running tests carried out, the Sabre fitted with a large three-bladed propeller and the single Gallay coolant radiator system down in the rear fuselage had a rearwards-facing efflux. All seemed well for an early maiden flight, but this was not made until after some lengthy delays in order to acquire AID and Civil Airworthiness certifications. Finally, on 12 June 1940, the flight was made, by the only available Heston test pilot that day, Sqn Ldr G.L.G. Richmond, who took off from the large Heston Aerodrome. A quite good take-off was followed by Richmond making a circuit, during which he noticed that the engine coolant temperature was climbing higher than normal. The pilot prepared to land, but after some level control problems during the approach, the 'Racer' stalled and hit the runway hard, so 'breaking its back' and one wing where a Dowty strut pushed through it.

Fortunately, the pilot was able to walk away with only minor scalds but, in the prevailing circumstances of wartime, any modifications after repair or a second attempt were soon both to be abandoned, much to Lord Nuffield's dismay alongside that of the DNS Board.

We feel justified here in pointing out that, in retrospect, by 1946 a new service prototype for the Hawker 'Fury Mark I', fitted with a fully developed 'Sabre VII' engine, had by then showed itself able to sustain a level speed of 490mph, which was quite sufficient for the record.

Under conditions of great security, frequent air raids and wartime blackout at night, painstaking development of the 'Sabre II' was continued by DNS in London and Luton while its producers, both in London and the Liverpool shadow factory, struggled to reach the targets set by the MAP for 'Sabre' engines to power a new fast Hawker Typhoon fighter. These were urgently needed to counteract the impact being made in hit-and-run raids over Southern England by the Luftwaffe's fast Fokke-Wulfe 190, fitted with four cannons for attack. The two Hawker Tornado versions, either with Bristol 'Centaurus' (a year late) or Rolls-Royce 'Vulture' (a year earlier but with problems) engines had by then both been cancelled in favour of the production Napier Sabre IIA-engined Typhoon.

The speed of the Typhoon had the edge over the F-W190, but because the airframe and engine were underdeveloped at the time of their RAF introduction into service in 1942, reliability was still low and so RAF pilot losses relatively high. The main engine problem lay in the distortion and wear that occurred with the 3/32in thick, 5in bore steel sleeve valves having four ports, they were then being produced at Acton and caused some seizures within the two magnesium alloy twelve-cylinder blocks of the 'Sabre'. The Napier research department, metallurgical laboratory and manufacturing methods men, looked in haste at all possible lubrication, material specification and surface finish variations. Eventually, they were wisely referred by Air Commodore R. Banks of the MAP, to the Bristol Engine Co. for detailed assistance in producing sleeves from a superior steel with nitriding treatment and a good bedding-down finish, plus centreless grinding that would resist any ovality. That company, as a result of their having previously laboriously 'mastered' manufacture of similar sized sleeve valves over the years, for such engines as their nine-cylinder 'Aquila' of 1934, or their then current fourteen-cylinder 'Taurus' radial engine of 1940, were finally willing to provide their fullest answers to DNS in the national interest. Suitable grinding machines were rapidly sent to the UK as cargo on one of the 'Queens', thence to DNS Liverpool works where production of sleeve valves began, more successfully, to this Bristol specification.

The 'Sabre IIA' engine became a standard for the 3,330 Typhoon IB fighter bombers constructed by Gloster Aircraft at the Hucclecote works, from 1942 to the end of Second World War. This engine, with a Napier-SU carburettor and double-sided, two-speed supercharger, was mass produced by Liverpool works. It gave a maximum power output of 2,180bhp at 3,600rpm when flying at an altitude of 4,000ft, this proved ideal in the ground attack role it assumed before and after D-Day 1944. A Typhoon fitted with four 20mm cannons as standard with a final addition of wing racks for eight rockets, or two 500lb bombs, made this aircraft into a most potent fighter bomber, or 'Bom-phoon', as the ground forces seeking air support came to know them. Flying for the Allied 2nd Tactical Air Force from D-Day, now from within France and Belgium, was further complicated by the need to take-off from temporary airstrips, that were often mud covered or produced clouds of abrasive dust on take-off which entered and harmed the sleeve valve operated 'Sabre' engines. This big snag was reported by Fighter Command, but rapidly solved by

'Sabre IIA' powered in 1942; a Hawker 'Typhoon IB' armed with four cannon at Napier Luton FDE. Inset is the Sabre's Momentum Air Filter.

Napier Luton producing an air-entry fitted 'Momentum Air Filter', a top priority job that was made and tested in one day, produced in quantity within one week and flown to Normandy for fitment to rebuilt engines, while causing only marginal loss of power. Just in time, the RAF Typhoon squadrons were back in business using their 'cab-rank' system of support to ground troops, who needed regular delivery of air support against the Nazis deadly Panzer and Tiger tanks. These hazardous short missions were mostly flown ahead of allied front line forces and sought out such well concealed enemy heavy armament and their supply columns, often on the move, as Typhoon pilots seldom left any undestroyed or in any kind of state to continue battle. One Belgian pilot wrote of this Normandy 'tank-busting' aircraft:

> It was probably the most versatile plane of the war, for it was used as a low level fighter, a long-range intruder with extra tanks, a dive bomber with two 500lb bombs under the wings, a low-level attack aircraft with eight rockets and an anti-flak shipping hunter. What a magnificent beast!

These later achievements in the battlefield had followed turmoil within DNS caused by the upheaval of establishing, and then managing, the large Liverpool shadow factory, from where 1,000 plus 'Sabres' per year for the MAP became increasingly vital to the RAF as the air war progressed. This rapidly changing situation now demanded a younger and more vigorous management board for D. Napier & Son than hitherto. Napier Flight Development Establishment Luton, had, by 1943, developed into a 'Mini Farnborough', with its 'Napier Squadron' of military aircraft on vital flight test work and new secret-listed prototypes within its airfield. Also the several smaller plants, such as Park Royal 2, were engaged in 'Sea Lion' marine engine production under Superintendent Bill Lewis, for which Winston Churchill later awarded him the MBE. Another was the Raynes Park light machine shops; these were acquired from British Salmson motors, along with its former skilled workforce and their machine tools. All were taken over en-bloc. Now, and at long last, the old family based DNS business, with around 2,000 employees, was transformed during the war into an expanding organisation that badly needed a more robust management than existed in 1940, the year when Ian Napier had resigned from their Board. Financier Sir Harold Snagge had steered the company well through the complex financial fortunes of DNS as its Chairman since 1932, and was now backed up by a new Managing Director, C.W. Reeve CBE, as of February 1940. Their fellow directors on the DNS Board were: the Hon. T.H. Brand, Chief Engineer G. Wilkinson, Assistant Chief Engineer W.P. Savage, Air Vice Marshall A. E. Borton, Deputy Managing Director A.F. Burke, Chief Designer F.B. Halford and Registrar R.C. Johnson. All were experienced: but some were ageing!

The War Government, and in particular the Ministry of Aircraft Production under the strong leadership of Lord Beaverbrook, stepped-in at the end of 1942, and recommended an immediate change in the composition of the DNS Board, at which most DNS Directors resigned their posts. This left the way clear for an almost new Board to be appointed from 1 January 1943, while at the same time D. Napier & Son Ltd was to be 'absorbed' into the English Electric Company Group, where it could be directed by a powerful E.E. Co. management team during the national crisis caused by the war. At this point, Sir George Horatio Nelson, Chairman of the E.E. Co., was invited to take over the chairmanship of the D. Napier & Son Board, while he was also allowed to appoint his young son, Henry George Nelson, as DNS Managing Director from the same date. As this young appointee was then at the same age and management level as the self-appointed Montague Napier had been in 1896 when he had then assumed control of DNS, there was little point in raising any objection within the company to this new boardroom family association. Although within the MAP ranks there were some early misgivings concerning the sudden appointment of this young, well qualified, former Cambridge University Engineering Graduate as the Napier MD! However, soon amongst many DNS staff, Mr Nelson's first initial 'H' had earned for him the good-humoured 'nickname' MD. 'Half-Nelson', this being coined by making a direct comparison to his distinguished father, Sir George, who then also headed the whole vast E. E. Co. Group.

The Nelsons were well supported in their wartime DNS Board by: Mr Percy Horsfall, Deputy MD A.F. Burke, Brigadier General Wade H. Hayes, G.A. Riddell – who became Chief Accountant, and Registrar Ronald C. Johnson – later to become DNS's secretary.

Fortunately, remaining within the technical ranks of DNS were some stalwarts, although the 'awkward' partnership between former directors Halford and Wilkinson was soon dissolved when George Wilkinson retired in 1942 after two decades of steady technical leadership. Frank Halford was soon to vanish from the Acton scene after his resignation as Chief Designer from January 1943, preferring to consolidate his working relationship with de Havilland at Stag Lane who were, by then, well into jet engines which Halford clearly saw as his own way forward in engine design. This left the solution of all 'Sabre' development problems in the hands of Chief Development Engineer Ernest Chatterton, in conjunction with Supercharger Chief Alfred Penn, plus Henry Tryon's widest experience. Before long there were introduced to Acton two significant new names: in 1944, with the war nearing its end, the widely experienced Herbert Sammons was made DNS Chief Engineer, he was soon followed, from the E.E. Co., by L. Frank Hall, who was to direct all Napier Research. Under the stalwart Works Management of Henry Baume, the next three years was to see the completion of 'Sabre' production orders, satisfying all MAP requirements.

The steadily increasing power output and reliability of the 'Sabre', achieved through concentrated development at Acton and its neighbouring works in the Greater London area, meant that engines of the Series IIB and IIC became available by 1944 to power the Hawker 'Tempest' fighter, itself starting life at Hawkers as the Typhoon Mk II. In this design, a much thinner aerofoil wing, elliptical in planform, permitted yet higher speeds without the onset of 'compressibility buffetting' as with the 5ins thicker 'Tiffy' wing. But this change meant also that the wing fuel storage space was much reduced, and for that reason a longer nose section behind the engine in the Tempest design contained an additional fuel tank in front of the cockpit. Incidentally, this gave some protection against the severity of 'Sabre' noise and fumes that hampered pilots in 'Tiffy' cockpits.

The prototype Tempest V was first flown by Hawkers' Phillip Lucas on 2 September 1942 from Langley when he immediately reported that it was 'a livelier, more precise and more aggressive fighter than the Typhoon'. This was good news for the RAF, who needed a faster fighter aircraft than the Spitfires of the time, and this very aptitude was to be of great value during 1944 when Tempests caught and destroyed over 600 'V1' flying bombs. The Tempest V had a 'Sabre IIB' engine giving 2,420bhp at 3,850rpm, with 11lb boost at take-off and for interception. Both Bill Humble and Roland Beamont claimed that it had a speed capability 'in excess of the 1939 Messerschmitt 464mph World Speed Record'. This fighter went into quantity production at Langley in time to see active service on and after D-Day in 1944. Also at home it spearheaded England's defence against the German 'V1 – Doodle-bug', which severely threatened London, and DNS Acton works where the ARP mounted a 'roof spotter' early warning system for the offices, shops and test houses.

At Napier F.D.E. Luton, a range of development engines were fully tested in modified 'Tempest' airframe installations, including the higher-powered Sabre IV and VA with RAE-Hobson bulk injection carburettors fitted to improve the aerobatic reliability of the Sabre engine over that with the original SU twin double choke, updraft carburettor unit. This then led to the 'Tempest VI' aircraft type that was produced by Hawkers from 1945 on, powered by the 2,600bhp Sabre VA engine giving it an improved air speed to 475mph. The 'Sabre VI' was designed at Napier F.D.E Luton, it had a front cooling fan behind the propeller boss, which gave a neat annular radiator 'Tempest' installation, and did away with the normal big 'chin' scoop that had contained air inlets for the updraft carburettor, oil cooler and Gallay

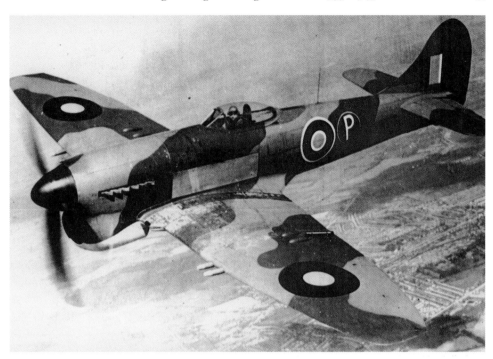

With thinner semi-elliptical wings, a prototype Hawker 'Tempest V' is captured in full flight out of Luton FDE, powered by a 'Sabre IIB' giving 2,420bhp at 3,850rpm.

radiator. A Luton-designed ducted spinner experimental 'Tempest' was also test flown in 1945; it aimed to further improve the entry of cooling air to its 'Sabre VI' of 2,600bhp at 3,850rpm with 15lb boost. After that, a twin 'Sabre VI' annular radiator installation was tested in a Vickers 'Warwick' bomber at Luton, a multi-engine arrangement with military or civil transport aircraft in mind and 5,000bhp on tap.

The 'Sabre VII' was another work under development, this engine had a larger supercharger giving 17 lb boost, with water-methanol injection directed into the supercharger eye along with the bulk-injected petrol fuel. This fully type-tested engine was then cleared for 3,000bhp for take-off, with a rated 3,055bhp at 3,850rpm, and medium supercharge, for combat at 2,250ft when it powered the fastest of the Second World War prototypes, the fine Hawker 'Fury Mark I' fighter.

The D. Napier & Son Ltd Company, who ended the war employing a peak of 19,500 personnel, had by the end of 1945 produced a total of just over 5,000 'Sabre' engines. This total included all types from Series I to VI of this engine, out of which a total of 1,500, including all the prototypes, had been introduced and manufactured in the Acton works itself, the balance of 3,500 'Sabre IIA, IIB and VA' engines had come from the production lines at Liverpool works shadow factory. During that same year the company had received Royal recognition when it was honoured that March by a visit to Liverpool by Their Majesties the King and Queen. Prior to this, DNS Liverpool works had received a visit during March 1944 by the Minister of Aircraft Production, the Rt Hon. Sir Stafford Cripps, who was able to tour that vast production works in the company of not only the

Rear equipment of the ultimate 'Sabre VII' engine giving 3,050bhp for take-off, showing flat supercharger casing bulk injected by two pipes for petrol and water-methanol.

A rare bird in profile, the Hawker 'Fury Mk I' fighter prototype having a neat annular fairing for its 'Sabre VII' power unit. Her level air speed could reach 490mph.

Nelsons, but of the newly appointed DNS Chief Engineer Herbert Sammons who was to become the technological leader of DNS during the expansive post-war period.

At the other end of the power scale had been the 'Sea Sabre' engine project of 1942 onwards, for which the basic 'Sabre V' bulk fuel injected engine was chosen, suitably de-rated to a maximum of 2,000bhp at 3,500rpm. This unit was 10ft long over its big marine gearbox with integral clutch and reverse gear with an output shaft set 10ins below the engine centreline. The large 45-knot, long duration, sea-going air-sea rescue launch, designed and built by British Power-Boats for operation in the Pacific Ocean theatre, had needed four 'Sea Sabres' giving an 8,000bhp combined output. After its prototype had been built and tested in the Solent, the special craft was cancelled, remaining issues being left to the US Navy.

Eventually it was the long-lasting marine 'Sea Lion' engine that was to get the 'last laugh' from 1945 at Liverpool, when all super-precision, high profile Sabre production had ceased after the war ended. The crews of triple 'Sea Lion'-powered RAF high-speed launches of the Air-Sea Rescue Service had pulled thousands of airmen from the open sea during the Second World War in Europe, working ceaselessly under their motto 'The sea shall not have them'. From 1942 a design of 68ft HSL, having greatly improved accommodation, had been introduced by the British Power Boat Co., 120 of this type were built, and became popularly known as the 'Hants & Dorsets', each launch yet again utilising triple 'Sea Lions' for its propulsion. After 1945 many continued in service, while others were converted to Rescue and Target Towing Launches (RTTLs), continuing in RAF use until the mid-1950s and requiring Napier spares from Acton and Luton works. This came at the same time as when fast RAF Tempest VIs with the Sabre VA engine were being used as airborne target tugs for RAF jet pilots in training, up until 1954 in

More roomy Air-Sea Rescue launches appeared during 1942, including 120 of these triple 'Sea Lion'-powered B.P.B. Co. 68ft 'Hants & Dorset' type with a 28 knot speed.

Sir George H. Nelson, the first Lord Nelson of Stafford who was long-term Chairman of the English Electric Co., and also the Chairman of D. Napier & Son from January 1943 to 1962.

the UK. Suddenly, while these RTTLs were being maintained in service (most still being fitted with triple 'Sea Lions' in the 1950s), a new batch of six Vosper-built RTTL 1As were laid down as late as 1956, these, surprisingly, also powered by Napier 'Sea Lions'. These engines were now being manufactured or just reconditioned by Liverpool works, ten years after the last newly built Sabre had been delivered from there. The twelve-cylinder Napier 'Lion' engine from a 1916 design, and in its twenty Series types had, by that time, been a product of the company for fully forty years! Could that service record ever be surpassed within DNS, or elsewhere? By 1946, with a new marine diesel about to come off Acton's drawing boards, could this one day become an equally strong contender for a Napier power unit longevity title? Well, perhaps such a record could repeat itself at DNS, but it would certainly take a very exceptional run of engineering successes within this same company to achieve such long service life again! Only time would tell whether, in this great power engineering business, history would ever be able to repeat itself.

D. Napier & Son had, throughout its earlier history, always proved exceptional for the 'value for money' it gave to its customers, plus in-service support. DNS Senior Deltic Applications Engineer Mr P.(Pip) Plant put it in a nutshell by saying this: 'D. Napier & Son has given more Good Engineering per Pound spent, than any comparable company'.

7

OCTANE EXITS AS OIL ENGINES EXCEL
1946–1956

With peacetime re-established at very great cost throughout the free world by the end of 1945, most wheels of industry now restarted, turning in rather similar circles to those they had done in 1939. But where the necessities of war had removed, or so changed, an industrial company's traditions of manufacturing and trading, to the extent that they had done for the 140-year-old company of D. Napier & Son, then perhaps the way forward was going to be set in a rather different direction. By 1946, both DNS and Marconi were relatively new, but highly significant, partners within the giant E.E. Co. industrial group which held influence throughout the British Isles. Apart from its E.E. Co. owned Napier production factory site in Liverpool, DNS was still situated mainly in the Greater London area. Now, back in peacetime, it also enjoyed the good fortune of sharing its own Chairman, Sir George H. Nelson, who had received his knighthood in 1943, with his wider E.E. Co. Group itself.

During the conflict just passed, the E.E. Co. had provided not only some wise counsel, but also considerable technical support. A number of tangible assets for DNS had been provided to assist in the Sabre engine production programme, in particular E.E. Co.'s newly designed and built Regenerative Dynamometers to test and run-in each Sabre, as these engine-driven units generated a lot of spare electrical power. This output had not only provided some power for each of the works at Acton, Park Royal and Liverpool, where these advanced electrical dynamometers had been installed in the test houses, but then fed any excess power from the Napier premises directly into the local national grid system. Now using modern test equipment, three hangers, a flight installation test bed and a tilting engine test stand, all these supplied by E.E. Co. to DNS during the latter part of the war, the Luton F.D.E. had emerged as the ideal premises for aircraft prototyping and flight test development, and so now stood with resources available to take on a wide variety of airborne projects. Similarly, DNS now had deep roots firmly entrenched, not only in London and Luton, but also in its Liverpool plant, with its great array of machine tools along with both assembly and test facilities. All in all, DNS was stronger and stood on the verge of exciting, potentially major developments. Clearly a lot of redundant staff and workpeople needed to be shed in the short term, but governed by the famously enlightened policies of the E.E. Co. regarding apprentice training, and staff re-deployment within its nationwide organisation, this gave the majority of highly skilled DNS employees some real security and fresh optimism for their futures in precision and power engineering.

Staff who were employed or under apprentice training in 1946 felt only too aware that they were engaged in mechanical engineering at the very cutting edge of contemporary internal-combustion engine technology. The Napier Company in its three main plants at London, Luton or Liverpool now, more and more, embraced the appearance and atmosphere of 'research establishments', in which almost every new design and project underway seemed to be of national importance, several actually being on the Secret List.

At Acton, under the Nelson Management Team from out of English Electric, apprentice training was, since the war, to be made a much higher priority than before it, with new investment in full-time engineer instructors working from within an apprentice training department. That is not to forget the starting of apprenticeships by David Napier himself in 1835 at Lambeth works, when just two years later his own son James started a ten-year apprenticeship, up until the DNS partnership was forged between father and son in 1847. In Spring 1944 an Acton draughtsman, Arthur Parker, was appointed by Works Manager, Henry Baume, to the new post of DNS apprentice supervisor, he to be responsible for the selection, instruction and education of DNS indentured apprentices within the London group of factories. He immediately established a training school in North Acton, with an intake of just seven apprentices, using temporary premises with workshop, lecture room, tool stores and an exhibition engine bond, these all standing in the former Elizabeth Arden cosmetics factory. His two instructors were Ted Shaylor for fitting and Charles Jones for machining, with a draughting course provided in addition, being run by Arthur Parker himself.

In the engine bond, at any one time, were five Sabre and two Rapier engines being prepared by the trainees as display sectioned engines, several going to the far corners of the world as well as into UK universities and military training colleges. The first annual 'Apprentice Presentation' was arranged in the new Acton canteen for January 1946, when the winner of the new Company Trophy was Alfred Harris, presented by Works Manager H. Baume while Arthur Partridge won the Foreman's Trophy via Works Superintendent W.E. Lewis. Managing Director H.G. Nelson then addressed the assembled apprentices and visitors, stating prophetically in New Year 1946 that:

> Britain has to face global competition of the fiercest kind, especially from new sources like China and India, where labour is cheap. We have, however, the advantage of being pioneers in engineering, and the object of the apprentice scheme is to ensure we maintain the initiative in the days ahead.

Meanwhile, the permanent training school had been built and equipped at Mansfield Road, Park Royal; it was opened in February 1946 with two additional instructors in Oliver Seymour and Frank Bonney, while apprentice numbers had by then risen to 130. From the summer of 1946 it was possible to engage a whole group as one 'apprentice entry' straight into this DNS training school, where all were given six months basic theoretical and practical engineering instruction together, and then tested for satisfactory workshop skills before entering the main works. Out there, according to each youth's

Seen in 1944, the first intake of Napier graduate apprentices with Arthur Parker the pioneer apprentice supervisor, and first green-collared Instructor Ted Shaylor.

aptitude, they were placed within the works, offices or test facilities, usually for periods of up to three months, to acquire new skills, gain experience and to benefit from real 'on the job' training. At this time day release for college studies also commenced, which augmented traditional evening class study to gain strong qualifications. Arthur Parker also introduced social and sporting activities for apprentices, including a summer camp, to help bond the lads into a closer Napierian team. Fortunately, in this period, the Napier Athletic Club had revived once more, along with its evening social events, after all the restrictions imposed during wartime, so that apprentices could progress into the established adult sporting activities, which took place at the large Gunnersbury Napier Sports Ground. A traditional, annual event had always been the 'Works versus Offices Football Challenge Competition' that had started way back in Montague Napier's day, when Acton works was known as the 'Napier Motor Works'. The trophy had changed hands many times over the last forty years, but was always fought for in a most sportsmanlike manner with the proceeds going to charity.

The apprentice supervisor's role was soon duplicated at DNS Luton F.D.E. By 1946 their apprentices passed through similar basic workshop training, either at Park Royal or in a Luton works training school, set up under Manager C.L. Cowdrey. The apprentice supervisor there was Bob Yule and his instructor team was geared to airframe work as well as engine technology. The first Luton presentation day was in 1947, when the 'Best Apprentice of the Year' award was presented to R. Woolfrey by Cecil Cowdrey, while the DNS Liverpool works soon had a similar training scheme to that 'down south'.

But reminders of wartime struggles to meet deadlines over the Sabre and Sea-Lion orders were still there, as design, research and manufacturing staff attempted to become involved with the challenges of entirely new products, some as yet without familiar shape or even a name. But, some engine types would not 'lie down and die' easily, particularly the Sabre aero-engine which was in its 'later-development stage' when the war ended. Advanced design type numbers for that superb engine still stood in design registers while the RAF flew the Tempest V and VI in service at home and abroad, in fact, it was flown wherever a fast, heavily armed fighter was needed which could take off from shorter colonial airstrips than any new RAF jet fighter was then able to do.

The main area of development for the Sabre that remained unresolved, was that of increasing power from higher boost-pressures at altitude, at the time this was achieved from two stage supercharging with inter-stage charge cooling. Design Nos. E118 /119 /122 all covered these developments, in which the higher power was to be absorbed by a pair of contra-rotating propellers, but of a smaller diameter than the 14ft, three- and four-bladed single propellers of the Hawker fighters of the Second World War. The engine type 'E122' of 36 litres, was to be the last bid to produce a fan-cooled, annular radiator, high-power installation, giving 3,350bhp at 3,600rpm, suitable for single tractor/pusher or multi-engine wing installations. By 1947, the prototype for the E122 project – destined to be the 'Sabre's Swan-Song' – was being manufactured for test at Acton works, while Napier Luton had prepared five-strong design studies for single-engine fighter planes that would accept the full 'E122' power output and size. This engine had been offered to outside

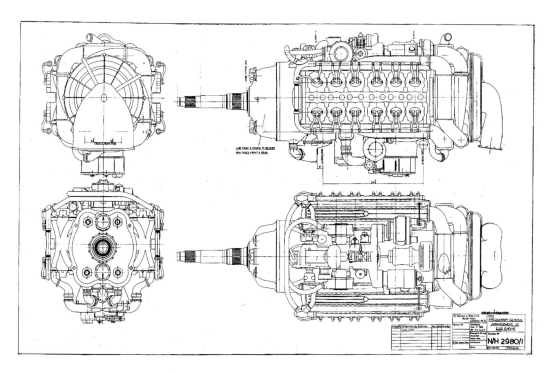

The 'Sabre' that was sheathed: four views of the 3,350bhp 'E122' engine of 1947 showing its two-stage supercharging with charge-cooling and contra-rotating prop-shafts.

aircraft firms, including Vickers, complete with power curves, the fullest specifications and an installation drawing prepared by DNS. Almost without prior warning, a high-powered delegation from the Air Ministry came into the plant, shut down manufacture of the engine and removed the 'evidence' to Rolls-Royce at Derby. 'Them-up-the-road' were about to introduce a large 46-litre engine of similar configuration, known there as the 'Eagle 22', which was designed to give 3,500bhp at 3,500rpm. Whether that Napier 'E122' did become of any help to Derby, no one knows! But this drastic move did at least do two things: it left the way clear for Rolls-Royce to submit their 'scaled-up Sabre' for the Westland Wyvern project, while remaining unchallenged by the E122. It, also left a more open road for DNS to make its late entry into the aero gas turbine engine field during 1947, with their first major type, the E128 'Naiad I' turbo-prop engine (see Appendices 3 f/ h/ i and 5).

Now to record several other 'Sabre-rattling' projects that were mooted in the 1940s, notably the new 'E113T', a two-cylinder, sleeve-valve, test-unit, with individual petrol injection, working on the two-stroke cycle. The unit was built and extensively run by the Napier Research Department at Park Royal, it caused huge noise pollution over the whole of the North Acton area from 1940 until October 1942, when this vee-twin unit, with a Sabre bore and stroke, was passed over to Ricardo's for development! Another, the 'E120 stretched Sabre' design of 1942, with thirty-two cylinders and a pair of long eight throw crankshafts, was probably never built despite its potential output of 4,000bhp. During Luton's Typhoon development work, the FDE was actively involved in a project to turbo-charge Sabre engines with units placed outside the fairings, the system employed two GEC-type blower units fed through two special exhaust ducts set above the wings. Apparently, the red glow these emitted while flying at night was found to more than offset any advantage in power and speed over any night adversary or 'flak' (as stated here), so the scheme was dropped there and then.

That type of engine exhaust-driven, power output booster-system had not been tried by DNS since 1926, but this interlude brought back an interest in turbo-supercharging of both petrol and diesel engines that was then actively pursued from 1947 at the express wish of DNS Chairman, Sir George Nelson. 'Express wish' appears a fitting expression to use here, because the expanding diesel-electric railway locomotive business of E.E. Co. was based on Sir George's knowledge of modernisation plans for UK rail locomotive power over the next decade and of impending railway nationalisation which made a growing demand for higher-powered express passenger diesel locomotives on Britain's railways seem inevitable. The existing four-stroke 12SVT engines of the E.E. Co. then needed to be boosted to higher power output for their locomotives; this required more efficient turbo-blowers, preferably of British manufacture, so Sir George turned to DNS to take on the task of designing and producing suitable centrifugal impeller turbo-blowers for their diesel engines from Acton. This new type of work was started on a commercial basis in 1947, under the leadership of the Chief Engineer of the Napier Aero Gas Turbine Department, AJ Penn, with Lionel Elford as aerodynamic designer of the centrifugal compressors and turbines within this new division. BT (Bertie) Bayne, the Chief Gas Turbine Performance Engineer, was made responsible for engine mass-flow requirements, and new methods of matching turbo-blowers to engine exhaust requirements, plus deciding the number of frame sizes needed in the new Napier turbo-blower range. These universally designed and adaptable units, giving a predicted increase of between 25% and 35% in engine power output – which would mean an improvement for the diesel engines of over 500bhp that were then planned to be blown, would also provide a marked fall in engine fuel consumption under long-term service conditions.

The early 'TS200' blowers were fitted in pairs to the EEC 12SV engine used in early trial locomotives, but it was soon realised that these lighter power units, with a 1,200bhp output, gave only the hauling power equivalent to a 'Class 5' British steam locomotive. In 1947 the very first two pioneer diesel electric main line 'Co-Co'-type locomotives were constructed by E.E. Co. at Rugby with their larger 16SVT engine of 1,600bhp, for trials on the London Midland & Scottish Railway, these being numbered 10000 and 10001. The plan hatched by the E.E. Co. was to donate them both to the LMS, this in fact was done with '10000', but the second was delivered after January 1948 as railway nation-alisation was implemented, so it was offered to the British Transport Commission instead for its evaluation. Now in the hands of the new British Railways Midland Region, their power was again found to be insufficient to take over the duties of Class 7 or 8 steam locomotives, which necessitated the two of them double-heading heavier trains on the West Coast Mainline, when hauling such services as the scheduled fast-train 'Royal Scot' from Euston to Glasgow. In future E.E. Co. pilot scheme main-line locomotives, their much heavier EEC 16SVT Mk 2 diesel engine was always used, this was again turbo-charged by no less than four small-sized Napier 'TS100' turbo-blowers, but which now gave the required output of 2,000bhp while driving a suitably enlarged E.E. Co. generator. Unfortunately, this led to extra weight in the engine room, which would then require two more riding axles under the locomotives; this became the normal Co-Co wheel arrangement for the BR 'Type 4' locomotives.

From this gradual beginning the successful Turbo-Blower Department set up in 1950 was developed, thus relieving the DNS Aero Gas Turbine Department of all their non-aero-engine workload, this enabled them to concentrate all their efforts on the design of the new Eland turbo-propeller engine. On the production front, Acton works was able to supply turbo-blower components, build units complete and provide test facilities up until 1950, when sizes and quantities grew much larger. At that point, DNS Liverpool works completely took over the production of blowers, now in greater quantity. By 1966, when DNS Acton works and design offices were about to be closed down, 2,000-plus turbo-blower units per annum were being delivered out of the DNS Liverpool plant, where 670 engineering personnel were then employed on turbo-blower production.

But the main thrust of DNS development work immediately after the war concerned two compression-ignition piston engines, both with very different design backgrounds.

To start first with the 'Senior Service's' requirement, which had been drafted in 1944 as a result of the findings of the Admiralty's 'Feddon Committee', this committee recommended that wooden-hulled light naval craft should not in future be propelled by petrol fuel engines. Rather, that lightweight diesel engines should be installed in them, providing still more power with greater fire safety in war service. After 1945, there was a keen contest for this contract between UK engine manufacturers, the E.E. Co.'s own designs were included, plus also a design submitted by DNS for a compact, high-speed,

Napier turbo-blower assembly shop at Liverpool works seen in the early 1950s.

lightweight marine diesel engine with about half the weight/power ratio of the others. Sir George Nelson and the Admiralty Board finally selected the revolutionary engine design from DNS, with its initial hush-hush detail design and development to be done at Acton. Earlier, triangular linking of three Junkers-type diesels had been proposed by the National Gas & Oil Engine Co. Ltd under some secrecy during 1942, but then the 1946 DNS triangulated design was further encouraged through a Mr Penwarden's cylinder-firing order scheme for the six-row, eighteen-cylinder engine, made out at the Admiralty Engineering Laboratory, West Drayton. That was now based upon the practicability of circulating firing orders and differing directions of crank rotation. Later on at Acton, with an inlet piston phase angle lag of 20degrees (Junkers had 11degrees) was then to be established, and the firing intervals between the three cranks in each triangular row was fixed at 40degrees. With a pair of rows firing in alternate sequence, within the eighteen explosions every revolution, this provided an impulse to one crankshaft every 20degree of rotation and so an almost constant torque.

At DNS the experience gained a decade earlier with their six-cylinder 'Culverin' aero diesel engine, was being utilised to immediate advantage for this new multi-cylinder design of ultra lightweight marine oil engine which was, likewise, to operate on the opposed piston two-stroke cycle. An in-line six-cylinder Junkers 'Jumo 205' engine had been exhaustively tested by BICERA during the war, when Mr H. Sammons had been involved there. Also, in September 1946, the Napier Research Department at Acton had put on display a part sectioned, Second World War-captured, and more highly developed Junkers Jumo 207B aero engine. This six-cylinder, opposed-piston unit of 16.6-litre capacity, had been found on test to produce 734bhp at 2,400rpm, when only boosted by its engine-driven supercharger. The Jumo 207B was, however, also fitted with charge cooling units plus, as an additional feature, an integral turbo-supercharger to maintain its power at high altitude, which could be switched in via a turbine waste-gate. That turbo-supercharging arrangement had clearly also been tested to give an indication of its possibilities, well ahead, for marine units fitted with a turbo-blower and charge-cooling, as used on Series 3 Deltic marine engines that eventually appeared on Acton drawing boards fifteen years later, in 1961. But this unit had been on extended test in the research department chiefly in order to evaluate its performance at sea level, which would then indicate its likely response when operating in the marine engine environment.

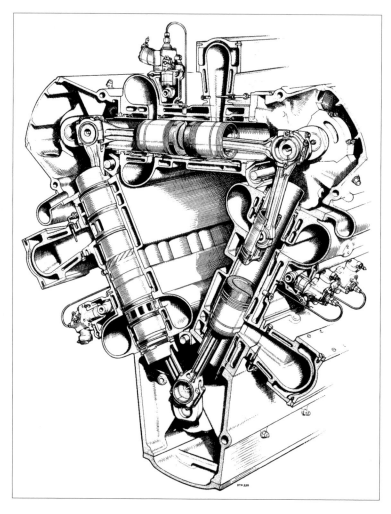

Napier 'Triangle of Power' in 3D: the 1951 mechanically blown 'Deltic' engine showing three scavenge blower drive shafts and Inlet and Exhaust pistons in three wet liners.

Design type E130 was laid down at Acton in September 1946. This being specifically for Motor Torpedo Boat propulsion, it had a $5^1/8$in bore for its eighteen long cylinder liners, in which its thirty-six opposed pistons each had a 7¼in stroke, giving the engine a swept volume of 88 litres. The proposed performance was set to be 2,500bhp at 2,000 crankshaft rpm, while from the marine gear box an output shaft was to turn a variable-pitch water screw at 850rpm. This '18-1' specification design work started in 1946 under Mr 'Ben' Barlow (an ex-Sabre designer), along with Mr George Murray, but the overall project was managed by young DNS MD Mr Henry Nelson, whilst the company's Chief Engineer throughout was again Mr Ernest Chatterton. By early 1949 the 'E130 18-4' MTB engine of 2,500bhp had an ahead and astern gearbox with a hydraulic clutch. This design work was led by DNS gearing specialist Len Snell. Also, strong, hardened and ground, straight spur gears within engine phasing gear cases were all of 3DP tooth size and delivered the input power from the three crankshafts, via idlers to the almost central output shaft gear into the marine gearbox, all of which were fed sparge-jet oil lubricant while the engine ran. Because this engine then finished up standing upon one apex of its equilateral triangular section, which otherwise was of Greek 'Delta' form, it was therefore named the 'Deltic' triangulated engine. All eighteen diesel injectors integral with pumps and control racks were thus reachable on its three cylinder banks, while four strong widely spread anti-vibration feet were provided below it.

Over ninety DNS design variants of the Deltic design type were to be schemed over a twenty-five-year period, including test units, all but one with the same bore and stroke as the E130 spec, but varying greatly in shape and power output when built; these possessed 3, 6, 9, 15, 18 or 24 cylinders, and intended for an assortment of applications (see Appendices 3n & 4d).

The earliest 'E130' eighteen-cylinder Deltic applications were for marine engines to fulfil the original Admiralty test programmes, following the prototype building work done by DNS up to January 1952, when there were six engines ready for Naval observed trials of installations in the Admiralty Test Houses at Acton and Park Royal sites, plus tests at sea. The first of those trials was carried out at sea in an ex-Second World War German E-Boat that had two of its engine room Mercedes-Benz MB511 diesels replaced by Deltic 18-11A units of an equivalent 2,500bhp sprint rating, installed in that Patrol Boat, renumbered P5212. Secondly, the two Vosper-built RN 'Bold Class' Fast Patrol Boats of 1953 carried out 'mixed power unit' trials, wherein a pair of D18-11As ran beside Metrovick gas turbines. Following these exhaustive, but successful, 1,000-hour trials lasting two months, orders from the Admiralty were then placed for similar production engines for the Royal Navy. That 'E130/D18-11B' type of December 1952 was then to be constructed at Liverpool works from 1953 onwards, to power the new RN 'Dark Class' A-Boat MTB of 1955, of which eighteen were built by Saunders-Roe, each with a pair of D18-11Bs providing 5,000bhp.

Heavily de-rated 'E130/18-7A' engines were also planned to power the RN 'Ton Class' minesweepers, with power output reduced to 1,650bhp at 1,500rpm for propulsion only. Also, with similar de-ratings, the 'Deltic 18-7B' type was designed in January 1952 for use in standby electricity generating units and even, perhaps, for rail traction locomotives.

Marine 'Deltic 18-11B' MTB engine on test in the Acton Admiralty Test House.

Gas turbine reaction end of a 'Nomad I' aero compound engine, showing six of its horizontally opposed diesel cylinder heads above its axial compressor and contra-props.

The earliest nine-cylinder 'Deltic' dates from 1950, when the 'E159/D9-5A' was designed for the RN as a Pulse-Generator driving engine, as used on board all 'Ton Class' minesweepers.

Were two such contrasting, yet both two-stroke cycle compression-ignition, engines ever developed under the same roof as the Napier Deltic and Nomad types of the 1940s? Both would have about a 4,000bhp maximum power output after full development, but these two engines, although approaching their power production from two very different thermodynamic standpoints, then both finished up as advanced compound diesel engine types, for very different military purposes. The Deltic, as an eighteen-cylinder, uniflow-scavenged marine power unit, with multiple applications giving it latterly a commercial sales value, was eventually turbo-blown and charge-cooled to produce 4,000bhp. Whereas the smaller capacity twelve-cylinder aero 'Nomad' was, by comparison, a purely experimental unit of unique design, a horizontally opposed, highly supercharged, compound diesel engine with a 6in. bore and $7^3/8$ in. stroke, employing the loop scavenged two-stroke cycle. This was, in fact, the first one of this diesel pair to reach that desirable 4,000bhp maximum power output during its later development, but by then with the aid of water-methanol injection.

This rapidly evolving aero engine had started life as the 'E124' Secret Project for the Ministry of Supply in 1944, when it was twice as large in concept as it finished-up, with twenty-four cylinders, from which it was required to develop 6,000bhp. This ultra long-range engine for transport aircraft was eventually, by 1945, redesigned by DNS at Acton as a twelve-cylinder unit, the 'E125 Nomad I'. This essentially 'married' a horizontally opposed, large-bore diesel engine with a diesel exhaust gas-powered turbine that drove an axial compressor unit to then supercharge the diesel cylinders. In addition, an auxiliary turbine drove a centrifugal compressor at take-off boost conditions, while extra fuel was burnt in the exhaust ducts to increase the flow of exhaust gas energy into the turbines. This rather long engine was test flown from Luton FDE installed in the nose of a 'Lincoln' bomber, which made a pass at the SBAC Farnborough Air Show with only the 'Nomad I' running, driving its contra-propellers!

Also from 1944, the M.O.S. required DNS to build a new axial compressor research station, in order to develop the axial flow compressors and turbines for higher altitude, and those for the Nomad in particular up to a flight altitude of 35,000ft. An adjacent site to the E.E. Co./DNS factory at East Lancashire Road, Liverpool was selected for this research: it was to be fenced-off from the main works for enhanced security and required a pass for entry. Construction began in 1947, which was not completed until 1953, but some limited unit testing was underway by 1951, under the management of aerodynamicist L. Alan Nevard from Acton, acting on behalf of the Chief of Gas Turbine Development A. John Penn.

With the arrival of the 1950s, the post-war consolidation of DNS at Acton, Luton FDE and Liverpool was gaining momentum. This was driven by changes at board level, where more changes and some additional new directors were appearing under the strong chairmanship of Sir George Nelson who operated out of English Electric House in Kingsway. Most significant was the departure from the DNS Board of his son H.G. Nelson in 1949, when he moved to Stafford to become the Deputy MD of the English Electric Group itself.

At this point in time, Herbert Sammons was appointed DNS Managing Director, he was the first experienced engineer to take up the position as MD of DNS since Montague Napier himself. Sammons then left the post of Chief Engineer which was divided between E. Chatterton over Piston Engines and A.J. Penn leading Gas Turbines. Much in keeping with the practice of DNS, joining the Board were representatives of the three major military services: Air Vice-Marshall Sir Conrad Collier, Brigadier General Wade Hampton and thirdly was Rear Admiral W.G. Cowland, he in an advisory capacity to the Board, on the sale of 'Deltic' engines to overseas navies, plus some turbo-blowers. Sir Archibald Hope soon became Director of Sales (Air), and the new Chief Accountant was T. O. Haselwood-Jones, while jointly representing the E.E. Co. Board was Percy Horsfall. The DNS Company secretary was now finally to be R.C. Johnson and he was given an assistant secretary, F.L. Parris. The D. Napier & Son Ltd ranks were now set for their full scale assault on power-unit world markets, with R & D and new design based mainly at Acton, all flight installation and development at Luton, while new large-scale production would be placed at Liverpool.

Exactly a century after the Great Exhibition of 1851, with its memorable displays of DNS products from Lambeth works, a somewhat similar exhibition of British industrial technology was planned to take place between June and September 1951. Its site was close to, if not actually standing upon, the ground site of the old DNS Vine Street works in Lambeth, where David and James Napier had designed and worked when manufacturing their precision-printing and coin-grading machines in 1851. This was the 1951 'Festival of Britain' exhibition at South Bank, with its 'Dome of Discovery', 'Skylon' and the Festival Hall.

However, due to the still fresh memory of the Second World War, all the exhibits were quite properly of an entirely civilian nature, not at all the 'products of war' of which DNS had been forced to be the manufacturer over the past decade. From the still new DNS attachment to E.E. Co., visiting DNS employees would now possibly be able to recognise a wide assortment of exhibits from various distant E.E. Co. works all over Britain, but anything by DNS was hard to discover. Whereas in the hall of transport alongside the almost new BR standard 'Britannia' Class Pacific steam locomotive *William Shakespeare*, there stood a new, but un-named, BR Southern Region-built, 135-ton Diesel Electric locomotive, which was numbered 10201. This pioneer locomotive had a '16 SVT', E.E. Co. 1,750bhp diesel engine within its shining black body standing upon Co-Co silvered bogies. While, almost completely hidden from view, visitors could have seen through an open-sided panel four early Napier 'T100' Turbo-Blowers, which were mounted high upon the massive E.E. Co. engine exhaust manifolds. So a new DNS product did visit the Festival, a hundred years on from 1851, above the same piece of Lambeth soil where precision balances and cars had once stood.

When H.G. Nelson as MD had departed from the DNS Board late in 1949, handing over the DNS Managing Directorship to Herbert Sammons, he saw to the provision of an ideal works adviser in John Paget, one of Nelson's Cambridge University and ex E.E. Co. colleagues, a silver medal-holding production engineer, who then took over as General Manager of the six DNS London area factories. These were at that time: Acton1 (on the original Main site), Acton2 (Stewart & Arden Offices), PR1 (Development Test-Houses), PR2 (Blade Shop, Investment Foundry & Apprentice School), the Coronation Road Test Tunnels and Raynes Park works (Control Boxes, Fuel Metering and smaller units).

Mr 'Half' Nelson had also left Acton a legacy, this fully in keeping with his new post of Deputy MD of E.E. Co. nationwide, with which he now planned a 'big breakthrough'.

As the UK's leading manufacturer of diesel electric locomotives, they were only too painfully aware of weight restrictions imposed on locomotive axle loadings by the British Rail civil engineers. He, with Sir George, had seen that lightening the diesel engine within the chassis, while increasing the power output required for rail traction, was the ultimate step forward in design. While at Acton it had become apparent to him that, despite its noisiness, the Deltic engine was fast becoming very reliable as a potential marine power unit, and could be de-rated as a highly reliable power unit for electrical generation which would make it suitable for locomotives. Thus, in October 1950, Ben Barlow had schemed out a new rail traction version of the eighteen-cylinder Deltic, to be known as the E158 engine, the D18-12A design type, interestingly this being specified as 'without an ahead or astern gearbox'!

Back at E.E. Co. Rugby, when the company realised what was afoot the D.O. of the Heavy Diesel Engine department soon protested that a lightweight high-speed diesel engine, coming from the south at DNS Acton, would be problematic to operate and was likely to be too delicate to withstand rail traction service, still less so alongside steam locomotives. With the large and heavy E.E. Co. Type 4, Co-Co locomotive of 2,000bhp now on their drawing boards for BR, this more powerful, twin-engined, but thirty-ton lighter main line locomotive proposal was not a very popular suggestion with Rugby D.O.

Free end with mechanical blower of a de-rated eighteen-cylinder 'Deltic' unit of 1,650bhp, seen at Netherton coupled to an English Electric 1.2 MW main generator for 'DP1' loco.

In order to prepare a design for this 'lightweight', a separate D.O. was then set up under H.G. Nelson's jurisdiction to investigate the 'shoe-horning' of a pair of E158 'Napier Deltic Oil Engines' into a BR loading-gauge chassis, able to transmit over 3,000bhp to the rails running beneath it. The roof-mounted cooling radiators above the engines required that the engine compartment deck be lowered between the six-wheel bogie units to receive the Deltics, while the eighteen-ton axle loading now possible was investigated for sufficient wheel to rail traction with 550bhp per axle.

Meanwhile, the 'E158' engine design was being developed at Acton and Park Royal, to ensure that it gave a 'continuous 1,650bhp' output to power an E.E. Co. 1,100kW flange mounted DC Generator for the drive motor current. With such a giant step taken in this advanced locomotive design, E.E. Co. had to decide how best to interest the conservative railway traction world, not by requesting orders, but by offering a locomotive for BR trial as a Private Venture loan unit, this likely to be well ahead of its final service acceptance.

The six years of anguish endured during the Second World War, and the constant demands of service had, by 1951, already taken their toll on the health of King George VI. After having passed many of his duties over to his elder daughter Princess Elizabeth, during his partial recovery from surgery, he then died early in 1952. Queen Elizabeth II, who had ascended the throne on 8 February 1952, had her Coronation delayed until 2 June 1953, which was then widely heralded as the start of a 'New Elizabethan Era'. This aspiration was to be reflected in a number of places within industry, but it was Napier FDE at Luton that, a year or so later named an Airspeed airliner conversion, now powered by two Napier 'Eland' engines – the 'Eland Elizabethan'.

Back in June 1951, a simplified redesign of the 'Nomad' aero compound was made at Acton in conjunction with the Piston Engine Development Department, under the direction of its Chief Engineer Chatterton and Gas Turbine Chief Engineer A.J Penn. This produced the better looking and lighter, 'E145' design for the 'Nomad II' engine. In this there was the improved 8.25:1 pressure ratio axial compressor recently developed by Napier Research Station (NRS), Liverpool. That was now powered only by three hot diesel exhaust-driven turbines, any excess power from these turbines above that required to drive this axial compressor supercharger was 'creamed-off' to add to the overall power output of the diesel crankshaft, that now driving a single propeller. The unit was to be servo-controlled at all flying conditions, excess turbine power being cleverly diverted to the crankshaft at cruising conditions via an infinitely variable ratio epicyclic gearbox system, which acted as a bypass for only the excess turbine power output. This engine, after prolonged unit rig tests, ran performance type tests on its dynamometer test bed at Park Royal 1, and then on propeller test stands at D.H.'s Hatfield airfield. DNS had been encouraged by two Royal visitors to Acton works in April 1952, when the Duke of Edinburgh and the Duke of Kent made a tour together; they showed great interest in the long-range 'Nomad II' engine project and also viewed the Deltic marine engine. Finally, in 1955, once again the 'Nomad' showed its compact Luton-built 'Lincoln' installation and its 'flying colours' in a daring display at SBAC Farnborough, while still not at its fully developed stage. That was the time when the Coastal Command Avro 'Shackleton' urgently needed a fresh long-range, low fuel-consumption engine to increase its maximum range and RAF service reliability.

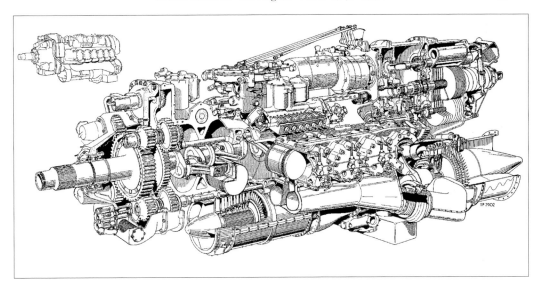

Cutaway of 'Nomad II' aero engine of 3,500bhp, with Beier VSG box top left.

At Napier Luton, full 'Nomad into Shackleton' installations had been designed and then carried out in two engine nacelles, while a single Nomad flight testing programme in a Lincoln had been concluded, reporting, 'We had no trouble during a series of two and a half-hour flights'.

On the test bench, the Nomad II had achieved the exceptionally low fuel consumption of 0.346lb/ehp-hr and a power rating of 3,640ehp at 2,100rpm, this while flying at 12,500ft. But as more development was still needed, especially with its slow running reliability, the whole experimental programme was unexpectedly and abruptly cancelled by the MOS late in 1955, after a decade of state-of-the-art Nomad compound engine advancement. This shock loss left a vast empty space within the piston aero engine ranks at Acton that the E.E. Co. found very hard to fill, while the target 'Shackleton' aircraft was re-engined once again by petrol Rolls-Royce 'Griffons', plus a pair of outer wing-mounted, thrust-boosting Armstong Siddeley 'Viper' jet engines which enabled reliable take-off with the much heavier aviation spirit fuel loads. Fortunately for DNS in London, 'Eland' turbo-prop development was going well at that point, plus the fact that a new gas turbine engine prototype for helicopter propulsion was, by then, well advanced 'on the drawing board'.

By 1951, Arthur Parker had left DNS for the CEGB, and he was replaced as apprentice supervisor by Frank Bonney who reported to John Radford from E.E. Co., now DNS Chief of Personnel and Training. He also worked closely with Mr Bill Lewis MBE, Acton's newly appointed Works Manager, after Henry ('Uncle') Baume had retired in 1947. A demand for, and DNS's supply of, apprentice places continued to rise, more than doubling in the three years up to 1954 at Acton works, in all of the three apprentice grades. The large annual presentation had far outgrown the combined works and staff canteen's space and the local and national ceremony now took in Acton Town Hall, with restricted seating for award winners only! Such was the importance of the scheme by 1955, that it set out to train young engineers, not only for DNS, but a wider sphere of engineering companies, the English Electric Co. included. Most numerous were the five-year Craft Apprenticeships in all skilled trades, from toolmakers, to sheet metal workers, to inspectors, when each trainee became C & G.L.I qualified in the theory and practice of his trade, and a fully skilled man. Next, but fewer in number, were Student Apprenticeships for older entrants, who aimed for professional qualifications and to work as an engineering designer or a draughtsman, a research project technician, or even as an Engineer Manager of the not too distant future! This four-year-long apprenticeship was for students who would at the same time study for a part-time engineering degree or for their HND/HNC qualification. The smallest of the grades numerically, was that of the Graduate Apprenticeships of just two years, in which entrants held an engineering degree, but came without the necessary workshop skill or office experience that would enable them to apply for an 'apprentice trained' position within DNS, or, when leaving the firm, out in the wider world of technology.

To give an example of how the Napier Apprentice Scheme operated for an individual, the author can recall in detail how he as an apprentice half a century ago, was helped to regain his confidence by being asked to 'make amends' for a company fault, after a test unit failure at Acton early in 1954, that could have caused him serious injury or worse.

As a third-year student apprentice attached to the research department, I had worked with Dick Burge on a small rig designed to access the fully lubricated 'metal to metal' driving qualities between an outer pair of steel flanged discs and three equispaced tapered steel discs running at high speed, and in deep mesh, between the two narrow flanges. In

MD Herbert Sammons presents the 'Company Shield' to student apprentice Edwin Knight at Acton's 1950 awards. On the right is Works Manager Bill Lewis MBE.

theory, an induced pressure oil film should prevent the two sets ever coming into metallic contact, thus giving a long, almost wear-free, life to this 'Beier Variable Speed Gear' system. After some weeks, I was then directed to assist in the full scale rig tests of the Beier infinitely variable gear (IVG) off the rear gearbox of a 'Nomad II' compound aero-engine, to be conducted in Test Cell 4. In order to access any 'slip' occurring between its triple outer sets of ten tapered discs and their driving set of eleven central flanged discs (these under high axial spring load), a large protractor quadrant and a pointer was attached to one set of pivoting outer tapered discs. This indicated its angular setting and hence the depth of mesh, while the three sets together were transmitting up to 180hp. An unstable servo-control system was under test at the time, so causing severe oscillation of the three outer sets' swinging arms, these having been moved under hydraulic control. This apprentice had, in previous tests, entered the test cell to read-off the pointer's angular setting on the protractor scale, but now with oscillation under load, the 'range of swing' in degrees needed to be read-off as rapidly as possible from within the test cell, before getting-out! Then, turning to leave the cell, the unit exploded, spraying splintered En31 ball-bearing steel discs through the magnesium Beier unit casing and into the brick walls and ceiling, rather like darts into a dartboard. When the smoke cleared, after a call 'Are you all right?' from the control room technicians, the unit was found to be wrecked, and this shaken apprentice realised how a second or two earlier I would have been 'in the firing line' myself. Later, the development staff from the P.E.D.D seemed more shocked than I felt, on seeing their urgent testing aborted in this way! By the next week, after a short inquiry in research and an interview with Superintendent Frank Bonney, I was once again studying back in college at Enfield Tech and continuing a sandwich course in mechanical and production engineering, while still not knowing the full reason for what had happened the week before, as our section leader Alf Dangerfield had been away from his research department office during those few days.

All was to be revealed, however, during the Christmas vacation fortnight, when the rule was that students should return to the works for those two weeks to do some short assignment. Thus, I was directed back to the research department. for a 'specially arranged task', when the director L. Frank Hall himself greeted me, and after giving a mild apology for the incident, told me of their findings from back in August. The En31 hardened tapered discs were splined on to their shafts, and close to the splines, but away from the working surfaces, the part number had been marked with a thermal pen! The thermal stresses set up had caused cracks back into the spline corners, so leading to the failure of the driven discs under those heavy oscillating loads. This serious fault had been overlooked by both design staff and AID inspectors alike for these 'development only' discs, but still it had led to that loss of development time and a dangerous accident on rig testing. My task, in the two weeks, was to devise a safe method of marking on the part number, still using the same region by the splines, that would not cause corner stresses and failure in service! By undertaking this corrective action for the cause of the catastrophic failure, I was able to gain in practical experience, while overcoming my 'near miss' anxiety in returning to the same division of the research department. How was that number marking method eventually replaced? By, instead, marking the part number letters and numerals, say 'NE 12345', by sand blasting them on to the hard steel, through an open 'NE 12345' cut in a circular rubber coated stencil box, able to locate and sand-shield each finish-hardened tapered disc. After trepanning out two 18swg circular blanks, the numbers were deeply engraved into one blank until piercing through, they having been set out in a small arc of the required ¾in radius.

The two thin steel blanks were then dished by hand, sufficient to accept and centralise a smooth Beier disc between them, then rubber coated on the outside to reduce the sand erosion during blasting. Finally, a light clamp was made and applied over the two halves. Holding the closed and clamped stencil under a sand-blasting nozzle in a cabinet, the part number was left printed, almost white in appearance, and in the specified arc close to the spline roots. The bright part number given, when micro-finish-tested with the tool room Taly-surf unit after the Christmas closedown, was not detectable in depth, only by sight!

This apprentice returned to his study the following week, rewarded, and much wiser from my experiences in rig testing, while also enabling DNS to identify taper discs without damage. The successful application of an ad-hoc method, after trying alternatives, was just part of the learning exercise. The manufacture and operation of the 'Part Number Stencil Case' had involved me in new processes and caused me to visit new departments in the works. When a tool number was finally taken out for the drawing, my 'vacation' felt complete!

Another incentive available to all apprentices was the company Merit Award Scheme, based upon a total combined mark given by the result of study, co-operation, timekeeping and practical progress within the works. Those apprentices with a higher level of total marks were, at the end of each year, awarded a monetary prize at the presentation event. It was therefore satisfying for the author to discover in the 1955 Merit Awards list that I topped the third-year apprentices, no doubt due in part to my 'fortunate' time in research leading to the workable solution to that Nomad disc marking problem. The '£9-0s-0d' I gratefully received from Bill Lewis in Acton Town Hall fifty years ago doesn't sound a lot now, but, in terms of today's UK money value, it was then worth over £300!

At the 1955 Presentations, Technical Personnel & Education Officer John Radford stated that 323 DNS apprentices were then undergoing training at Acton alone, and the number was rising. He commented that they regularly produced their own well-informed publication – *The Napier Blower*, this being the official organ of the Napier London Apprentices Association, while another separate journal was also being published by the Napier Luton Apprentices. He added that, after a recent review, it had been established that 188 ex-apprentices now held responsible positions within the DNS Company. Proof enough, as if it was needed, that the 'University within Napier' was now well established.

While writing here of part numbers in the 1950s, it is worth recording how DNS had devised a very useful D.O. system of letter prefixes to their drawing numbers after the Second World War. By that time drawing numbers were multiplying, particularly for Sabre and SeaLion engine components and assemblies, these needing to be separated from those for the more recent engines. In order to identify their number sequences, a series of meaningful letter prefixes were introduced to differentiate between the drawings relating to each Napier engine, product or type of unit. Some of these codes are here listed, as follows.

Prefix 'ND' – for Napier Turbo Blower Units, these for 500bhp output plus diesels

Prefix 'NE' – for Napier Aero Engine Units – e.g. On Nomad II and Eland engines

Prefix 'NM' – for new Napier Marine Engine Units – and all types of Deltic engine

Prefix 'NC' – for Napier Compressor Units – Within Eland and Gazelle engines

Prefix 'NT' – for Napier Turbine Units – Within Oryx, Eland and Gazelle engines

Prefix 'APJ' – for Aero Project Schemes – design schemes for new aero engines

Prefix 'SK' – for all engine build 'sketch' numbered sheets, these all for reference

Prefix 'T' – for all in-house jig and tool drawings, special cutters and assembly fixtures

Prefix 'ACP' – for anti corrosion protection processes applied to specific components

Prefix 'NRE' – at Napier Luton F.D.E for Rocket Engine Units – e.g. Scorpion engine

Prefix 'PLS' – for Test Plant Schemes – e.g. a PR1 Nomad Test House engine coupling

By the 1950s the DNS Design and Drawing Offices in Acton had expanded to a point where the space within the first and second floors of the 'New Concrete Building'(NCB) at 211 The Vale was fully occupied by the Tool Drawing Office, the Manufacturing Development Department DO, the Test Plant DO and both the Piston Engine – PEDD and Gas Turbine – GTDD Development Departments. During the Second World War 'duplicated' drawing offices were established next to the Napier main site in the former Eastmans cleaners building, spread over three large floors. This laundry building was as old as the DNS Motor Works of 1903, as an early photograph of the 1905 workforce, standing behind six-cylinder car chassis, shows it clearly in the background. The main detail drawing offices, for prototype and production components and assembly drawings were situated there all through the 1940s, 50s & 60s, but to many draughtsmen, it seemed too remote from the main works itself, and required 'a step' in bad weather to reach the canteens on the top floor of the NCB. Whereas, at DNS Luton, the DO was more fortunate to be self-contained in the newer, and then extended, two-storey Napier building originating in the 1950s, set high above the Vauxhall Works, and set on the corner of Percival Way, adjacent to Luton Airport.

Behind this modern building were many of the DNS workshops and extensive test areas, while stretching out on to the airfield perimeter were sited the original three large hangers for completing flight aircraft.

The early 1950s atmosphere in the three main DNS plants had now become one of new expectancy, particularly in the Deltic marine engine building shops in Acton and Liverpool, there was a 'more buoyant' feeling than hitherto, even approaching one of 'riding on the crest of a wave' – to mix two nautical metaphors in a single sentence. By 1955 Napier Marine Engines were at last in regular service with our Royal Navy, and DNS Liverpool production works was fully tooled-up and staffed by skilled craftsmen and technicians, who were ready to deliver in quantity the hundreds of eighteen-cylinder and nine-cylinder Deltics to meet the Admiralty orders for engines to power the remainder of the 'Dark' and 'Ton' Class coastal defence vessels. The fast 43-knot HMS *Dark Aggressor* (FPB 1102) was one of the first of the eighteen of these A-boat MTBs to be commissioned, all eventually being given most threatening names by the Admiralty Committee when entering service from 1955. Thus for example, a *Dark Biter*, a *Dark Killer* and a *Dark Highwayman* roamed the seas as either Motor Torpedo Boats or as the RN's first type of Fast Patrol Boat, some of which could lay up to nine ground mines. All but one of these craft were built by Saunders-Roe Ltd with a timber skinned, black painted, 67ft hull over aluminium alloy framing. The RN described the Dark Class as: 'Noisy and lively – but generally successful'.

Meanwhile the first 'Deltic'-propelled example of the placid and, by comparison, almost stately 'Ton' Class minesweepers, had been launched on 2 June 1954; this was the M1130 named HMS *Highburton*. She was built by Thorneycroft, with a 140ft timber hull over an aluminium alloy frame, and was powered by a pair of 18-7A 'Deltic' engines giving her a combined output of 3,100bhp, with a maximum speed of 15 knots. All were named after some lesser known small towns and villages set in the English countryside, those whose names happened to end in 'ton'. Such as: No. M1149 HMS *Badminton* built by Camper & Nicholson, M1175 HMS *Quainton* built by Richards Iron Works, and the last, M1208 HMS *Lewiston* built by Herd & McKenzie and not launched until 3 November 1959.

Those earlier built '29 Ton Class' vessels, had Mirrlees diesels with less power, but most were then re-engined with Deltics during their refits by the time they were sold-on to Commonwealth navies during the 1960s, usually for similar duties. The minesweeper Pulse-generating engine used by all the 'Tons' was a DNS nine-cylinder, generator-drive, D9-5A Deltic engine of 800bhp, and was located separately from the pair of propulsion engines.

One such early Ton Class was M1115 HMS *Humber*, she was RNVR commissioned, with Mirlees engines, and was launched on 19 March 1953. She was then re-fitted in 1963 with 2 Deltic 18-7As' as a mine-hunter, and also renamed HMS *Bronington*. Still as M1115, known popularly as 'old quarter past eleven', this mine-hunter was then commanded by HRH Prince Charles during most of 1976 when he served as a Lieutenant-Commander in the Royal Navy Coastal Forces. Although intended primarily for inshore and coastal duties, with their adequate power the Ton Class boats were well able to make long ocean passages when service required it. M1115, HMS *Bronington*, is now in preservation and on public display in Manchester, on that city's ship canal.

RN Dark Class MTB *Dark Aggressor* powered by a pair of 2,500bhp Deltics.

First 'Deltic'-engined RN Ton Class minesweeper HMS *Highburton* in 1954.

At the vast DNS/E.E. Co. production works on the East Lancashire Road, Liverpool, where the E.E. Co. had previously built its domestic appliances, the DNS turbo-blower quantity production and testing facilities had been established away from Acton by 1952. They were joined in 1954 by members of the 'Deltic' production department, who helped to fill the remainder of that wartime plant area, while utilising further much of its special machinery. When both products had begun to flow from these workshops and test bays, DNS proudly put on public works tours of their two-part, model factory. This was a clear flash-back to that 'open invitation' given to buyers to tour Napier Motor Works at Acton some fifty years earlier. By 1950, such an opportunity at Acton, which was involved in 'cutting-edge' development projects, was out of the question for London's general public. Excepting, that is, the parents and friends of apprentices about to receive awards on each presentation evening who, many escorted by their own sons, could enjoy a tour of the more general engineering workshops where they had worked during their training. Liverpool, however, had a much freer hand over its regular tours, which gave an insight into types of work and the conditions of service there, often to prospective employees.

Mr J.L. Hignett, Works Superintendent on 'Deltic', recalls the highlights of such a tour.

First place in a typical visit was the impressive 'Deltic' Assembly Area, complete with a full-size working engine cross-section to be seen in action. This was followed by a quick visit to the Test Houses, to witness a completed engine on test in one of the eight test cells. From that very noisy atmosphere, they would proceed to the quieter and larger machine shops, to inspect the gear cutting and Maag machine precision involute grinding of some hardened Deltic phasing gears, before seeing the machining of connecting rods from forgings, going on finally to view these highly polished rods. Next, they would go to the turbo-blower assembly area to see the finished article, with a sectioned blower there for explanation purposes, before visiting the blower sub-assembly shop with many finished components and built up rotors to admire. Finally, before refreshments in the visitors' canteen, a visit to the test and development section for turbo-blowers, that had been 'imported' from Acton works with its equipment. A well-earned cup of tea then followed.

More than 1,500 personnel were being employed in DNS Liverpool works by the 1960s but, after that time, many changes were to occur both within and without both companies.

While reviewing DNS at Liverpool, the large and finely equipped Napier Research Station was constructed, from 1947 to 1953, by Napier/E.E. Co. in order to provide a uniquely powerful test and development research facility for the then developing axial compressors and turbines being designed into the new aero gas turbines nationwide. A plan worked out by Chief Engineer A.J. Penn, along with DNS's aerodynamic designer Alan Nevard at Acton, was to install sufficiently high steam turbine-driving power at the NRS, to make it a place where compressors up to any foreseeable size could be tested and analysed, both for in-house and for outside customers. The NRS had three main blocks; centrally placed were offices for administration, test-unit design and much research data analysis, for which EEC's advanced 'Deuce' mainframe computer at Stafford was used. Then, on one side was a block containing the Gas Turbine Plant for development work, the in-house machine shop and the instrumentation shop. In the block on the other side was a complete Yarrow Steam Turbine Compressor Plant removed from a Hunt Class Royal Navy Destroyer, with two 300lb/sq. in superheated steam turbine drives of 10,000hp, which could be linked to deliver its full 20,000hp at up to 20,000rpm when this was required. In these conditions Napier's big axial compressor was developed for the original pre-Nomad 'E123' engine of 6,000ehp, and after which the compressor was then sold-on to the General Electric Co. in the USA. Before the new 'E141 Eland' compressor, there had been the large one tested under contract for de Havilland's 15,000lb thrust 'Gyron' turbo-jet engine, the world's most powerful at the time! But also in the compressor test block at NRS Liverpool, and first

Meeting of the GTCC at Napier Park Royal Research Station in 1946, with DNS engineers A.J. Penn and H. Sammons on the left-hand side, and J. Paget and E. Chatterton at the rear on the right-hand side. Air Commodore Frank Whittle is third to the right of white-coated MD H.G. Nelson.

to be there, was the ex-Park Royal 1,500hp, Electrical Compressor Drive test plant, plus its airflow laboratory and the NRS fitting shop. This E.E. Co. built and supplied electrical test plant could deliver its 1,500hp drive at shaft speeds up to 25,000rpm, it was used earlier at PR1 for developing Nomad and Naiad axial compressors, but at NRS was to be used, in time, on compressors for both Oryx and Gazelle units. The whole NRS was managed by Alan Nevard for all of its fifteen years.

Down south, DNS Luton FDE managed by Cecil Cowdrey, had by 1955 expanded its flight test and development programmes well beyond both the Nomad I & II compound piston engines with their gas turbine features, to now embrace the Napier turbo-prop and other companies pure-jet installations that were to occupy the next decade. Increasingly, their work had come to involve the control of 'icing problems in-flight', for which they were developing a solution on behalf of the E.E. Co. Bradford, they eventually produced a cyclic electrically powered, thermal de-icing system, which became known as 'Napier Spraymat'. This resinous coating with interior conductors, was then applied to both airframe control surfaces and to engine air intakes of several civil and military 1950s aircraft, such as the Bristol 'Britannia', and with considerable success in terms of improved all-weather safety and commercial gain.

General engineering continued to be the theme of the research department at Acton, where many projects under examination were directly from E.E. Co. contracts for pure research. DNS, as a precision mechanical engineering company, picked-up research programmes in keeping with its traditional output, those at Acton under Frank Hall's direction being in connection with bearings and gearing in particular. A Bevel gear-testing rig was a long-term project in order to perfect gear meshing after gear cutting had been closely checked on a specially designed Napier bevel gear profile measuring-machine. A heavy bearing rig was built to develop large pad-type bearings for ship or alternator shafts under up to 120-ton thrust loading and at speeds of up to 4,500rpm. Small gas-bearing testing sharply contrasted sharply with this situation.

With almost perfect timing in Autumn 1955, and so appropriately just after the radical British Transport Commission Modernisation Plan for the railways of Britain had been announced, the time had arrived for the emergence of that high powered, yet lightweight, E.E. Co. locomotive designed back in 1952. This came a while after the futuristically styled rolling chassis for this private venture DP1 had been completed at their old Dick Kerr works in Preston. It had a lowered engine room floor that would support its pair of Deltic 18-12A engines, in order to allow the radiator fan drives above them to clear the roof and to fit within the BR main line loading gauge. Each engine would drive its 1,100kw generator, flange mounted to its phasing gear case, with a 45kw auxiliary generator arranged above it. This was a six-axle Co-Co locomotive chassis, with an eighteen-ton max axle load achieved by the fact that the combined weight of its two aluminium alloy high-speed Deltic engines would be less than a single iron bodied, medium speed diesel engine, as employed by the E.E. Co. to power their heavier 'Type 4' locomotives of 2,000bhp about to enter service. These Type 4s would have a 'whistling' exhaust note – not too unlike a BSA 500cc. DBD34 'Gold star' motorcycle of the same period – due to having within them a quadruple installation of tuned Napier T100 turbo-blowers pressure charging their big sixteen-cylinder diesel engine. These circumstances led to the blowers causing that most individual sound. After DP1 had been towed by rail to DNS works at Netherton, for the installation and load testing of her power units (these having arrived from Acton by road), she was out-shopped and, to everyone's surprise, was seen to be carrying the name of *Deltic*. This was boldly and centrally sign-written over her 'royal blue and gold lined livery', and was probably more in keeping with her mission to sell E.E. Co. locomotives powered by the lightweight DNS generating engines to overseas markets, then to British Railways' management's wishes.

Deltic first moved under her own 3,300hp on 15 September 1955 and was then handed over 'on loan' to BR Midland Region at Liverpool Edge Hill Depot for extensive trials on the West Coast Main Line, and later down to Euston in London for service on fast passenger trains. It was foggy on 15 December 1955 when she left from near Speke Junction hauling the heavy 'Merseyside Express', but before arriving at Euston she had easily reached her permitted speed of 90mph and had shown 'an extraordinary capacity for making up lost time'. This trip was made with Acton's own technicians Frank Yellen and Jimmy James on board, 'to see that all went well' on the run, before she, and they, were met in London by the glare of excited media plus railway officials. With the publicity generated, Mr 'Half' Nelson had certainly succeeded in making that 'big breakthrough' for his and Sir George's E.E. Co. group, which was

Water spray research Lincoln aircraft at Luton FDE, forming water droplets for 'Spraymat' ice protection development and insecticide spray work by small gyroplane.

On chassis completion outside E.E. Co. Dick Kerr works, Preston in 1955, the 'DP1' prototype loco awaits its 2 'D18-12A' engines and the bold name of *Deltic*.

soundly based upon a joint venture with DNS. The *Sunday Dispatch* newspaper sold a forty-eight page supplement – 'Pictorial History of Railways' – featuring a massive headline picture of the *Deltic* locomotive on its front page extolling it as 'The world's most powerful diesel-electric railway engine – the *Deltic*'.

After a shake-down period, from 4 June 1957 BR agreed to utilise *Deltic* over a seventeen-hour running day covering four duties, so as to build up her in-service mileage more quickly by hauling fast trains 4,320 miles per week. From 13 January 1959, *Deltic* was transferred to the BR Eastern Region, York Depot, for more extensive load trials on the East Coast Main Line, between Kings Cross and Newcastle, covering freight as well as express passenger workings. But by 16 March, now based at Hornsey Depot, she was given her head hauling heavy crack expresses over the ECML, where *Deltic* became their star performer. But it had taken three years of testing before BR had placed an order with E.E. Co. for a batch of twenty-two production version, Type 5, Deltic 18-25B-engined locomotives for their accelerated and modernised ECML services. Deltic prototype DP1 was kept running right until the delivery to BR Doncaster works of the twenty-two Type 5s, from E.E. Co. Vulcan Foundry works, that had begun in Spring 1961. At this point, with no further British or Canadian interest being shown in her type, *Deltic* was retired after more than 450,000 miles of running on BR tracks, then to be restored to pristine condition at Vulcan Foundry. Following the death of Sir George Nelson – the first Lord Nelson of Stafford – in 1962, the new Chairman of the E.E. Co., Mr H.G. Nelson, then presented the *Deltic* locomotive to the Science Museum in London on 28 April 1963. This was quite near to the DNS Acton works, and a unique Napier exhibit was thus made in the transport hall there alongside the passenger-hauling *Rocket*, built in 1829 by Old George Stephenson.

Making a giant step forward in 1956, the prototype axial compressor charged exhaust gas turbine-assisted 'Compound Deltic' engine awaits an Acton test house, in which it then produced 5,500bhp. Air intake is at upper right, with exhaust on the left.

Although Deltic had now been silenced, Napier Deltic power unit development was about to mushroom further over the next two decades, with the advent of Series II and III turbo-blown marine engines being developed at Acton, to give up to 50% more power. But an earlier design of March 1954, for an eighteen-cylinder 'Compound Deltic' marine engine, the 'E160, C18-4', had then set out to overtake these later turbo-charged engines for power output, using gas turbine technology to boost the two-stroke diesel, just as it had done in the aero Nomad. For, into that triangular void within the three Deltic cylinder blocks, there was put an axial turbo-compressor set, this replacing the usual mechanically blown centrifugal scavenge blower of the Series I Deltics. With power recovered from the 88-litre diesel exhaust gases when running at 2,000rpm this, when geared back to the phasing gear case, would total 5,000bhp or more. By July 1955, three further 'Compound Deltic' designs had been produced: the 'E185/ 86/ 89' engines, incorporated hydraulic drives to and from the turbines, giving anticipated 5,500bhp outputs for marine sprint applications. This 'hush-hush' development work was being coordinated between Penn's and Chatterton's departments, within an Admiralty contract for engines giving ultra high power with very low fuel consumption, so as to improve naval mission durations. The first successful test house run by a Compound Deltic in Autumn 1956, according to E. Chatterton's report, produced a staggering 5,600bhp at 2,000rpm, so keeping 6,000bhp well in sight, and this in spite of miserly diesel fuel consumption.

But by then the Admiralty had, of course, another 'iron in the fire', namely the Bristol 'Proteus' gas turbine engine with a similar power output, but with a high specific fuel consumption and a dependence on aviation kerosene. The complex, less developed 'Compound Deltic' installation would be heavier, but because of the much lower weight of the diesel fuel required by it, any Fast Patrol Boat (FTB) would in fact be more lightly loaded, and so faster at the start of a mission with these engines. The lighter 'Proteus' gas turbine engine installation, plus the weight of their very large fuel load would make such an FTB heavier when setting out on a mission but, following its rapid fuel consumption out from base it could, in fact, become the lighter craft during a later engagement.

Disappointingly for DNS, the Admiralty's choice was for the simpler and lighter Gas Turbine installation, and that selection of new type of prime mover would then be applied to all future Royal Navy FPBs. This hard and emphatic RN decision now left D. Napier & Son's advanced low fuel consumption 'Compound Deltic' contender without its future funding or any prospective buyer, which then almost immediately led to its premature cancellation, without any further development, late in 1956. This was a most notable and innovative marine engine which was to remain the most powerful piston engine that the Napier Company was ever to manufacture.

But then, quite soon after, an overseas FPB market needing real quantities of the DNS 'Series 2, Turbo-charged Deltic' engines was to appear from across the seas, this being just in time to sustain the Liverpool production line throughout the next decade. This was also to coincide with a time when the whole future of the Napier aircraft engine business was to become threatened, both from within and without the E.E. Co. Group.

8

GAS TURBINE AND ROCKET ENGINE GALAXY 1957–1967

After 150 years the late 1950s were going to prove to be a climax to the innovative work of D. Napier & Son Ltd and their still growing influence in the modern post-war world. That celebration would occur in Summer 1958, but a deepening awareness of the long tradition within DNS was by 1957 reaching to the surface of everyday activities. One such item was the launch in Summer 1957 of an in-house magazine *This is Napier* and Volume 1 – No. 1, showed three speeding RN 'Dark Class' Motor Gun Boats planing across its front cover, while inside was a boardroom photograph and message from the Chairman of the English Electric Group of Companies, Sir George H. Nelson Bt. After welcoming this new publication, he stated: 'To a select band of readers it will present the personalities and personality of the Napier organisation and the story of its work in an informal manner, thus helping to make more close and more cordial the relationships between the company and those with whom it has dealings.' It certainly had a good effect on staff morale over its run of just ten issues, and provided ordinary employees with fairly up-to-date information and photographs about DNS projects and its customers. Never had the rank and file of DNS been so aware of the growing importance of their engineering work to the British Nation. *This is Napier* then, surprisingly, continued as Volume 1, right up to what was to be its very last issue, No. 10, distributed early in that fateful year 1961, when a new Managing Director appeared inside the cover, Mr H.E.C. de Chassiron. The editor then posed the question: 'Will he have a policy – and if so, what will his policy be?' No clues were given, apart from statements like 'his dynamic leadership', 'esprit-de-corps' and 'with his background' – a background that in fact was not actually stated, as it was E.E. Co. So, readers were left only to guess at what might be to come later that year, leading to changes that were to affect both the buoyant aero gas turbine and flight development divisions of DNS. Let's review the work of these teams up to mid-1961.

Prior to 1956 DNS engineers had chiefly been preoccupied with piston engine types of prime mover, plus their turbochargers. Bit by bit the greater importance of this more traditional and popular product range was eroded by that of the gas turbine engine in one form or another. It was the very diversity of gas turbine design and development at DNS that usually set it apart from its rivals; this department was led for thirty years by Arthur J. Penn. It had been his early mastery of centrifugal compressor design that had boosted the power output of the supercharged Lion, Rapier, Dagger, Sabre, Nomad and Deltic engines. His association with F.B. Halford up to 1942 had, apparently, later resulted in the efficient single sided supercharger impeller for the Sabre VII being 'scaled-up' for use within the centrifugal compressor of the DH 'Goblin and Ghost' turbo-jets, this after Halford had become DH Chief Designer in 1944. Similar centrifugal compressor technology was further needed, and was eventually fully applied in the first Napier Turbo-blowers of the 1940s and '50s and, in a highly developed form, remains in vogue today. But thereafter, for all single shaft aero gas turbine engines from Acton, it was invariably the axial flow compressor that was embodied in Napier engine designs throughout this period up to 1962. Reasons for the early change to a higher pressure ratio axial compressor are well worth exploring, as these were responsible for outcomes that were soon to affect the very future of DNS.

Firstly, the MOS contract awarded to DNS in 1945 for the long-range 'Nomad' aero engine, was matched by another contract for an Axial Compressor research programme in conjunction with the E.E. Co. DNS engineers under A.J. Penn, at first concentrated on improvements to his well proven centrifugal type then in service, after which Lionel Elford and Alan Nevard were then asked to concentrate their efforts on the relatively new axial compressor type at the start of this research at Acton, at Park Royal I, and later from 1950 at the Napier Research Station in Liverpool. Nevard, as AJP's Technical Assistant, looked after the aerodynamic design of both axial compressors and turbines, while Elford worked on initial mechanical design. The original twenty-four-cylinder 6,000bhp Nomad engine's axial compressor had been started by the time the smaller 3,000bhp version had been approved for development from the MOS, thus giving a 'scaled' pair for calibration and comparison purposes. All calculations were kept secret and done within AJP's office, he himself checking all figures and results when at home! With ever higher pressure ratios being achieved, and the 'surge line' speeds now diverted away from optimum efficiency drive turbine operating speeds; the axial type was fast becoming the more compact rival for the centrifugal type, especially in DNS's slim, future wing-buried gas turbine engines.

A Gas Turbine Collaboration Committee (GTCC) had been set up in 1941, by Dr Roxbee Cox, on which two representatives of all companies were allowed, those for DNS being A.J. Penn and Chief Designer, R. Chamberlain. At the 1946 GTCC meeting, hosted by DNS at the Park Royal I Research Station and chaired by Dr Roxbee Cox with Air Commodore Frank Whittle, attendees included Dr A.A. Griffith of Rolls-Royce, Air Commodore Rod Banks (he then admitting 'the Napier axial compressor did better than expected') and DNS's MD, H.G. Nelson, these luminaries being among a forty-five-strong gathering of most of Britain's aero engine chiefs of the time. D. Napier & Son Ltd was to act as host for two further GTCC meetings in 1951 (again at PR I) and 1960 (at the NRS), when Alan Nevard, NRS Liverpool Manager, fully represented DNS on the GTCC.

The resulting compound E125 'Nomad I' engine had an eleven-stage axial compressor feeding into a centrifugal one; these were driven by three turbine stages and the engine was first run in October 1949. In contrast the E145 'Nomad II' engine had a twelve stage axial compressor only, powered by a three-stage turbine and was first run late in 1952. This unique compound unit was often treated primarily as a gas turbine engine at

DNS, its big twelve-cylinder, two-stroke diesel acting chiefly as an exhaust gas generator, with thermodynamics similar to a 'Free Piston Engine'. By January 1945, an 'E126' free piston engine design had been proposed at Acton, with its main units the same as those for the Nomad I.

The first recorded design for a Napier propeller aero gas-turbine engine was carried out at Acton from May 1945, when a small 'E127', 500shp Propeller Turbine Engine was proposed as a light prototype unit, which was generally known as the Napier 'Nymph'. The project was bench-tested only, in that its turbines were required to produce 1,500bhp in order to provide 500shp for its propeller shaft, plus the usual 'times-to' power figure (1,000hp) for its axial compressor.

A contract for a 1,500shp single shaft propeller turbine was given by the M.of A. to DNS in 1945, probably as a replacement for the known future loss of 'Sabre' development work. This became the E128, 'Naiad' engine from an October 1945 design, and was built and tested before the 'Nomad I' in 1949. Its small axial compressor was based on an existing Nomad type, with twelve stages giving 5.5:1 pressure ratio, running at 18,250rpm during take-off. At the 'hot end' it had a two-stage turbine providing the power within this slim 28in maximum diameter engine, which, by the end of 1948 was giving 1,590ehp in bench tests at Acton and in Coronation Road Test Tunnels, this included 240lb jet thrust at the take-off rating. This 'Naiad I' gave 1,050ehp when cruising with turbines at 17,000rpm. Luton FDE had installed a 'Naiad' engine to fly in the nose of a 'Lincoln', which it did on reduced power at the SBAC Farnborough show, while a Luton model shop mock-up installation of a 'Naiad' in a Vickers airliner nacelle was exhibited on the DNS stand.

Coupling a pair of 'Naiads' through a double gearbox, to reduce drive speed down to a single propeller shaft formed a most compact 3,000shp engine, which was proposed as 'E129' (then altered by the Air Ministry to 'E128D') for a Fairey 'Gannet' carrier-borne anti-submarine aircraft. This contract then went to Armstrong-Siddeley's 'Double Mamba' engine instead, leaving DNS with only castings for airflow tests at Luton.

At the 1948 SBAC show, DNS exhibit their advanced 'Naiad' turbo-prop engine of 1,600bhp. The open cowling one was for the 'Viscount', plus a Double-Naiad' model.

Subsequent, and far more damaging, was the loss of the turbo-prop engine contract with Vickers for the four-engine Viscount Airliner, to the lower-powered Rolls-Royce Dart engine. This, with a two stage centrifugal compressor and just 1,200shp output, was bigger and 25% heavier than the Naiad engine, which had a prototype airliner-airframe ready for engine installation at Brooklands. Sir George Edwards, Chief Engineer of Vickers, not able to trust the state-of-the-art axial compressor within the Naiad, was then finally persuaded to select the bulkier Dart installation from Rolls-Royce. That decision provided them with an enormous long-term order to power over 400 Viscounts. This blow to DNS was to have a permanently adverse effect on the company's aero gas turbine prospects within the civil aircraft market in the UK, which never fully recovered from this loss of revenue and prestige. In future, firms in the USA and Canada were to be Napier's best customers.

Dr A. W. Morley had joined DNS in 1946. He arrived from the RAE Engine Research Establishment and in the future was to develop many design proposals for unconventional gas turbine propulsion from within his highly secretive 'Forward Projects Office' at Acton. He was joined there by Dr A.R. Mortimer, who was another theoretical thermodynamics expert and original thinker, and both were able to explore new propulsion systems and so push forward the boundaries of DNS technology. We can mention a few examples that are by now well off the 'secret list', but these are no doubt patented and hence unavailable.

The rotary wing aircraft, in all its variants, was often investigated at Acton, with multiple lift rotors, both within stub wings and arranged at the extremities of helicopters. Also, the tip-jet reaction drive of helicopter main rotors, by means of rocket, steam jet or combustion chamber, the latter chosen for the big Fairey 'Rotodyne'. Some creative schemes reached the aero design office at the 'APJ' layout stage, where engine type numbers were then allocated to these power units. A notable example is Number 'E138', a Turbo-Ram Jet Engine, comprising three units discharging into a common re-heat chamber and jet pipe, giving 15,000lb thrust at sea level static conditions', this design was taken-up in July 1949. Going by sketches of the installation, such a small manned aircraft would surely have travelled just like a space-rocket!

At about the same period, when the 'Cold War' was beginning to bite, a series of eleven Napier-designed pure turbo-jets was formulated at Acton in response to tenders from Vickers Aircraft at Weybridge, the parent E.E. Co. at Warton, and other companies. These are all shown in Appendix IIIj, they spanned an eight-year period, and vary from 'E181', a small single shaft turbo-jet of 1,100lb thrust, to the big 'E149' two spool compound, two shaft turbo-jet of 20,000lb thrust, that similar to high thrust, two spool jet engines that were then being developed by Armstong-Siddeley, Bristol Engines and Rolls-Royce.

The Vickers 'Valiant' V-bomber design exercises showed layouts for that aircraft with installations of three, four and even five Napier turbo-jet engines in 1950. However; these jet engine designs, although impressive on paper as installation drawings and as artist's impressions meticulously drawn by Harry Heritage of Napier Technical Publications, were never to be constructed at Acton works, or even at Luton FDE from George Dicker's fine model shop, as the 'Double Naiad' engine had been for display purposes. Somewhat later in the Cold War period, in 1954, Morley and Mortimer made a report for DNS regarding a 'Cruise-type missile' propulsion engine, described as: 'An Expendable 2,500lb turbo jet engine, using a supersonic counter-rotating compressor'. Single and double engine type missiles were illustrated with high-speed capability. All such militarily sensitive work was covered by the Official Secrets Act at DNS, and so, as it was an M.O.S engine project it was, possibly, entered into the design register in 1956 as 'E237 – SECRET'. If this form of axial compressor was ever developed further, the findings were not released.

Once again, almost as if a more straight-forward project offered too little challenge, a gas turbine-driven gas generator engine had been on the stocks since 1952, listed as the 'E146, Oryx' aero engine. As early as February 1951, a turbo-gas generator used for helicopter propulsion had been envisaged, in connection with Hunting Percival Aircraft (HP), the long standing airfield neighbours of Napier Luton FDE. To the MOS, Napier at Acton must have seemed the ideal research establishment to develop such a gas turbine, this was an equivalent to the far better understood 'free piston engine', but likewise had no output shaft of its own, and delivered its power output described in terms like '750 gas horse power'. A new helicopter division had been formed at HPs by 1950 when they were looking into the best use of gas turbines to power some new rotary wing aircraft, and looked to the ejection of the whole exhaust from a gas turbine through the tips of their rotor blades. This would much simplify its mechanical design by eliminating the need for anti-torque measures and the complexity of gearboxes. In November 1951 DNS and HP joined forces to design the 'E146, Oryx' engine and the 'P74' helicopter respectively, and a

An original design of reaction helicopter gas producer, the Napier 'Oryx' gave 900ghp, with an auxiliary axial compressor seen left of the upper gas collector box.

contract was issued on 8 May 1952 for a test bed helicopter fitted with two 'Oryx' engines. In conjunction with NRS Liverpool, Manager Alan Nevard decided on a gas turbine engine driving a rear mounted auxiliary axial compressor to produce cool air to mix with the gas turbine exhaust, before delivery via a collector box to the helicopter's overhead rotor. With a twelve stage main compressor of 9.0:1 pressure ratio, running at 21,900rpm, which supplied five combustion chambers and two stages of turbine to drive it, the 'Oryx' then drove from a common single shaft, an additional four stage auxiliary compressor of 1.8:1 pressure ratio, this provided lower pressure cold air to cool the combined gas collector box and mix (bypass style) with the hot exhaust gases.

Such a pair of engines, when installed, could theoretically pass to the rotor blades 29lb of gas/sec. at 9lb/sq.in pressure and at a temperature of 400 degrees Celsius. A single one was then type-tested successfully at these performance figures for the P74, and also at the higher 825ghp to suit a proposed larger Percival P105 helicopter project to follow that. This 'Oryx' engine had been fully aerodynamically designed in all its units, including its non-throttling valve and collector, by the NRS at Liverpool. Unfortunately, at HP they had made some wildly inaccurate assumptions regarding lamina airflow within the P74 helicopter's rotor blades, so that on its tethered tests on Luton airfield in May 1956, it achieved exactly nil vertical lift-off from the ground! Despite a very hasty HP redesign, which called for a large increase in power due to the unforeseen airflow losses, the whole programme had its funding withdrawn by the MOS, as they then wanted to centralise all helicopter manufacture elsewhere. So DNS had provided the engine power all to no avail.

Staff activities at Acton had continued unabated during 1956, with a thriving Napier Sports and Social Club. A motor club, tennis, bowls, rugby and association football teams all remained competitive in their local leagues. Matches between both senior and apprentice teams from Luton and Acton factories were always played with zest, as was the 'Local Derby' for the football Challenge Shield, between Napier and CAV teams. In 1956 Works Manager Bill Lewis presented this trophy to the Napier Athletic team's Captain.

Stanley Gardens, situated between the DNS and CAV works in Acton, was still the scene for lunchtime meetings outside the Napier middle gate, and provided opportunities for the AEU Shop Stewards Committee to address the local engineering craftsmen during some short local disputes. When locomotive men belonging to ASLEF came to call on Napier AEU members to support their strike in 1953 the gathering was large, long and heated; it ended without any unanimous result being reached amongst the local Acton engineers. Every Napier apprentice had signed an agreement with DNS management to remain out of all union affairs, or any dispute, until his indentures had been awarded. So, during a dispute within the factory, each apprentice reported for duty as normal under his foreman, who would personally supervise his day's work, or direct him to cover any more urgent tasks.

With, no doubt, very different main objectives in view, a few CAV and DNS men met at lunchtimes for prayer in the YMCA opposite the works, this was encouraged by the Christian leadership of Henry C. Tryon who was still active in the Napier Research department. Several bolder workmen and apprentices would then stand in Stanley Gardens to lead this group in singing a hymn or two, with accordion accompaniment, or to 'give a short word from the Gospel' to the lunching men on the pavements, who could listen as they chewed their sandwiches. It was later in 1956 that a Napier 'Christian Fellowship' was started, within the works itself, as a result of Henry Tryon's long influence at management level. The first meeting brought together forty staff and craftsmen, including General Manager Sir John Paget and Works Manager Bill Lewis, both of whom lent support to the group's aims.

The two most successful Napier aero gas turbines came last in their short line, and were likewise named after fast and nimble antelopes following on from the little 'Oryx'. The 'near miss' scored by the earlier 'Naiad' propeller turbine engine into UK airliners, was soon to be redressed from Acton works, NRS Liverpool and Luton FDE by the very determined design of a far more powerful and competitive engine from 1950, the E141, named the 'Eland'. This time, fully supported by the E.E. Co., DNS had designed an enlarged turbo-prop as a Private Venture engine, aimed specifically at the civil airliner market worldwide, where the radial piston engine had reached almost the limit of its now supercharged development, with it now capable of giving power outputs up to the 2,500bhp mark. Hence, the prototype single shaft turbo-prop 'Eland I' was designed to produce a minimum of 3,000ehp at the comfortable 12,500rpm of its ten-stage axial compressor and three stage turbine, this driven by hot gases out of six combustion chambers. Recent compressor tests at NRS, still under Air Ministry contracts, had developed a ten-stage unit giving 7.0:1 pressure ratio with a high 83% efficiency. This compressor was then scaled-up to pass 31lb/sec air mass flow at 12,500rpm for the Eland compressor, so large that it required testing and calibrating on the big 20,000hp steam-driven test unit at NRS Liverpool. Variable angle inlet guide vanes were devised so that 'surge' condition could be moved at lower revs, thus permitting the engine to be accelerated from 9,500rpm to 12,500rpm in just 2.5 seconds. The first 3,000ehp Eland engine ran in August 1952, and passed its MOS Acceptance Test in September, with a maximum continuous rating of 2,340ehp at 12,000rpm, with a fuel consumption of 0.48 lb/ehp/hr and a weight/power ratio of 0.52lb/ehp. The 'E141B' engine soon followed, this was the 'Eland 2' up-rated version, which developed 3,250ehp at take-off and proceeded to be flight-tested from Luton FDE in a Napier registered Vickers 'Varsity'. Following wing-nacelle design modifications by Luton D.O. and a trial installation there, testing

Versatile 3,500bhp of 'Eland' engine power was made available for fixed wing and helicopter types, most spectacularly in a pair for the Fairey 'Rotodyne' prototype.

was speedily begun in 1954 in the hands of Napier Chief Test Pilot Mike Randrup. This was initially undertaken with one gas turbine engine asymmetrically installed opposite a piston engine, but then with an 'Eland' pair, after which the 'Eland-Varsity' became extensively used as a twin 'Eland' flying test bed, with full onboard instrumentation which was constantly monitored during flight.

DNS prepared designs for greatly up-rated Eland engines over a ten-year period, from an E150, 'Double Eland' of 1953 which provided a 6,440ehp unit, to the E187, Eland design of June 1955, with an 8.5:1 pressure ratio compressor, an air-cooled, three-stage 'hot' turbine and a predicted output of 5,500ehp. (See Appendix IIIk for fuller Eland details.)

The conversion of an Airspeed Ambassador British airliner, from a pair of radial engines, to twin Eland power was next undertaken at Luton and was to have trials in BEA service. This aircraft, named the 'Eland Elizabethan', was to become the sole re-engined British commercial aircraft by DNS, and despite general approval after a strong, silent display at the Farnborough Air Show, sadly for DNS and BEA it was learned that further 'Lizzie' conversions were not likely to be needed, with de Havillands ending their manufacture.

Drastic action was called for, so DNS purchased an American-built 'Convair 340' airliner, complete with its Pratt & Witney R2800 radial engines. The plane arrived in 1955 at Luton Airport for a full Napier conversion design and installation and was to be powered by a pair of 'E141A, Eland 6' engines of 3,500ehp, with over-wing exhaust reaction ducts. This done, with the full support of Britain's Air Registration Board, a flight test programme commenced from off Luton's grass and Cranfield's concrete, in order eventually to gain

Overseas re-engining of piston engine aircraft was done by assembly of 'Eland' bolt-on 'Power Eggs', seen open at Luton FDE and showing the neat 'E141' installation.

USA Federal Aviation Administration (FAA) approval for flight in the USA. The three twin 'Eland'-engined aircraft flew 'around the clock' to amass flying hours, up until a fresh 'Convair 540' turbo-prop conversion was flown across the Atlantic to the USA by DNS pilots. Then on to Santa Monica where American PacAero engineers were to carry out conversions under the direction of Luton's Chief Engineer Ken Greenly and some of his mobile FDE staff; these included, amongst others, John Rickard, Basil Cheverton and Napier Test Pilot Mike Randrup. After lengthy FAA scrutiny, during which patient DNS Luton staff were able to satisfy many special conditions, on 22 August 1958, the FDE Manager, Cecil L. Cowdrey received a cable from USA to – 'MONEYER LUTON':

CAA TYPE CERTIFICATE NUMBER SA4/582 FOR NAPIER ELAND CONVAIR ISSUED AT 1620 HOURS TODAY FRIDAY AUGUST 22 STOP.
OUR TEAM IN SANTA MONICA SENDS ITS THANKS FOR THE MAGNIFICENT SUPPORT FROM LUTON IN OUR MUTUAL ENTERPRISE

– GREENLY

The seemingly impossible had been achieved: a British Napier turbo-prop engine – a type unknown till then in the USA – was now certified to replace American piston aero engines in American Civil Airliners. An unwanted airliner engine in the UK in the face of fierce British competition, it was now earning dollars in the USA, and would later do so in Canada too! Many more conversions were carried out in the USA, fitting 'Eland 504A Pods' delivered by air from Luton FDE, where they had been finally assembled and fully bench-tested, into 'Convair 440 airframes', to give the greater performance and economy of the 'Noiseless Napier', once again, in the turbo-prop 'Convair 540' airliners of Allegheny Airlines. Twelve new airframes were then ordered by the Royal Canadian Air Force, 'Eland 504' powered, known as 'Canadair CL66' transport planes, similar to the C540 conversions.

Ultimate success of the 'Convair 540' airliner, as built new with 'Eland' power by Canadair for the RCAF as their 'CL66' transport from 1960.

Meanwhile, two rather less expected applications of the versatile 'Eland' engine were about to be explored by Acton DO and adapted for users within the British rotary wing aircraft field. A pair of Eland engines would now provide 7,000shp, this was sufficient power to lift much larger helicopters and VTOL aircraft than had hitherto been possible. Back in 1953, an 'E151 modified Eland' engine had been designed for a startling new Fairey Aviation project – the 'Rotodyne VTOL Airliner', powered by a pair of Elands. This machine – being part fixed wing and part rotary wing – was to be 'lifted-off' as a helicopter by its big Eland-powered rotor, before transferring power to two propellers on stub wings, through which it would fly conventionally, whilst the lift-rotor auto-rotated above the fuselage. DNS manufactured the 'E151' engines at Acton. These models had a forward propeller shaft and rapid hydraulic clutch system which engaged a large auxiliary axial compressor, mounted between its now bifurcated exhaust ducts at the rear end. Fairey built the airframe and 90ft-diameter, four-bladed, high-tensile steel rotor through which pressure air produced by the installed 6,000hp passed to its ends from the Eland-driven auxiliary compressors. Here, four kerosene burning jet-reaction units were mounted at the blade ends, these four rather loud 1,000lb-thrust jets provided constant rotation during its vertical lift-off and descent to the ground. This forty-four-seat, or 4.5-ton load, aircraft was first flown by Fairey in 1958, followed by successful 'transitional flight' tests; it was then demonstrated that year at the SBAC show at Farnborough, before it travelled between London and Paris town centres. In 1959 this prototype 'Rotodyne' flew at the Paris Aeronautical Show, after it had, on 5 January that year, set a World Record Speed for rotary wing aircraft of 190.9mph over a 100km closed circuit, that capability being well in advance of any contemporary 'pure' helicopter.

The setting up of Westland Aircraft in 1960 was to kill-off both the fine Rotodyne project (even after BEA had been an interested customer), as well as Westland's own heavy lift 'Westminster' helicopter. This, the 'Sky Crane', which was seen lifting a 7-ton load at

Showing an early transitional flight of the big 'Rotodyne', with wing-mounted 'E151 Eland' variants supplying air to the fuel-burning Fairey Tip-jet units on the rotor.

Farnborough in 1958, had first flown on 15 June that year and was also powered by a pair of 'derivative' design, Eland-type engines. These roof-mounted engines had only a rear shaft drive output via a clutch and gearbox powering the 72ft-diameter main rotor of the 'Westminster'. If, in an emergency, this helicopter was forced to fly on just one of its 'E229A Eland' engines, that unit could deliver a 3,650shp short duration output, which would give the pilot 2.5 minutes to make his safe landing. A prototype thirty-nine-seat passenger 'Westminster' version had also been built and tested at Yeovil. This trio of large British-designed and Napier-powered helicopters had been advanced for their time but, sadly, were then cancelled after the formation of Westlands, the first of several government rationalisations in the aircraft industry, with new 'Napier Aero Engines Ltd' likely to be the next.

The question must be asked, did the 'Eland' engine private venture pay-off for DNS? Certainly they had produced, albeit in limited quantities, a reliable, versatile and powerful aero gas turbine that had beaten their American counterparts 'to the post'. With the financial backing of E.E. Co., Napier R & D had proved themselves adequate and their design teams had shown themselves competent, so the whole exercise, although then to be cut short for DNS, was a confirmation of their true engineering excellence and technological standing in the 1950s British aircraft industry. Without the Eland engine, Napier Engines Inc. in the USA, under John C. K. Shipp and Admiral Pflum, would not have existed, and the RCAF would not have had the CL66 transport. At Napier Luton, the great Eland export achievement, under the close scrutiny of the FAA, would not have happened in 1958, which had added 'gloriously' to the DNS 150th Anniversary celebrations. That outstanding, all British, 'Rotodyne' programme could not have taken place without the ideal adaptability of the Eland turbo-prop engine, as Rolls-Royce and Bristol had no engines available or even suitable for that prototype. Above all, the Eland airborne private venture, with full E.E. Co. approval and support, had demonstrated, once again, that the British E.E. Group could, using Ken Greenly's expression, succeed in 'our mutual enterprise'.

Yet another innovative, joint private venture was being designed during 1956 between E.E. Co. Preston and DNS Acton, this showed real progress from the earlier private ventures I have already referred to. From the double success of the DP1 locomotive and the Eland aero engine, it was seen that a new blend of these two projects could produce a Gas Turbine Locomotive. In fact, the finished locomotive turned out to have more of a 'steam locomotive' outline, carrying its fuel in a tender behind it, while its 4-6-0 layout, six large coupled driving wheels were gear driven. But that's where any similarity ended, for under its bonnet was the 2,700bhp EM27L gas turbine unit, which had an advanced eight-stage axial compressor which supplied combustion chambers and four stages of power turbine, in which two turbines powered the compressor, and two were 'free-turbines' providing shaft drive to its gearbox mounted above the centre driving axle. This was where DNS came into play, as the compressor and turbines had been developed at the NRS Liverpool, while its compact forward and reverse reduction gearbox was designed and manufactured at Acton. The prototype locomotive was delivered in July 1957 to the Rugby Locomotive Testing Station of British Railways for full evaluation on its rolling-road dynamometers. Here its transmission was 'shaken down' successfully, reaching 97mph on the rollers, before beginning extended running trials on the Midland Region's lines.

But first this gas turbine loco entered London from Rugby via the old Great Central route into Marylebone to attend the Institution of Locomotive Engineers' Exhibition there, carrying the E.E.Co. logo and number 'GT3', as it followed two earlier G.T. types that had been tried by BR Western Region, but who now refused further gas turbine experimentation. Despite promising results during track testing on the Great Central section and the WCML over Shap Fell while hauling heavy loads at speed, this unique British development ended there by 1962, as electrification of BR Midland Region lines spread. Exercising the strongest competition imaginable, the Eastern Region had then taken delivery of twenty-two Type 5 'Deltic' locomotives!

The age of record breaking was not quite yet over for DNS, with another great record being achieved by the courageous engineering staff of Napier Luton FDE late in 1957. At that establishment two 'Top Secret' development programmes had been undertaken by Manager Cecil Cowdrey, in the field of high-speed flight by Ram-Jet and Rocket-Engine in the later 1940s. A National Gas Turbine Establishment (NGTE – Pyestock) contract for a long series of Ram-Jet Test Vehicles (RJTV) had been accepted by Luton FDE in 1950. Over thirty RJTVs were built up until 1958, their performance was recorded by Napier technicians when fired from the Aberporth Test Range in Wales out over the Irish Sea and were powered using a wide variety of fuels through fuel feed turbo-pumps. Up to eight solid propellant booster rockets were needed to launch each of these 20ft-long Napier-NGTE test vehicles, which accelerated to a high enough forward speed for the internal ram-jet engine to start to function and to generate its thrust.

The Napier Luton-based liquid fuel rocket programme for the MOS, led to the design and development of twenty types of Napier rocket engines in all, numbered from NRE 1 to NRE 20, with thrusts ranging from 100 to 40,000lb. The first design dated from 1951 and was a mono-propellant rocket with a thermite-igniter burning ammonium nitrate fuel to produce 1,000lb of thrust. By the end of 1952 the first design, NRE 5, for a High Test Peroxide (HTP) and Kerosene bi-propellant rocket engine fired by thermal ignition, had been built, to a capability of 8,000lb thrust and been tested within a concrete airfield bunker.

The NRE 11 version of 1954 gave 3,000lb thrust as a 'Red Shoes' ground-to-air missile sustainer engine, this for an E.E.Co. missile, that was later known as the 'Thunderbird'.

This type of rocket engine was further developed under Chief Engineer Walter Shirley as the 'NRE 14 Single Scorpion' thermal ignition rocket engine, intended for use in the 'high altitude booster-rocket package' of English Electric 'P1B Lightning' interceptors. These 2,250lb thrust, re-lightable rockets were then paired to give the 'NRE 15, Double Scorpion' unit of 4,500lb thrust within the 'Lightning' booster package, to be mounted under its fuselage, which contained the two Rolls-Royce Avon jets. Napier Luton had employed an MOS-issued Canberra bomber as a flying test bed for their double-chamber NSc1-2 engine at all altitudes, including fast initial climb after take-off, as demonstrated at Farnborough. But the Scorpions really came into their own above 50,000ft when the pair of Avon jet engines were becoming starved of oxygen. On such a test flight, on 28 August 1957, Pilot Mike Randrup, with Walter Shirley as flight observer, wearing pressure suits, flew this 'Canberra, WK163' from Luton airfield, to high above the open sea south of the Isle of Wight, to snatch for Great Britain a new World Altitude Record of 70,310ft (13.5 miles), away from the USA. This they had done by firing their 'Double Scorpion' rocket

Seen mounted in the bomb bay of E.E. 'Canberra -WK163', the Napier N.Sc-2 'Double Scorpion' rocket engine, designed and developed at Luton FDE. Re-lightable at any altitude, in 1957 the unit boosted WK163 to a World Altitude Record of 13½ miles.

engine from 45,000ft while maintaining a steep climb, a feat for which they were jointly awarded the 'Britannia Trophy'. The Napier Luton engineering team were congratulated by the DNS Board, while the company were credited with the World Altitude Record and held the certificate of the 'Federation Aeronautique Internationale'.

For D. Napier & Son Ltd, the year 1958 was fittingly to prove the pinnacle of the 150-year-old Company's success, with it then being fully engaged in producing power units for the most modern modes of transport by land, sea and in the air. The company in that year celebrated one and a half centuries of high-quality production since David Napier had arrived by ship in London to seek out precision engineering and then displayed an extraordinary genius in practising it. A tribute to his early achievements needed to be given, as well as to those of his brilliant son and partner James. He had been followed by David's grandson Montague, who had displayed his painstaking genius for mechanical design, development and manufacture in the field of internal combustion engines to drive boats and road vehicles. The tribute was made by staging a range of events in the main DNS centres of central London, Luton and Liverpool.

The main touring exhibition was then mounted in each centre by rotation, starting out in the Tea Centre in Regent Street, London, on 3 June, when the then Minister of Supply, Aubrey Jones, opened the exhibition, while Sir George Nelson spoke about some notable Napier achievements from 150 years of high-quality engineering.

Many examples were on display, from a ram-jet test vehicle standing in the entrance hall to the fine Schneider Trophy which had been won twice by aircraft powered by 'Lion' engines. Then, several historic dioramas depicted early Victorian products from Lambeth works; others showed many racing activities of Napier-powered vehicles, boats and aircraft. The Napier family was represented by Mr Selwyn Napier and his sister as members of Montague Napier's own family. With Napier trophies and photographs of record breaking on show, all telling the story of the quite unbeatable Napier precision engineering from its 150 years, the 10,000 visitors who attended savoured and learned from the exceptionally wide range of general engineering products that had come from the works of DNS. The complete exhibition then moved on to the Luton and Liverpool centres, where new exhibits and displays of local interest were added for the many visitors who had connections with DNS.

Such an occasion couldn't pass without a Meeting of Napier Cars and their proud owners. This took place on 7 June in London, with a rally in Regents Park, followed by a short tour in London traffic via Regent Street, Pall Mall, Piccadilly and Oxford Street. The eleven Napiers involved, ranging from 1900 to 1922, then proceeded to the Royal Aero Club, for a luncheon where the guest of honour was Mrs Myra C. Edge, the widow of S.F. Edge, and a Vice-President of the Veteran Car Club. In her speech after the luncheon, Mrs Edge said of him: 'S.F. Edge was a brilliant and fearless driver – I think that is generally acknowledged – but those who might have been distressed if he had met with an accident always consoled themselves with the knowledge that those who drove Napier cars ran the fewest risks.' Also at the rally, in school cap, was a young David Napier, great-great-grandson of the founder of the company, who was photographed at the wheel of a car designed by his grandfather, the eminent engineer Montague Napier.

The 150th Anniversary called for a permanent record in book form of DNS history and achievements, this was provided by two contrasting publications during 1958. The first was in the form of an attractively designed manual of D. Napier & Son Ltd past and present, with the title *This is Napier; more power at lower cost*, a detailed fifty-eight-page technical record of most current products, company facilities available and listed the sixty company offices and overseas representatives throughout the world at that time.

Secondly came a well illustrated, hardback book entitled *Men & Machines – D. Napier & Son 1808 – 1958*, written for the E.E. Co. by a pair of authors, C.H. Wilson and W.J. Reader, and published in 1958 by Weidenfeld & Nicolson Ltd. Although carefully researched for historical matter and general technical information, a wealth of financial detail was included at every phase of DNS history. Perhaps this over-emphasis was offset by the *This is Napier* technical brochure published that same 150th Anniversary Year.

The only DNS happenings that could add anything to those celebrations concerned members of the Napier Board of Directors. Firstly, Sir George, the Chairman, in 1959 was made a Baron, to hold the title Lord Nelson of Stafford. Almost immediately he invited his son, the Hon. H. George Nelson to become his DNS Deputy Chairman. The second person joining the Napier Board as a new Director was Robert Andrew Inskip, alias the 2nd Viscount Caldecote, who joined DNS from the Board of the E.E. Co. A third was also a new directorship, this time for a former E.E. Co. graduate apprentice, Sir John Starr Paget,

DNS 150th Anniversary celebrations at the Napier car rally in Regents Park, and the liking for the 1914, 15hp Gentleman's Estate Carriage of the Hon. Patrick Lindsay.

who had started with DNS at Liverpool during the Second World War, rising to be their Chief Works Superintendent and finally the Assistant Manager, to Liverpool's then Manager Mr F.R. Smith, who saw to the production of the bulk of Sabre engines from there. Board member Sir John Paget then remained the DNS General Manager in London and its Works Director throughout the 1960s. Lastly, after long and accomplished service with DNS, Alfred John Penn was made the company's new Technical Director in 1959. It now appeared to most staff that Napier gas turbine engines had finally 'won the day'.

However, the first senior technical member of DNS staff to be lost by resignation, in January 1959, was the Chief Engineer of the Piston Engine Division, Ernest Chatterton, after his long, distinguished career with DNS-leading Sabre, Nomad and Deltic developments.

Clearly, by 1960 the blending of management between E.E. Co. and DNS was complete, while the dire events of 1961, yet to arise, were still well within the 'political arena'. It was perhaps timely that the highly respected DNS Engineer and MD, Herbert Sammons retired from the Board in December 1960, following A.V.M. Sir Conrad Collier in May that year. The new MD was another E.E. Co. man, Mr H.E.C. de Chassiron from Stafford.

A further Acton figurehead of long standing within DNS to 'be retired' at that time was the immensely popular Works Manager Bill Lewis MBE, who left DNS Acton with much regret, but was at least spared the pain of holding office during the traumatic times ahead of 1961/62.

D. Napier & Son as an individual aero engine manufacturer was still one of the 'Big Four', they having supplied many of the RAF's power unit needs since the First World War, along with Armstrong-Siddeley, Bristol Engines (both radials) and Rolls-Royce (in-line engines). DNS, as the senior company exhibitor, had of right occupied 'Stand A' at each SBAC Farnborough Show, and in recent post-war years had regained fully their old credibility as engine designers and builders 'par-excellence'. The Napier Company had risen to the challenges of the late 1940s, when the aero gas turbine was new to their experience but, with the ability and help of the NRS at Liverpool, state-of the-art axial compressors were tested and made available for in-house and outside customer use. The combined 'Blade Shop' and Napiercast Precision Investment Foundry at Park Royal 2 works, in Mansfield Road, had been the envy of other companies, for their output of Nimonic cast and machined turbine blades as much as for their forged and machined aluminium bronze compressor blades. These were finished to tight aerofoil and root tolerances on Napier-developed, hydraulic 'PF' or precision finishing machines. Much sub-contract manufacture had been carried out, and would still be, for others within that

The helicopter 'Gazelle' engine seen on its tilted test bed at Coronation Road.

'Big Four'. Despite having had to resort to aero engine development as a private venture, competitive engines kept coming along from old DNS, the very last of which – the 'Gazelle' – was by 1957 powering squadrons of gas turbine-driven military helicopters for both the Royal Air Force and Royal Navy. That old Napier 'Lion' from off the DNS shield and logo of the Second World War would just not 'lie down and die', although there were those at the Air Ministry who had wished for it to happen from 1950.

Back in 1953 the Bristol Aeroplane Co. had suggested to DNS that a free-turbine shaft-drive 'Oryx' variant could be matched with a development of their 'Bristol 173' tandem-rotor twin-engine helicopter. Acton DO prepared designs for the E152, Oryx 2 of 650shp and the E153, Oryx 3 of 900shp output free-turbine engines that year. The former was suitable for the commercial derivative of the Bristol 173, and the latter was to be tailored to the Bristol 191, a heavier machine intended for the Royal Navy. Although the 900shp was adequate for all normal twin-engine helicopter operations, a one-hour rating of 1,100shp, plus at least 1,260shp for two and a half minutes for when one engine cut out was required. DNS decided that to adequately cover this '191' requirement, and that for the even more advanced Britol 192 model, they would design a completely new engine, with a far greater mass flow than the Oryx compressor gave, that engine became the 'E156, Gazelle'.

So, for the climax of DNS aero engine design and development, we now turn to the unique, 1954-designed free-turbine power of the 1,500shp Gazelle helicopter engine. Being able to draw upon the strength of compressor and turbine research within the NRS, the Gas Turbine Division's designers at Acton were, in this case, able to make full use of an existing, highly efficient Research axial compressor of $11^5/_{16}$ in diameter with eleven stages, which delivered 16lb/sec mass flow at a 6.37:1 pressure ratio. After the Ministry issued a design and development contract, the serious design work for the Gazelle free-turbine was then started in June 1954. So rapid was the uptake of work that the first unit ran on the bench and was accepted, on 3 December 1955. By the 14 December it had then delivered its full brochure performance of 1,260shp – all achieved in eighteen months by Acton.

Because of its helicopter main rotor direct drive application, the E156 was designed to run in a vertical installation, but could also be mounted at any angle required of it. All testing was done either vertically or at various angles, a variable rig having been designed by the test plant DO to simulate the overhead rotor drive position. The Gazelle axial compressor, which fed six combustion chambers, was on a single shaft driven by the first two stages of the turbine, while the third turbine stage was 'free' and drove the rotor above it through an epicyclic reduction gearbox and coupling. This transmitted 1,260shp to each rotor in the prototype Bristol 192 tandem rotor helicopter that first flew on 5 July 1958. When the thirty RAF version Belvedere aircraft went into service in 1960, they were powered by two up-rated Gazelle 2 engines of 1,650shp, with a lifting capacity of over 2 tons or space for eighteen fully armed troops or up to twelve casualty litters. These general-purpose aircraft were, at the time, the largest military helicopters built in Western Europe with a maximum speed of 138mph. Their service in RAF squadrons took place over a wide area in Home, European and Middle Eastern operations during the 1960s.

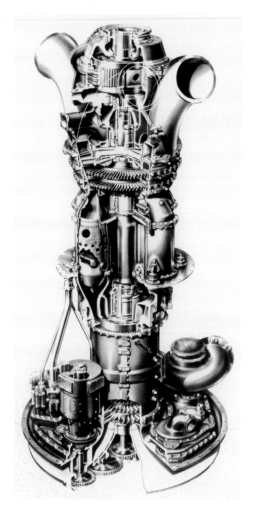

Left: Revealing cutaway of the 1,450bhp 'Gazelle' engine, showing its free-turbine disc sectioned at the top, this driving upwards via an epicyclic reduction gear to the rotor.

Opposite above: At RAF Odiham, a Bristol 192 'Belvedere' tandem rotor helicopter of 1958, powered by front and rear 1,650bhp D. Napier & Son 'Gazelle' free-turbine engines.

Opposite below: A quartet of Royal Navy Westland S58 Wessex HAS1 helicopters, each in service in 1961 with a single D. Napier & Son Gazelle 161 engine of 1,450bhp.

Just as, if not more, versatile was the single-engined Westland 'Wessex' military helicopter that was a British development of the Sikorsky 'S58', then built under license by Westlands from 1960 onwards. The prototype was flown utilising an S58 airframe, with its radial engine replaced by an inclined, nose-mounted 'Gazelle' engine of 1,250shp, whereas the Westland-built production HAS 1 helicopter, which was first flown on 20 June 1958, had the more powerful E201, 'Gazelle' free-turbine engine rated at 1,450shp. With a speed of 140mph, and sonar buoy submarine detection equipment, the HAS 1 became an essential part of the Royal Navy's carrier-borne anti-submarine and 'search and rescue' airborne forces. The later Wessex HAS 3 version equipped the RN's large '737 Naval Air Squadron' on board six Cruisers, including HMS *London* and HMS *Fife*.

These longer range helicopters, known as the 'camel-backs'- due to an upper 'Radome' behind the crew's cockpit – also carried strike weapons in the form of air-to-sea missiles.

Napier Luton FDE played a prominent part in the flight development of later Gazelle-engined Wessex variants for the Royal Australian Navy, namely the HAS 3A type.

Napier Luton, as part of their rocket engine development work, produced a helicopter rotor tip-jet booster system. This operated from the decomposition of high test peroxide into superheated steam and oxygen at 600 degrees Celsius, over a silver metallic catalyst, with the gases being ejected through de Laval nozzles. Applied to small army piston engine 'Skeeter' helicopter rotors in limited numbers, it greatly increased the rate of climb to 1,400ft/min. These NRE 19 tip-jet units were supplied in six sizes to suit larger machine rotors also, such as the Westland 'Whirlwind' helicopter. At Luton, DNS had made ample use of this catalytic generation of superheated steam to operate the turbo-pumps within their rocket engines of all sizes, its high temperature also being the source of thermal ignition for kerosene.

From 1958 on, every two years at the Farnborough show, a remarkably varied display of Napier-powered helicopters took to the air during the flying display, becoming known as the 'Napier Helicopter Flying Circus', with a type to suit almost any customer! These could include the big Westminster sky-crane, a RN Wessex, the Rotodyne airliner, those tiny boosted Skeeters or the tandem rotor Belvedere taking on loads and troops.

Although there were a few extra orders from the military, the commercial outcome for DNS was very limited as, one by one, these projects were cancelled by their builders. The future shape of the helicopter was certainly there, and in the air, but overseas alternatives eventually broke into the larger military and civilian markets leaving these well advanced early British developments of gas-turbine rotary wing aircraft without a home market.

DNS Luton had, after a decade of R & D by 1960, become the UK Centre for aircraft thermal de-icing systems, under the name of 'Napier Spraymat', which by that time was being applied to control surfaces, propeller spinners and rotors of most major new British aircraft, plus many overseas. Also, many of the 'Spraymat' heater mats and conductors were now being manufactured for the UK and USA in Japan. For the effective anti-icing and de-misting coatings of all aircraft windows and cockpit canopies, the products of the Sierracin Company of USA were now being applied to these aero transparencies and sold under license by DNS, who now used the names 'Sierracote' and 'Sierraglo' for them in the UK. Eventually both companies came to a mutually profitable arrangement, whereby D. Napier & Son and Sierracin Corporation shared their licenses for Spraymat and these coatings and their joint sale of each others products across the Atlantic, well into the 1960s. Luton FDE had also continued constant flight testing of DNS and other' company's engines.

Above all, the Napier 'Gazelle' had proved to be a resounding success in the heavier military helicopter field. At the Liverpool production plant, by 1960 the manufacture and test of turbo-blown Deltic engines and turbo-blower units produced for diesel engine customers, had been recently joined on the shop floor by smaller batches of 'Gazelle' parts. These then awaited assembly either at Liverpool, or at Acton, before the final testing was carried on as normal on the dynamometers at Coronation Road. At the Park Royal Blade Shop, the night shift had been withdrawn back in November 1959 due to insufficient orders for the 'Gazelle' free-turbine engine, and only limited 'Eland' orders from USA. At the time there was a real fear that should the then growing government-driven rationalisation programme be implemented, it could perhaps force the closure of DNS aero engine manufacture altogether. At a time when the 'Gazelle' was so heavily relied upon by the RAF and the Navy it would be lost for the British forces, not only to the DNS Company. Clearly it was time to hatch some far-reaching strategic plan of action that could safeguard that engine and maintain those already in service in the immediate future. Such action could happen, despite particular needs at DNS who had produced the unique 'Gazelle' engine at just the right time, to meet fully several British military requirements.

At board level both E.E. Co. and DNS shared a majority of their leading executives, from whom a carefully contrived plan of action was beginning to take shape, under the unified Chairmanship of the 'Nelson Team' and the two other joint directors.

But behind the scenes were politicians, ministerial chiefs and directors of Rolls-Royce. Their first objective was clear-cut: to release the unique Gazelle free-turbine from DNS control and place its future into the hands of Rolls-Royce. This was to be done in such a way as not to antagonize the senior Napier staff, who would possibly be needed later to lead the engine's development. Secondly, with that done, the Ministry would be prepared to see the remaining aircraft-based business at DNS Acton and Luton permanently closed down, while leaving the other main DNS activities at their three sites to continue under a much revised DNS Board of Directors, but with the company as a whole to remain a subsidiary of the parent E.E. Co.

The details of a plan rapidly worked-out between E.E. Co., Rolls-Royce and the Air Ministry in 1961 involved a number of steps. It followed correspondence on 15 February 1961, marked 'Secret', and some meetings held between the Hon. H.G. Nelson, DNS Deputy Chairman and the Rt Hon. Peter Thornycroft MP, Minister of Aviation, in which it was proposed that either Bristol-Siddeley or Rolls-Royce should take over the development of the 'E 219 – Gazelle 18' engine of 1,750shp, designed at Acton in June 1959, for use in the Westland Wessex HAS 3 helicopter. By 23 March it had been agreed with Rolls-Royce that their company was to be responsible for the development, DNS Acton was to be used as the centre for this, but both DNS Liverpool and Luton were to be excluded from that programme. The M of A confirmation for this plan was received by DNS on 30 March 1961, but it was firstly to involve the floating of a new company bearing the Napier name, this was formed by neatly and inexpensively re-naming an old, dormant company 'Napier Business Vehicles Ltd'. Historically, that company was formed on 10 March 1913 by Montague S. Napier from re-naming 'Napier Motors Ltd', itself incorporated only on 17 April 1912. By 21 July 1913, D. Napier & Son Ltd was then incorporated; this was to be Napier's only motor vehicle company, thus leaving N.B.V. Ltd dormant with just £100 capital. Now forty-eight years later, this was to be re-incorporated as Napier Aero Engines Ltd (NAE). The NAE capital was initially to be the £100,000 (£99,900 being additionally needed) that was contributed by E.E. Co. finances agreed on 12 May 1961. But it was soon to be doubled to £200,000, from 11 September 1961, with a further £100,000 from the Rolls-Royce Company, who would then become joint owners of NAE and have directors on its board. These initial steps were quietly taken and signed-for during the spring of 1961, during DNS Board meetings all held at English Electric House in the Strand, convened by DNS Chairman Lord Nelson and Deputy Chairman Hon. H.G. Nelson, with just DNS secretary R.C. Johnson in attendance. Then, with the new NAE Company incorporated from 2 May 1961, a general notice was prepared as a press release, but 'Not till after Midnight on 31 May'. This was to be given to DNS staff by MD Mr H. de Chassiron the following day. He was quick to emphasise the new bond between DNS and Rolls-Royce, as they were now about to share the more powerful 'Gazelle 18' engine's development and manufacture, plus their joint interests within NAE Ltd at Acton, without which the Ga.18 engine would not be ordered at all. By some miracle, so it seemed, 'Them up the road' had suddenly moved in 'Next door' to DNS, this after all those years of rivalry in the motor car and aero engine industry, since the 1,000-mile trial of 1900 when S.F. Edge and Hon. C. Rolls shared the honours. That general notice, jointly issued from E.E. Co. and Rolls-Royce, concluded with an assurance – 'I am certain that these arrangements are in the best interests of all employees of the firm. It removes recent uncertainty as to our official position in the aero engine field and gives every reason for confidence in the stability of future employment.'

Several staff transfer notices from DNS to NAE were then given out on 30 June by R.C. Johnson, to be implemented from 17 July 1961, while other DNS employees were also notified about their change of employment through Works Director Sir John Paget. Meanwhile, the transfer of information from the DNS Aero Gas Turbine Division to NAE Ltd continued throughout the year, involving the change of ownership of designs and drawings for the Ga.2, Ga.13 and Ga.18 engines, the Eland engines and the E151 Eland-Rotodyne – Rapid Action Y100 Hydraulic Clutch. The transfer of engines and spares in stock also took place steadily from 15 July; this comprised 208 of the earlier Gazelles, which were either complete or under manufacture at Liverpool, and initial orders for just twenty-seven of the Ga.18s.

When the Board of NAE was announced, it comprised: Chairman – Mr J.D. Pearson (Chief Executive and Deputy Chairman of Rolls-Royce), Deputy Chairman – H.G. Nelson (Deputy Chairman of E.E. Co. and DNS), Managing Director – Mr H.E.C. de Chassiron (DNS Managing Director from September 1960), plus Viscount Caldecote (MD E.E. Aviation), Mr F.T. Hinkley (Commercial Director of Rolls-Royce Aero Engines), Mr A.A. Lombard (Rolls-Royce Aero Engines Director of Engineering), Sir Archibald Hope (DNS Director of Sales), Sir John Paget (DNS General Manager) and A.J. Penn (DNS Technical Director).

With such a line-up of high ranking talent, clearly the future of the new company was expected to remain bright, despite having to base its entire development work at Acton.

During this management upheaval within the aero engine business, 'old' DNS itself continued with its busy 1962 production schedule for turbo-blowers and turbo-charged Deltic marine engines at Liverpool works, along with all further development of these for future markets, both at the Acton site and at development test houses, Park Royal 2.

More was to come, however, as Sir George Nelson, the Lord Nelson of Stafford, died on 16 July 1962. He was deeply mourned at D. Napier & Son and throughout the English Electric Group of Companies. His son, the Hon. H. George Nelson, now took the reins at English Electric House, under the title Chairman and Chief Executive, while G.A.(Sandy) Riddell, the Controller, and Bernard Banks, the Commercial Director, became Joint Deputy MDs, both men having served his father Sir George Nelson faithfully over a long period.

Soon after, on 2 August 1962, a confidential letter was sent by NAE Chairman Mr Jim Pearson, addressed from Rolls-Royce at Derby, to Mr Sandy Riddell at the E.E. Co. regarding a recent letter he had received, dated 31 July, from Mr F.J. Doggett, the under Secretary (Air B) at the Ministry of Aviation. In this, he had argued that, in view of the future smaller requirement likely for the 'Ga.18' engine in the Wessex HAS 3 helicopter, the employment of Napier Acton works for its development and manufacture would now become uneconomical for the M of A to support long term. Whereas, similar facilities within Rolls-Royce, where the later 'Twin-Gnome' engine for the 'Wessex 2 & 5' was being now produced as a safer replacement, would also be a more economical option for the single 'Ga.18' engines as well. Certainly for Rolls-Royce this arrangement would thus give a double benefit, leaving them the sole big helicopter gas-turbine engine supplier to the services. Doggett had left Pearson in no doubt that the future of the 'Ga.18' engine would itself be conditional on the move of its development from NAE Acton works to a place within the Rolls-Royce organisation. So it was not long before it had been agreed within the NAE Board, who now felt a degree of secrecy and urgency, that in order to once again accommodate the M of A on financial grounds, the change of site from NAE Acton to that at Rolls-Royce Hamilton in Scotland for all such limited Gazelle work should be actioned as soon as possible. The recently installed new Lord Nelson, still deputy NAE Chairman, was too fully occupied with the ultimate leadership of the E.E. Co. he had just inherited, to object further to that decision. So, very suddenly, on 22 August 1962, the notice of an urgent meeting to be attended by all senior DNS and NAE Staff, Heads of Departments, Superintendents & Foremen, was circulated by John F.A. Radford, Manager, Personnel and Administration.

That meeting was held on 24 August in the general works canteen, on the top floor of the 'New Concrete Building' at 2.45 p.m., when the NAE Chairman, Mr J.D. Pearson (Rolls-Royce Chief Executive), addressed the assembled staff and announced 'a planned and phased run-down of work' at the sixty-year-old DNS/NAE Acton works. This was to lead to the eventual closure of all the London area sites, except for Coronation Road test tunnels which would still be needed by Rolls-Royce for 'Gazelle' engine testing from Scotland for the foreseeable future. He predicted that some 2,500 people would be affected by this run-down over a nine-month period. NAE Ltd had now become finally integrated into the aero engine division of Rolls-Royce Ltd, but this was in respect of one main Napier product only, and that was to be progressively superseded by an alternative Rolls-Royce engine for the 'Wessex'.

Pearson ended his statement to the badly shaken meeting, by very hopefully adding that: 'The business of D. Napier & Son Ltd, whose establishments are in Liverpool, London and Luton, is not affected by this decision; neither is the N.A.E. Company's modern foundry which produces alloy steel castings to precise limits by the investment process.'

By 29 August 1962 redundancy payments had been scheduled for many staff, these being effective from 31 December that year for former NAE employees. By March 1963 the scale of the exodus from Acton of younger employees and existing apprentices was increasing, so necessitating an adjournment debate 'Napier Aero Engines Ltd (Closure)' held in the House of Commons, at the request of Philip Holland, MP for Acton, on 7 March and reported in that copy of Hansard. The outcome was a signed letter from the Prime Minister Harold Macmillan to Holland, a copy of which he then sent to J. Radford at NAE Ltd. In this the PM wrote that as early as 15 February 1960, Duncan Sandys had stated his government's policy towards the aircraft industry, that was to create just 'five major groups; two making fixed wing airframes and guided weapons, one making helicopters and two making aero engines'. Certainly a major step towards this had been taken through NAE's sudden dispersal from Acton, the PM then concluding that 'while one sympathises with the employees affected, there is no reason to doubt that the decision is in the national interest, and there can be no question of the government seeking to reverse it.' That Prime Minister's phrase 'You've never had it so good!' could hardly be applied to engineers in Acton in 1962–63, but he was generally correct in his forecast that in their search for other suitable work he 'did not expect any serious difficulty'. Staff at Rolls-Royce, who were involved at the time, have since then expressed the view that they 'were given the job of doing the government's dirty work for them' – believe that if you will! They have also reported that disappointingly only five Senior NAE Design Staff re-sited themselves up to Derby on the 'Gazelle team', whereas a whole group of ex-Acton men were to meet up again later, after joining the Rolls-Royce Small Engine Division at Leavesden.

By the end of 1962, a valuation of five acres of the Acton works site had been made, but there were 'no takers' at the asking price of £1.4 million for its future redevelopment into unit workshops, but the sale to a development company was agreed by 7 January 1963. The final handover of all gas turbine materials was completed by 14 September 1964, in readiness for the eventual plant clearance and final land sale during the next two years. The profitable NAE owned investment foundry at Park Royal was sold as a working unit to Westlands at Hayes (formerly Fairey Aviation), on 2 September 1964, where it was re-established and operated as a viable plant for components using the lost-wax process.

It was intended that NAE Ltd own the Luton FDE, but, although it had no engines to flight test, its unique range of aircraft de-icing products and high-precision facilities had been robustly defended as the last DNS airborne stronghold by Cecil Cowdrey, its Manager since 1940, who utilised its former D. Napier & Son Ltd letterhead in trading to the very last. His decisive press release of 1961 proclaimed: 'I have given considerable thought to this matter, and I have had several discussions with the Managing Director, and it has been agreed that so far as Luton is concerned we remain outside the new grouping (NAE) – in other words we are still D. Napier & Son Ltd'. By 1962 the revised plan here was for the busy Luton plant to become part of the E.E. Co. Aircraft Products Division, which was again resisted by the Luton management up until their retirement. When, at long last, the Luton FDE site and plant was acquired from DNS/NAE by the E.E. Co. (along with its several manufacturing licenses) the date had moved on to 8 April 1965. That was a full week after all NAE trading activities had ceased on 31 March 1965 and from which time Rolls-Royce Ltd had taken over the complete Gazelle business from NAE and now held

The former DNS Acton works and offices site outlined for disposal in 1964.

a 'Ga.18' development contract. The winding-up agreement for NAE Ltd was now simply a formality to conduct between its joint owners the E.E. Co. and Rolls-Royce Ltd, so this document was prepared and eventually signed by both parties on 15 July 1967.

The final outcome of the 1961 aero industry rationalisation plan for DNS resulted in D. Napier & Son Ltd outlasting that 'company of convenience' NAE Ltd well into the 1970s. The rebuilt DNS Board set up in 1961, aiming to continue their diesel engine and turbo blower businesses, was constituted with some new and some well-known directors. The DNS Chairman was again the Hon. H. George Nelson, P.J. Daglish was the new MD, H.E.C. de Chassiron and the Rt Hon. Viscount Caldecote both continued on the Board, with G.A. Riddell from E.E. Co. as the new Deputy Chairman, plus Mr P. Horsfall and F.L. Parris the DNS Assistant Secretary, who quickly resigned his position in Dec 1962.

The Deltic high-speed diesel business now continued to be fairly brisk, with the Liverpool production shops kept well occupied with a variety of power units on order. By early 1962 BR Eastern Region had taken delivery of its twenty-two 3,300bhp 'Type 5' English Electric-built and Napier 'Deltic'-powered locomotives from its Vulcan Foundry works at Newton-le-Willows. These main line machines, using a BR officially permitted top speed of 100mph on the East Coast Main Line Anglo-Scottish express trains between London Kings Cross and Edinburgh Waverley stations, were each powered by a pair of E 169 design type, Deltic 18-25 engines de-rated to 1,650bhp at 1,500rpm, they were controlled either singly or as a synchronised pair at the higher speeds. These locomotives soon became known as the 'racehorses', owing to their speed being higher than other diesel locomotives on BR, and also the fact that eight had been given the names of former Derby winners. This fleet of twenty-two was split into three groups, eight at Edinburgh-Haymarket, six at Gateshead, the remaining eight at London-Finsbury Park, stabled in purposebuilt depots, while their maintenance was the subject of a five-year contract between BR(E) and the E.E. Co.

By January 1961, the first production version of the Type 5 locomotive, No.D9001, arrived with a pair of 1,650bhp 'Deltic' units, seen here at Kings Cross before naming.

This 'Deltic fleet' introduced high-speed Inter City rail travel to Great Britain during the 1960s and '70s, along with their high traffic availability and outstanding reliability. In 1966 a 'Super-Deltic' locomotive of 4,400bhp was designed by E.E. Co., this time to be powered by a pair of 'E171 turbo-blown Deltic T18-27' engines, but head-and-tail diesel units and popular railway electrification had both reduced that locomotive market.

Over the horizon and out to sea, DNS exhaust gas-driven Deltic turbo-machinery in the form of the 'E239 turbo-blown Deltic T18-37K' marine engine giving 3,100bhp at a 2,100rpm sprint rating, had been in demand for a class of Norwegian designed and built FPB craft since 1958. As a result of DNS Deltic Applications Engineer, Mr 'Pip' Plant, working in co-operation with the brilliant young Naval architect Jan Linge of Boatservice at Mandel, this Fast Patrol Boat design was developed with a vee-drive twin-engine Deltic installation, which, to quote Pip Plant's words, could at last really 'take advantage of what Deltic engines had to offer'. By 1962 this Tjeld Class FPB was ordered in good numbers for the Norwegian Navy, with an installed power of 6,200bhp giving them a speed of 45 knots. This situation required three Napier engineers to be resident in Norway. At DNS these craft were to become known by the rather inept name of the 'Nasty Class'; they were fitted with a variety of torpedo tubes and armament to equip them as fast MTBs and were used by a dozen or so friendly Navies worldwide, including the two 'Hugin Class' versions for the Federal German Navy. Perhaps their crowning glory was when four of the 'Nasty' MTBs were bought and successfully tested by the US Navy, after which they part-built their own timber hulls at the John Trumpy Yard, with Harry Gardner from DNS in residence to oversee the installation of each pair of T18-37Ks. This led them to design their own all-aluminium hulled 'Osprey Class PTF23' Boats, built in the USA by Sewart Seacraft, each of which enjoyed its two T18-37Ks delivering 6,200bhp through direct drive. By the end of 1966, DNS in Liverpool works had built their 500th Deltic!

Alongside the Deltic production line at Liverpool works, was a similarly active one for Napier turbo-blowers employing 670 personnel in 1966. The range of different type and sized units had by then reached twelve, up to the largest and newest 'TS610' for bigger

An early Norwegian-built 'Nasty' Class MTB dashes over the sea, powered by a pair of turbo-blown T18-37K 'Deltic' engines, delivering over 6,000bhp for 45 knots.

merchant ship diesels, seven of these units having been delivered in 1966, compared with 931 of the medium capacity TS200 type blower. The annual total that year was 1886 of all sized units sold and built at Liverpool works, whereas the grand total manufactured since the turbo-blower business had started at Acton in 1948 had then reached 18,774. The outstanding commercial success of the turbo-blower division, set up at the request of the E.E. Co., initially for its railway locomotive business, in 1966 remained a profitable one, which had kept well abreast of its competitors on the continent of Europe and in the USA.

All of the three DNS centres, Liverpool, Luton and London, had been endowed with highly equipped mechanical research facilities since the end of the Second World War. These were then available to the wider E.E. Group of companies and other local industries, as much as they were made use of for DNS projects and in-house R&D work in connection with engines. The NRS at Liverpool had during the 1950s/60s been the backbone of high efficiency gas turbine and compressor development, not only for aero-engines, but also for Napier turbo-blower testing and development to keep it ahead in that most competitive market. Napier research work continued in the metallurgical, aerodynamic, fluid-dynamics and stress-analysis fields, with a particular interest shown in the development of new bearings and their lubrication, including high-speed gas-bearings and shaft-sealing techniques. For instance, an E.E. Co.-built 100MW steam turbo-alternator set running at 3,000rpm was to be directly cooled by low-density hydrogen gas, in order to remove heat while minimising the internal windage losses. The seals for the 16in diameter shaft against hydrogen loss, at up to 30lb/sq.in pressure, were designed and then developed in the Napier Acton Research Department. with testing done at the PR1, DTH site the 1950s. This led to successful ring type and face type oil lubricated seals, but for atomic energy power stations where oil was unacceptable, DNS developed types of gas lubricated shaft seals lubricated by air. After loss of aero engine work in 1962, development work for the U.K.A.E.A. was taken on at Acton works, through the busy E.E. Co. atomic power division at Whetstone, from new welding techniques within reactors to remote handling devices for radioactive materials.

Despite having moved their offices from 211 to 47-55 The Vale, Acton, DNS lived on actively for another decade, but increasingly beneath the sign 'under new management'.

9

MOVING FORWARD UNDER NEW NAMES 1968–1992

Exactly 160 years after the foundation of an engineering workshop in London by David Napier, his immensely influential company was now about to leave the British capital for good. Over the intervening years it had excelled in many fields, especially those of mechanised printing, money manufacture with great exactness of weight, motor vehicle development which overtook the continent's best and, latterly, the widest possible variety of engine design and construction powering almost all forms of transport. The remaining DNS staff still in London worked either in offices at 47-55 The Vale (this formerly termed Acton 2 site), were testers in the surviving Development Test Houses at Park Royal 1 or were operating at Coronation Road Test Tunnels where 'Gazelle' free-turbines were put through their paces. These were the 'Rolls-Royce badged' engines that had been built in Scotland.

The voluntary liquidation of Napier Aero Engines Ltd as an independent company had been legally arranged by 14 March 1968 between its joint owners the E.E. Co. and Rolls-Royce, so it only remained for its residual directors to formally approve that the NAE Company be wound-up at one more board meeting. That was chaired by Lord Nelson himself in London on 19 September 1968, just six days after his E.E. Co. had agreed to merge with Lord Weinstock's G.E.C. The whole sham NAE episode was then deemed closed, with apparently some relief to all concerned, with departing Secretary R.C. Johnson left to see that all NAE records were destroyed after a two-year waiting period. Whether that was in fact done remains unsure, as ample documentation of that infamous company remains to this day, some now in the hands of the Napier Power Heritage Trust, while other copies are, naturally, still held in the possession of Rolls-Royce at Derby. From that date the Napier name was 'grounded' from the aircraft power industrial scene, after an all too brief fifty-year period, but, to put this in perspective, this was only one third of the total life of D. Napier & Son Engineers.

Throughout the second half of the 1960s, Mr P. J. Daglish, formerly the Commercial Director, had become the new DNS Managing Director. In his able and resolute hands the DNS Chairman Lord Nelson could at last safely leave the future prospects of the now smaller but still widely spread Napier Company, while he had to grapple with the growing storm arising from various takeover bids for his giant E.E. Co.

They knew that in time the high market value and technically excellent two main DNS products manufactured at the Liverpool works, turbochargers, or 'blowers', and the high-speed diesel engines – the 'Deltics', would both also be threatened as the result of any new merger or change in the overall control of their parent E.E. Co.

The battle to make a profitable merger with the chiefly heavy electrical engineering based E.E. Co. had continued since 1960, the time when the E.E. Co. itself was pressing the G.E.C. to combine with it (in the event unsuccessfully). Later, after the E.E. Co. aero division at Warton had itself been coaxed into rationalisation by a powerful combination of the British Aircraft Corporation, Bristol Aeroplane and Vickers Armstrong, E.E. Co. under the chairmanship of the younger Lord Nelson was being hurried into new merger negotiations during 1968. By then G.E.C. had combined with the A.E.I. Company in 1967, forming a strengthened electrical group under Arnold Weinstock's leadership. By the next year electrical mergers once again made the headlines, when the Plessey Company suddenly proposed that it should merge financially with the giant E.E. Co., in which DNS were operating as a subsidiary firm. But soon the G.E.C./A.E.I. group, being more prominent in the lighter electrical industries, were also considering the same tactic, with the E.E. Co. as their target, to thus form a much better balanced electrical business. Lord Nelson became perplexed by the aggression of Plessey's management throughout, and by Autumn 1968 held secret meetings with Lord Weinstock in London, with whom he formed a working understanding and a plan for their combined companies. On Friday 13 September 1968, Plessey was the bidder having all the bad luck, while E.E. Co./G.E.C. quickly and publicly announced their intended amalgamation – which was, at the time, the largest merger in British industrial history.

The story now returns again to the surviving D. Napier & Son Company (DNS), which remained a fully owned subsidiary of the still individual English Electric Company beyond October 1968, in order to review its development and trading activities during the latter part of the 1960s. February 1967 saw a total Napier Company workforce spread between its London and Liverpool plants of 1,632 employees. By that time practically all the new development and production of diesel engines and turbo-blowers was to be found within Napier Liverpool works on the East Lancashire Road, which was sited alongside the large E.E. Co. plant that both produced and stored their popular domestic appliance range. The contrast in engineering disciplines and technological standards that existed between these two plants, living under the same roof, as it were, was then most striking, although in both instances the quality was exceptionally high within their own product market areas. The workforces there were also quite different in character, ranging from highly trained, fully skilled operatives and technicians working within the DNS machining, assembly and testing shops, to the wider variety of mechanically and electrically skilled shop-floor personnel just next door. Side by side the two workforces both brought in much revenue for the E.E. Co., gained from very different customers and via very different routes within the commercial world, while both sets of customers were demanding the best of British high quality in machine design, finish and performance.

The DNS Company had required that many Acton based staff and technicians be removed from London to their Liverpool plant, with the consequent family upheaval. This was in a very similar manner to that in which NAE staff had been rather unsuccessfully

Free end of a top-of-the-range CT18-42K marine 'Deltic' engine, emphasising the size and complexity of the turbocharger and charge-coolers leading into three manifolds.

urged to relocate to Derby only five years previously, when only five Napier staff families moved 'up-the-road' to the north. At least, for this latest exodus north to Liverpool, their long standing DNS Company loyalty need not be broken, only their loyalty to London.

Naturally, many chose resignation instead of relocation, and found alternative employment for themselves in West London's industries. For one long-serving Napierian, Mr Geoffrey McGarry, it was not essential to move elsewhere on either count, as he was appointed the London representative for the Napier turbo-blower business. While, typically, another, Mr Alan Tovey, stayed with DNS and its Deltic engines after making two such relocations, firstly from Acton to Liverpool, but then in late August 1968, another from Liverpool to Davey Paxman at Colchester. This transfer, within the English Electric Diesels grouping, was in preparation for the Deltic engine production to be relocated there soon after the then anticipated E.E. Co./GEC merger, which in fact took place in the following month.

It was about this time that the Series 3 Deltic engine range came into its own, based upon the 'E263' charge-cooled, Acton design of 1961. With the usual eighteen-cylinder and 88-litre swept volume capacity, these now worked at a high brake mean effective pressure of 129.6psi (Series 2 – bmep 108.5psi) after combustion, owing to a turbocharger boost pressure of 19psi and the cooling of its scavenge air charge now down to 62 degrees Celsius (Series 2-126 degrees Celsius) before admission through the inlet ports.

With the same crankshaft speed of 2,100rpm as the Series 2, but now with a greater weight of diesel fuel injected into the denser air charge entering combustion spaces between its high conductivity Hidural copper alloy piston crowns, an increase in the marine sprint power rating to 3,700bhp was achieved. Quite naturally, it was not long before testing of these 'CT18-42K' engines at the DTH Park Royal test house under DNS Chief of Engine Test Ken Quinney, produced a sustainable 4,000bhp output from a Deltic unit just 3ins longer. This 4,000bhp maximum power output made this ultimate batch of production Deltic engines the most powerful units DNS had ever built in any numbers for sale to a military customer, and superior even to those remarkable, high-revving 36-litre aero and marine 'Sabre' variants from the Second World War era. The CT18-42K Deltic was finally specified by the Indian Navy, after keen competition from German and Russian engines, for their Delhi-designed flotilla of four fast 'Seawards Defence Boats', MGBs, which thus had a total power output of 7,400bhp per boat. This batch of eight engines was finish-built at Colchester, their sets of parts having been earlier produced at Liverpool works with the DNS tooling. These engines were up until then the highest powered that Colchester had tested, and were supplied to a Lt-Com B.R. Menon, Marine Engineer Overseer for the Indian Navy, for installation in the MGBs at Calcutta; this after all Deltics had transferred to Paxmans at Colchester.

Later in 1978, Paxman Diesels Ltd publicised this engine for the GEC Diesels group, with a low weight/power ratio of less than 4lb per hp, when it then developed 4,140bhp!

The green door of 'D. Napier & Son Ltd Engineers, The Vale, W.' closed for the last time during the spring of 1969, by which time the Acton 1 main site had been sold for industrial re-development to the Brixton Estates Company. The slow demolition of Acton workshops for this re-development took place gradually over the next twenty years, by which time most of the site had been built up with unit workshops, all fronted by their offices, so forming the new Acton Industrial Park. The DNS tool room, with one wall facing The Vale, was the last shop to be demolished, while the final ground level building to go down was the Research Department's rig shop in Stanley Gardens, this having been rented by Lucas-CAV for use as an extra fuel injection test facility until 1995. So today there still remains, set back along The Vale, the old 1903 office block and drawing office, where the 'Piccadilly Circus' engine display area was later installed, plus the tall four-storey New Concrete Building, all externally re-styled in garish modern finishes.

Before vacating the New Concrete Building itself, which fronted the Uxbridge Road, the DNS Management, incorporating its strong E.E. Co. complement of directors, had, during the 1960s, prepared a large bronze plaque, mounted on an English Oak facia, this mounted on the right hand wall inside the new ground floor front double doors. Engraved with filled white letters set under the last DNS Company Lion-rampant logo, it reads:

BETWEEN 1903 AND 1963 THESE AND THE ADJOINING PREMISES HOUSED D. NAPIER & SON LTD WHO STARTED IN LAMBETH IN 1808. HERE THEY ROSE TO ENGINEERING FAME AND JOINED IN 1942 THE ENGLISH ELECTRIC GROUP OF COMPANIES

It then went on to list just eight 'World Records gained by Napier engines manufactured here' between 1919 and 1947, these all being with power provided from 'Lion' engines.

Certainly records achieved through 'Lion power' over those twenty-eight years had almost eclipsed some of those made by Napier cars before the First World War, but the few records made in the gas turbine and rocket eras would also have been worthy of mention here, right up to 1960.

The E.E. Co./GEC joint company was initially led by Lord Nelson as its Chairman, and a GEC Managing Director, while the newly created Lord Weinstock just monitored progress of this giant electrical company from 'the wings' and introduced some unpopular economies on the way. By 1970 their joint constituent diesel engine businesses were being re-centralised, partly at the former Napier Liverpool works but also at Colchester as Ruston Paxman Diesels Ltd, now a subsidiary of English Electric Diesels Ltd. It was not long, however, before the GEC name replaced that of the E.E. Co. for this combined group, as by 1972 that same Paxman Diesels Ltd was a subsidiary of GEC Diesels Ltd.

About the same time, a similar grouping was made for all gas turbine development at the big Ruston plant in Lincoln. There then took place an exchange of work between these towns' plants, during which Ruston's range of diesel engines moved both into Liverpool and Colchester, this almost as an 'exchange deal' for the Napier turbocharger plant, as this then moved from Liverpool down to Lincoln, in order that they could be manufactured alongside the Ruston gas turbine products. This last move proved to be a very successful one for the old established Napier blower business, as the Napier turbocharger brand name has prospered there for almost forty years, under a variety of new owners.

But by far the most important change for DNS occurred on 16 December 1974 when the by then GEC Gas Turbines decided to officially do away with the old company name of D. Napier & Son Ltd. This was fully 127 years since that father and son family partnership with that name had been set up in 1847, at Vine Street works in Lambeth. To accomplish this change in the company name, the title Napier Turbochargers Ltd (NTL) was then incorporated instead of DNS. This still included the Napier name in order to build upon the existing goodwill and solid reputation of this Napier brand, with its widespread applications for pressure charging locomotive, generator and marine diesel engines throughout the world. As a clear example of their utilisation in the UK, many of British Railway's diesel electric locomotive fleet had relied on Napier turbochargers from the outset of its traction modernisation plan in the mid-1950s. Early onto the scene were the heavy 'Class 40' type with the E.E. 16SVT Mark II engine of 2,000bhp, each one with four 'whistling' Napier MS 104 blowers. With 200 of these locomotives built by the E.E. Co. in railway service from 1958 – 1985, the 1,000-plus long-term order for this application was quite significant for DNS. This class was followed by a shorter, lighter 'Class 37' type of 1960, and many of the 309 that were to be built remain in service to this day. Their E.E.12 CSTV diesel engine rated at 1,750bhp, was turbocharged by a pair of Napier HP210 turbocharger units, again realising orders for DNS of at least 1,000 units over the years. The widespread use of the light 'Class 20' type for freight, these often run in pairs, and for local passenger work, started back in 1957 from which time 219 of these E.E. Co. locomotives were constructed. Each had the E.E. 8SVT engine of 1,000bhp with a pair of Napier MS104 turbochargers to boost its power output, whilst giving to it that well-known 'tinkling' engine sound. Another successful E.E. express locomotive was the 'Class 50' type of 2,700bhp which used their 16CSVT engine, boosted by four Napier HP204 turbochargers, there being fifty of this class built between 1966–67, when they were allocated to the Midland Region, before being switched to the Western Region to augment their ever troublesome diesel hydraulic locomotives. All those original turbo-blowers for the above types were supplied by DNS Liverpool, but by the time the new 'Class 56' freight locomotive type was delivered in 1976, its pair of Napier SA085 turbochargers would have been manufactured and supplied by Napier Turbochargers at Lincoln. In fact, fifty-six of these machines were constructed, both at home and abroad, for British Rail, all powered by the Ruston-Paxman 16RK3CT engine of 3,250bhp; they lasted until the 1990s. Another very significant order for NTL was the supply of well over a hundred, SA084/DP turbochargers for the power-cars of the 125mph High Speed Train diesel-electric multiple units of the '253 and 254 Types' in the 1980s. Each power car (later 'Class 43') had a twelve-cylinder Paxman 'Valenta' 12RP 2,000L engine pressure charged by a single NTL SA084 which causes, when running at 28,000rpm that familiar 'whine' within an otherwise deep exhaust note. The HST125s replaced the throb of the Class 55 Deltic locomotives on Kings Cross – Edinburgh trains from 1981, but in doing so ensured that another higher Napier tuned exhaust note would remain audible within most areas of the British Isles.

At that time, before the demise of the twenty-two Class 55 locomotives on the Eastern Region of British Rail, a new phenomenon swept through the world of railway enthusiasts in the UK. Now, to those DNS men who had daily to endure a continuous staccato roar from the Deltic diesel exhausts on a 1,000-hour test, or to a lesser extent the penetrating treble note of Napier blowers while on development tests at the Acton, Liverpool, Colchester or the Lincoln plants, those sounds had become part of the background noise they met on arrival at their plant most working days. But in the post-steam era of the 1970s and '80s, for a large number of UK followers of railway operation, the audible sound and performance of some modern diesel traction locomotives had taken deep root in their affections. The four Napier blowers' 'whistling' exhaust note of the E.E. Class 40s was one, but much more so was the emotive sound that was audible, as well as often visible, from exhaust emissions of the Class 55's. It was partly due to such sensorial factors that hundreds of their followers had been prompted to form a Deltic Preservation Society in 1978, in order to raise a fund of money to purchase one working Deltic locomotive when it was due for withdrawal from the Eastern Region's stock in the next few years. By 1981, when many of these fine Deltics were being withdrawn, the membership and a fund had grown to such an extent that the society purchased from Doncaster works not one, but two of these locomotives for preservation. Such was the popularity by 1982 of the Napier Deltic engine in these 100mph railway locomotives that thousands of enthusiasts 'mourned' their loss, while phrases such as 'Farewell to thy greatness' were often to be seen and heard. Within two years, a third Class 55 locomotive 'Tulyar' had been added to their collection, while yet another group, this known as the 'D9000 Fund', had similarly purchased two more locomotives out of the twenty-two that had been built at E.E. Co.'s Newton-le-Willows works in 1961. The National Railway Collection held in York Railway Museum had been allocated locomotive No. 55002 named 'The Kings Own Yorkshire Light Infantry', this being in addition to the other five then in private ownership. With professional railway engineers much involved within these two societies it then seemed possible, but in the event took fifteen more years of effort, for some of these six machines to re-appear in running order on the mainline railways in the UK. Help from Colchester's engineers would also be needed.

The widespread use of NTL turbomachinery was repeated, and continues, on the high seas, where both four and two-stroke marine diesels have been successfully turbocharged in the UK, and frequently in shipyards abroad. Napier turbo-blowers have long been used by Fiat, Doxford, Sulzer, Gotaverken, Harland and Wolff, as well as Ruston and Paxman marine types of diesel engine. Most of the later types of marine Napier Deltic engines, as were being supplied by English Electric Diesels Ltd of 47-55 The Vale, Acton W3 from 1968, were already being constructed with a DNS designed integral turbo-blower. Their production from Liverpool works continued into the early 1970s for E.E.D. Ltd, until all modification, installation and refurbishment work for Deltics was transferred to the GEC Diesels-managed Paxman Diesels works in Colchester. Here, Deltic applications flourished in mobile electric alternators and large rotary pumps, as in the New York Fire Department 'Superpumper', and were engineered and maintained over the next quarter century. There the Deltic continued, very much as an original DNS-designed product, but then further developed by a dedicated team of former Acton-trained and experienced design and installation staff, led by Chief Applications Engineer Mr Pip Plant.

By the early 1970s, the Royal Navy required a new state-of-the-art 'Mine Counter Measures Vessel' (MCMV), incorporating the many improvements by then available, to replace their large flotilla of wooden-hulled Ton Class minesweepers that had been ordered with Deltic propulsion and pulse generator gear back in the early 1950s. To this challenge the Napierians still in office at Colchester rose with distinction, upgrading and uprating the nine-cylinder Deltic engine to perform both these functions, without recourse to the heavier eighteen-cylinder type for the vessel's main propulsion system. Their designs were to be based on the 1950 mechanically blown 9-5A propulsion engine and on the 9-5B pulse generating 'Deltic' engine, the latter as used on the 'Ton' minesweepers. Two 1965 designs (later revised) for both of these had of course travelled with them from Acton, one being the E280, 9-59K, 950bhp propulsion engine, subsequently to be fitted with an integral hydraulic 'creep-speed' motor. The other was the 750bhp E276, 9-55B for electrical pulse power generation, with the new option for the fitment of four hydraulic pumps for the additional services needed by the Navy when slowly progressing through mined waters. Both these Deltic types were now needed with low magnetic signature plant within the vessel's engine room, for which requirement all newly specified low-magnetic signature steels were selected for most of the working components as was operationally safe. Even crankshafts, cylinder liners and conrods were re-designed in austenitic steels to suit.

A Paxman Diesels–built, mechanically blown 'Deltic 9-59K' propulsion engine of 1980, showing a big ahead and astern gearbox, plus (left) hydraulic creep-speed motor.

Siemens Industrial Turbomachinery-built, modern Series 8 Napier 'NA298' turbocharger unit, showing its 'blisk' turbine and fine-bladed centrifugal compressor.

Following the same glass-reinforced plastic hull construction of HMS *Wilton*, the MCMVs of the 'Hunt' Class have 197ft GRP hulls, with three nine-cylinder Deltic engines below decks in the engine room at the stern, and are fitted with Plessey Type 193M Sonar and bow thrusters to ease docking. The first entered service in 1979 as HMS *Brecon*, coded 'M29' for trials, whereas the last of the thirteen Hunts built appeared ten years later in 1989, the Deltic-powered M41 HMS *Quorn*. Probably the very last new RN boat to have Napier engines, this 650-ton vessel with 1,900bhp of propulsive power on board can reach a speed of 17 knots. These highly versatile vessels saw much service during the Gulf War, and elsewhere on the troubled high seas. In their fishery protection and coastal patrol roles, their service life is now planned to extend to at least 2010.

By 1997 the ownership of the Colchester plant was titled GEC Alsthom Paxman Diesels Ltd, which then changed after a sale of the plant to MAN of Germany 2003. The provision of Deltic spares and rebuilds for all types of the engine will probably rest with Rolls-Royce.

English Electric Aviation Products had taken over the former Napier factory at Luton Airport when the Napier name was taken down in 1964. This business was then to pass to Rotax, who continued to produce the Napier Spraymat type of cyclic thermal ice protection system and their Sierracote aircraft transparencies for the home and USA aircraft markets during the 1970s. At this time, under the direction of E.E. Co. appointed Mr John Rivett, many of the former Napier staff continued at Luton in their former roles, until GEC then took managerial control, before handing the plant over to Lucas Aerospace in 1990. From then on, now under Mr Philip Barrington's management, the new company, Aerospace Composite Technologies Ltd, grew to be the leading UK producer of aircraft transparencies, including one-piece cockpit canopies for some of the world's fastest jet fighters. Finally, after a period as part of the Westland Aerospace organisation in the mid-1990s, this former Napier plant was managed by Mr Philip Harris, with the name of GKN Aerospace Transparency Systems, who produce not only thermal de-icing systems, but now the optically precise cockpit canopy for the present-day Eurofighter 'Typhoon'.

But it is with the Lincoln plant that this popular 'new names game' must finish, for here in the former Ruston works of 1854, in that great cathedral city, the Napier brand of medium-to-large turbochargers are today still produced. As a result of years of computer based design, research and rig testing, plus customer-run diesel engine trials, the internal aerodynamic design of the present-day 'blower' has been developed to give much higher pressure ratios up to 5.2:1 and overall efficiencies exceeding 70%, with extended service lives from this modernised Napier Turbocharger range.

In 1990 Napier Turbochargers Ltd had played a key role in regaining the 'Blue Riband' of the Atlantic Ocean for Great Britain from the USA; the new speed record for the Atlantic crossing was just three days, seven hours and fifty-four minutes. Richard Branson's 74ft *Seacat* wave-piercing catamaran was the craft, powered by four Napier-turbocharged Ruston 16RK270 diesels, developing a total peak output of 19,500bhp continuously, to beat the time set in 1952 by the 52,000-ton liner *United States* by almost three hours. Napier turbo-power had reliably completed its task!

In October 1991, GEC-Alsthom formed European Gas Turbines (EGT) at Lincoln, at which point the Napier brand name was temporarily dropped, until it was realised that customers wanted 'Napier turbochargers' by name to continue as the product brand they purchased and trusted. By 1994 the Managing Director of the plant, Mr Neil White, had persuaded their French European owners to allow Lincoln to continue the Napier brand name on all unit build plates. In the event, EGT was to be replaced in 1998 by Alstom Power-Napier Turbochargers, who then continued under Alstom Power UK Ltd in Lincoln until 2002, while the Napier turbocharger plant had been managed in turn by Messrs Andy Bellamy and Ken Winn. But then in 2002, the whole Lincoln industrial gas turbine plant was purchased by Siemens, while all Napier-brand turbocharger units continued to advance in design and efficiency. Their new German owner initially traded under the title of Demag Deleval Industrial Turbomachinery Ltd. Once again the Napier turbocharger plant was to be rejuvenated by another new General Manager, Mr Andy Thacker, at which time the name of the entire Lincoln plant was again changed to Siemens Industrial Turbomachinery Ltd during the year 2005. The modernised, and now highly mechanised, Napier Turbocharger group within that company then employed 130 personnel, and by now produces upward of 500 new turbocharger units per annum.

10

SAVING NAPIER'S HERITAGE JUST IN TIME 1993–2008

For some inexplicable reason, the fame of the Napier Company had faded to such an extent by 1990 that it was often difficult to trace definite information or data relating to its foundation or technological achievements outside of the annual Napier staff reunions, that had continued to meet since the final closure of the Acton plant in 1968. Only ten years before that, the company's 150th Anniversary book *Men and Machines* heralded a new and prosperous Napierian era for its London, Luton and Liverpool works. That book, which had never been written for the 'man in the street', had at the time been somewhat criticised by Acton's Technical Publications Department, who themselves had the responsibility of carrying out the research required for those 1958 exhibitions staged in all three towns. Certainly the aircraft press at the time had done a magnificent job of collating all Napier designed and built aero engines; the supplement in June 1958 by *Aeroplane* entitled 'A Century and a Half of Power', and that in *Flight* listing 'Napier Aero-Engines', both made fine references then and since that peak time in DNS aero engine activity.

But ten years later, in 1968, the puppet company Napier Aero Engines silently slipped away from the aircraft industry for good, leaving the marine engine, airborne thermal de-icing and turbo-blower businesses of D. Napier & Son all firmly gripped within the still fast-expanding E.E. Co. The last chapter has already referred to the constantly changing ownerships of these still viable products, as well as that merger with GEC, who had no traditional regard for DNS's work, least of all for its one and a half centuries of steady development in mechanical engineering precision, most of this not associated with any electrical projects, apart from ignition and, of late, control servo-systems. Perhaps the very diversity of output and innovation from DNS through their long history had blurred its importance within any one consistent field, the longest unbroken run to date being for its marine engine output spread over a whole century, albeit under more than one name and overall ownership. The frequent export of DNS major products had given the company a wide range of markets across the globe, but their usage was often by official establishments and the military services, while at home Napier car customers had often been the wealthy rather than the general public. Had these factors somehow contrived to leave the British man-in-the-street unaware of this manufacturer's extraordinary engineering achievements and the great reliability of DNS products when in regular use 'behind the scenes'?

Even more surprising in researching this book was the apparent lack of awareness and regard for the achievements of David Napier in the spheres of technical literature and the engineering institutions. Could the effects of the 'shipbuilding David Napier' (famous cousin of David Napier of DNS Lambeth, also in London at Millwall during roughly the same period) have confused the historians regarding their dual Victorian engineering progress? Had the 'David of DNS' ultimately failed to succeed in establishing his own identity in the general precision engineering field? Perhaps, but was this then the reason, back in 1990, why the name of Lambeth's David Napier had been omitted from the book index of the great Cambridge University Library, and that of the Institution of Mechanical Engineers? The marine work of David Napier of Millwall, whose time was comparatively short-lived in the English capital after Glasgow, was far better recorded. Apart from one well-thumbed copy of *Men and Machines*, listed under Napier D., there existed then no other significant reference. But, of course, the 'David of DNS' had, regrettably, chosen not to associate himself later with the 'young' I.Mech. E, that had itself been founded in 1847, the very same year the D. Napier & Son partnership had been formed. With his productive time fully taken up establishing this DNS Lambeth Company with his son James, and carrying out his later patented engineering designs, David Napier had by necessity then left institution membership for his son and partner. Much the same reason could be advanced for Montague Napier during the early 1900s, who, before his health failed, had been kept fully occupied with his rapidly expanding company now at Acton, while under constant pressure from S.F. Edge to develop yet higher powers.

In more recent times, many former Napierians have noticed the lack of appreciation of DNS's achievements during much of the twentieth century, both before and after integration within the E.E. Co. (Christmas 1942). The very existence of D. Napier & Son Ltd after 1961 was seriously questioned by many, while Rolls-Royce had erroneously shown on its published family tree, the amalgamation of DNS with its own company that very year! That had been spotted during a design course at the Cranfield Institute in 1983, at a time when the author was powerless to take any action, until the true facts of the matter were investigated after the foundation of the Napier Power Heritage Trust (NPHT) in 1993. Mr Mike Evans, Chairman of the Rolls-Royce Heritage Trust (RRHT), on realising the error, saw to it that all Rolls-Royce publicity was amended to indicate that Napier Aero Engines Ltd had been formed jointly with Rolls-Royce in 1961, while the original DNS Company continued its separate business existence as a subsidiary member of the E.E. Co. group. Also in connection with the Rolls-Royce Company, it had been noted that an RAF Bristol 192 'Belvedere' tandem rotor helicopter of 1960 was illustrated in their *Leader of the Skies* publication of 1981, this inferring that it had Rolls-Royce engines, instead of its two Napier-Gazelle engines. This mystery was to be later unravelled as a result of some very helpful co-operation that has taken place between the two heritage trusts. This has been a real highlight for NPHT during the last fifteen years, and continues untarnished today.

Words can frequently be more devastating than cutting tools, as many omissions and errors in expert books have proved, some 'writing out' Napier engine achievements on land, sea and in the air over the years. All writers will have their favourite subjects and themes they wish to emphasize, but any popular author who eliminates historical facts by simply not referring to them, alongside others of equal merit, shows bias and does harm. Errors can be made, as in a particular 1938 volume published for the RAF, in which the winning Supermarine 'S5' aircraft of the 1927 Schneider Trophy contest was stated, in error, as having a Roll-Royce engine. As no mention of the winner of the 1922 race was made (another Napier engine success), this left the RAF and readers to conclude that only Rolls-Royce had achieved Schneider Trophy successes up until their 'outright' 1931 win. Such a distortion of the true facts in this case stripped D. Napier & Son of its hard-won victories, outlined in Chapter 5, all in conjunction with R.G. Mitchell of Supermarine or H. Folland of Gloster Aircraft, who had both selected purely Napier power until 1929.

Another spur that convinced us Napierians of the need to form our own dedicated Napier heritage group occurred in 1990, when the Chairman of the Leavesden RRHT branch, the late Douglas Valentine, a former Bristol Engines Co. man, questioned the author as to 'why it was that you Napierians had left it to our RRHT branch to procure former Napier aero engines for display at Leavesden?' His enthusiasm for all engines was soon apparent, and one was challenged to assist by joining up and advising their group of volunteer restorers. In the event, the Rolls-Royce Leavesden Small Engine Division soon closed and their collection was moved to the Bristol works at Patchway, where five Napier engines were on display from 1994 alongside many Blackburn and de Havilland examples. Their enthusiasm was contagious and persuaded several Napier men to take up the challenge within a few years at Brooklands, in the museum and technical college.

Napier motor carriages have been preserved meticulously down the years at home and abroad by many discerning owners of distinction, but as far as one could tell in 1990, there was no Napier Owners Association. Naturally, the Veteran Car Club of Great Britain (VCC) acted as the chief body to which Napier car owners belonged. But some members lacked information regarding the company who had built their car chassis in the early 1900s, this despite the loyal and dedicated research work carried out by Mr Derek Grossmark, a former President of the VCC, who had owned six Napiers himself. Could any newly formed Napier Trust be effective in rallying together all the Napier owners worldwide for the approaching Car Centenary in the year 2000?

Each of the aforementioned challenges begged for accurate Napier based information to address it as, since around 1968, this information had become dispersed 'to the four winds'! This was the challenging 'Heritage gathering task' that members of any future NPHT would have to face, and the one for which they prepared themselves in 1993 at the inaugural meeting. All ten present were former or active Napier staff members, but even when combining their knowledge of the company and its products, they very soon had to conclude that after thirty years of silence, a huge DNS information gap had opened up.

That meeting had followed an informal tea in Hanwell, near Acton, in the home of Miss Joyce Finch, a former Acton works secretary, who had organised DNS reunions on the first Friday of December each year, since Acton's green door had been finally shut in 1968. This small gathering in October 1991 was between just three of Acton Reunion's friends: Joyce, Geoff McGarry and the author. Here, the name 'Napier Power Heritage' was chosen and an oval lapel badge showing the old *Napier* logo in green, on a cream background, was designed. This was then manufactured in enamel and made available to 1991 s reunion visitors, and later to all Heritage Trust members.

It will be of note that the Trust's use of this old *'Napier'* logo was later to be challenged by a car designer, who was in the process of buying the copyright for the logo from the Patents Office at that time. Napier Turbochargers' legal department then investigated the matter, but found that this old logo was not needed by them any further, and so could well be up for sale. Exclusive registration of the logo had not been maintained by either the DNS Company or E.E. Co. Sadly, that new car has never appeared, to date, but the logo is used solely on our badge.

Quite unknown at this time to former Acton staff, a large reunion lunch for the Napier Luton FDE former staff had taken place during May 1991 in Luton, as the result of an initiative by Mike Cowdrey (son of Luton DNS Manager Cecil Cowdrey) and their very supportive reunion secretary John Rickard. When this was realised, one of their number, Mr Oscar Ballard, was then able to represent Luton FDE at the first formal meeting held to look at the priorities and objectives of a Napier heritage group, then aiming to be formed from DNS staff and enthusiasts. This would exist quite independently from the large company backed RRHT that had already been in existence for ten years; they recorded just ninety years of Derby-based engineering since that company started in 1904. This exploratory inaugural meeting was called from amongst Napierian friends who had already shown a strong interest in reviving the long, 185-year history of DNS as a most urgently needed action. It took place informally in Aston Clinton on 13 Februrary 1993 when Mr John Crow, a then current employee of Napier turbochargers at Lincoln also attended, and the meeting made a firm decision to found a Napier Power Heritage group with constitutional aims to: 'Stimulate a wider awareness of the merits and applications of the many types of engine designed, developed and built this century by D. Napier & Son Ltd'. That day Geoff McGarry accepted the post of NPH Chairman, with Alan Vessey as the Secretary.

Within the reunions, several thought that this NPH idea would be 'too little: too late' to redeem the situation, as most DNS company records, drawings and data had been either destroyed or lost in those moves from Acton, Liverpool and Luton fully twenty-five years earlier. But others responded by offering a wide selection of DNS ephemera that they had wisely kept safe from out of their own offices and workshops, when these had to be shut down. So the DNS records and technical data began to appear once more. One NPH Vice President, the former Service Manager Bill Cottee, passed to the archives information on his work as a Napier rep. at Langley, RAF Odiham in England and R.U. Wevelghem in Belgium, while servicing the Sabre engine for our Hawker 'Typhoon and Tempest' fighter bombers during the Second World War. Another VP, Mr Pip Plant, the former Chief Installation and Applications Engineer at Acton and Colchester for all the types of Deltic engine, provided his large collection of photographs, reports and manuals for those engines. But the key document with which he was then able to endow the Trust was a copy of Acton's '1903 to 1968 Napier Engine Type Register'. This had stood as a backbone for all Acton works engine design and development over its sixty-five years of intensive piston engine and gas turbine design. From Acton's Technical Publications Department, former personnel such as Harry Heritage and Ken and Vi Steele contributed much pictorial information with which they had been personally involved for thirty years, plus photos of historic Lion engines of the 1920s.

NPHT was most fortunate to also have Acton TPD's Frank Regamey from the 1940s, a founder member who not only designed all the Trust's artwork but then, as an accomplished aircraft artist, painted over a dozen fine Napier-engined aircraft and launch pictures, which have been passed to the Trust's exhibition collection.

Another key element in the retrieval of Napier history came after an urgent telephone call in 1996 from a DNS Luton colleague, then with Aerospace Composite Technologies centred within the former Napier factory at Luton Airport. He informed NPHT that a JCB digger had broken into a long-closed storage area the previous day, revealing most of the photographic records of DNS made there since 1940, by Wallace Harvey's cine film and photographic department. If we removed them that very day, the building work could be delayed while this was done. Some two-tons of material were shifted out that day, comprising cans of Luton FDE cine film, and nearly 40,000 glass plate negatives covering engine flight testing, thermal de-icing research, plus all Napier rocket engine development there. The sight of Typhoons with early Napier Sabre engines in the Luton Squadron was good to see once again. After sorting through this discovery, NPHT was initially fortunate to find limited storage for these within the archive store at Brooklands Museum up to 2000. That autumn the river Wey flooded that store, unfortunately destroying some of these films and negatives, after which they were once again moved, into the private store of NPHT and former Luton FDE member Trevor Brockington. He, by image reversal and scanning of negatives on to a DVD, has produced some good prints and slides from this vast collection, for which the negative registers were also retrieved in 1996. This all took place with the kind permission of ACT's Mr Phil Harris, who has twice hosted the NPHT Luton Reunion within the old Napier plant canteen, followed by a nostalgic works tour.

Whereas Acton works staff and design teams had mainly dispersed out of West London after 1963, many staff of the Luton plant stayed on during the transition period to E.E. Co. and several changes of ownership and name followed that event, as outlined in the last chapter. Today therefore, a coherent group of enthusiastic former Napier Luton staff have remained in touch within the Bedfordshire area. So much so, that under the leadership of Basil Cheverton, former Napier Chief Flight Development Engineer, a fascinating and accurate record of the life and times of DNS and their staff at the FDE was compiled in 1998, having the quite emotive title 'Portrait of a Unique Aviation Establishment'.

While having any conversation with a former Napier designer or R&D staff member, there always comes to light new facets of DNS practice and products, their colleagues with whom they worked then later often provide additional information as further enquiries are made. 'Too little: too late' sometimes proves to be right, as one by one former Napier staff fall by the wayside, victims of old age or infirmity, usually present at a reunion, but sadly absent the following year. Two former senior managers were approached in the early years of the Trust, one being Sir John Paget, formerly manager of DNS London Group factories, who expressed his delight and interest in the idea of NPHT, only to die from a fall one week before our meeting to recall and discuss his twenty years at Acton. The other was the Lord Nelson of Stafford, otherwise the Hon. Henry George Nelson MA, F. Eng. FICE, Hon.FIMechE, HonFIEE, FRAeS, formerly DNS Managing Director from 1943, then Deputy Chairman and finally Chairman, during those trying DNS years in the 1960s.

Lord Nelson had also been Chairman of the E.E. Co. from his father's death in 1962, and then forged the merger with GEC in 1968, after which the old DNS Company was divided up between other parts of his joint E.E. Co. – GEC empire. The author still holds the very early reply he received from Lord Nelson dated 3 February 1992, regarding his support for the formation of a Napier Power Heritage group. His response turned out to be non-committal, yet showed his general approval, stating that he wished us every success. An extract from it reads:

> May I say that it is very heartening to learn that there are still, after so many years, those who not only remember the great achievements of Napier's and its wonderful team but are also sufficiently interested to wish to ensure that its many contributions to outstanding engineering successes are not forgotten.

He continued:

> What I believe must be done is to ensure that our museums retain a proper presentation of what has been achieved in the past and how such achievements have contributed to today's technological successes. It is also important to ensure that libraries of reference in the Professional Institutions, the Universities and Technical Colleges have on record documentation for reference when required. In this way future generations can be properly informed and our technical heritage is not lost or forgotten. It is encouraging that organisations, like Napier Power Heritage, are doing this before those who know the background are no longer available.

It was then signed by Nelson of Stafford, who died early in 1995. A Service of Thanksgiving was held in St James' Piccadilly on 21 March 1995, at which NPHT officers represented all Napierians. Those points that Lord Nelson raised within his letter have influenced the approach to education that the Trust has then adopted since 1996, when it became registered as an educational charity.

In particular, the management of EGT – Napier Turbochargers in Lincoln has strongly influenced NPHT, right from the time in 1993 when their MD, Mr Neil White, suggested that the NPH group should become a charitable organisation, in order to enable them to support its aims and its work. NPHT's charitable status was achieved on 20 April 1996, when its title became 'The Napier Power Heritage Trust', registered as No. 1053078. This status has had some advantages for its membership and for its administration, but has also ensured that the many valuable artefacts held within the Trust are secure by law from a 'takeover' by any similarly interested group that is not also a registered charity.

True to their word, the illustrated quarterly newsletter, *Napier Heritage News*, has been printed by, and circulated from, the offices of Napier Turbochargers to all the Trust members, institution libraries and museums since the winter issue of 1992. This slender NPH publication has been the means of keeping members and the world informed of new Napier heritage discoveries, lectures & events arranged by the Trust, latest developments in Napier engine restoration, plus the sharing of many staffs' recollections of their years as DNS employees, at Napier plant locations in the UK as well as overseas.

As more engineering institutions and groups have heard of NPHT with its information, a stream of invitations to attend their sessions with personal slide or video presentations and lectures covering some aspect from those two centuries of Napier creativity, have been extended to and accepted by NPHT officers. Over a hundred talks have now been delivered to transport enthusiast clubs and at exhibitions, or more seriously as lectures for the learned societies, such as the Royal Aeronautical Society and the Institution of Mechanical Engineers at branch meetings. On three occasions it has been a pleasure to address groups within the Rolls-Royce Heritage Trust on the products of their oldest rival D. Napier & Son Ltd.

A major aid to building up the membership of the Trust, to in excess of 300 persons, was the early participation of its members in the Model Engineer Exhibition in London that follows Christmas up to the New Year. When visitors to Olympia, Alexandra Palace or Sandown Park, many of whom are formerly engineers or even pilots, catch sight again of the Napier name, they invariably press for more information on the D. Napier & Son Company or their highly varied and unusual piston and gas turbine engines. One special visitor to the Trust stand in January 1999 at Olympia was Mr David Napier, a direct descendent of the Scot of that name in 1808, and the grandson of Montague Napier, of Lambeth and Acton motor carriage fame who was the originator of the 'Lion' engine.

Quite similar interest has usually been apparent from visitors to Brooklands Museum, Air Shows at Shoreham, Duxford Imperial War Museum and at the Shuttleworth Collection at Old Warden Airfield. At such venues, enthusiasts and model builders have wished to learn of Napier engines, acquiring their drawings and diagrams which have been made available by the Trust on its stands. The Trust's book *Napier Powered* from this publisher, compiled in 1996 by this author, contains over 200 pictures of DNS car and engine products, their applications and the records made during the twentieth century, and has proved a popular souvenir.

From amongst its Napier staff membership, NPHT has been able to form an engine restoration team which has, up to 2005, been responsible for the external restoration of no fewer than four types of 'Lion' engine. First was a Lion XIA of 1931, similar to that in the Napier Railton car at Brooklands, alongside which it is now displayed. This actual engine had been involved in the World Long Distance Flights of the Mark II Fairey Long Range Monoplane up until 1933. Then followed the final re-assembly and finishing of a Racing Lion VIIB engine, that had flown in the 1927 Schneider Trophy Gloster IVB biplane entrant, but had retired when lying second to the winning Supermarine S5, that had a similar engine. This exhibit is on loan to the Solent Sky Museum in Southampton.

For the National Maritime Museum, the supercharged Racing Lion VIID from the fast hydroplane *Miss Britain III* was renovated in 2000, the two now stand side-by-side at Greenwich. Lastly, in 2001 the Imperial War Museum found an early Lion IB of 1919 that badly needed a full strip, missing units supplied and paint restoration, for exhibition at Duxford. This extensive job was completed by Bill Mongar's team at Brooklands College in 2005 to a high standard of finish.

Future restorations may well include a Gazelle free-turbine engine, the last aero Napier to be flown in service.

Notable meeting at Olympia in 1999, between a tall Mr David Napier, grandson of Montague S. Napier seen in the centre photo, and NPHT's President Geoff McGarry.

The NPHT in 2005 owns, and displays five former Napier engines at prominent museum sites. Three are HTP/Kerosene liquid propellant rocket engines, developed at Napier Luton FDE in the 1950s, two are Double Scorpion units, of which one is sectioned (that is on display at Hendon RAF Museum). The other rocket was coded 'Red Shoes', later E.E. Co. Thunderbird, ground-to-air missile-sustainer motor, developed by DNS for the E.E. Co.'s Guide Weapons Division, also then at Luton Airport. The Schneider Lion VIID, unfortunately partly sectioned by Manchester University before the Second World War, is displayed at Solent Sky after NPHT's restoration at Brooklands. By far the largest engine is a charge-cooled 'Deltic CT18-42K' marine engine unit of 3,700bhp output. This monster exhibit was accepted in 1995 from the National Maritime Museum into the NPHT's charge, after which it has been on show with the Military Power Boat Trust at Marchwood on Solent. It has now joined several other historic eighteen- and nine-cylinder Deltic engines at the Barrow Hill rail traction depot of the Deltic Preservation Society Ltd, near Chesterfield.

Despite the ongoing public appeal of several veteran Napier motor carriages in the UK ,and Deltic engines in service with the Royal Navy and in Heritage Locomotives on the mainline, the aero engine range from Acton remains the firm favourite of most twenty-first-century engineers. In conjunction with the British Aviation Preservation Council (BAPC) of which NPHT is a member group, an aero engine list has been prepared and published by them, recently revised again for 2005. In this document the aero engines of DNS in preservation in the UK and Ireland are stated, plus the locations where they are stored or on public view. This listing contains the details of thirty-four Napier aero piston engines and twenty-three Napier gas turbine and rocket engines, which includes all those referred to above. Such popular Napier engines as the Sabre, are most likely to be found in the London Science Museum, the Hendon RAF Museum or at the Solent Sky Museum in Southampton.

The NPHT has been fortunate to inherit a fine selection of highest quality, large-scale model engines that were built at Napier Luton FDE under the direction of George Dicker. These include ¼ scale models of the Eland and Gazelle aero-gas turbines, and a fine Deltic T18-37K turbo-blown marine engine. This latter, along with an original large model of the Irving-Napier Special *Golden Arrow* car of Sir Henry Segrave in 1929, was donated to the Trust by the Managing Director of GEC-Alstom Diesels, Colchester, after a party of Trust members had enjoyed an interesting visit to his works there in 1999.

A further memorable visit, also arranged by Mike Baker of Colchester works, was to the RN Portsmouth Dockyard to make a tour of inspection of a 1979 Hunt Class MCMV, M30 HMS *Ledbury*, when her engine room revealed those three nine-cylinder Deltic power units installed.

The dawn of the twenty-first century in the year 2000 coincided with two centenaries relevant to the motor car industry within the UK. The first Napier motor-carriage had been built in 1900 at Lambeth, while its participation in the UK 1,000-mile trial of that year had also provided a landmark for D. Napier & Son, when it had finished second overall in the trial, driven by S.F. Edge. Thus in the year 2000, a re-enactment of the 1,000-mile trial was made by three Napier veterans in April. The two-cylinder 'G20'

Four assorted Napiers on Brooklands banking at the Car Centenary in 2000.

model of 1900, driven by its owner Christopher Thomas, not only cruised the course, but received the mechanical reliability award. Both the very contrasting four-cylinder 1902 Napiers of Clive Boothman and Johnny Thomas also did well in the trial which, as in 1900, had over sixty entrants from both home and overseas. June that year saw in the paddock at Brooklands the largest group of Napiers ever mustered, twenty-eight in all, assembled to celebrate the full Centenary of the Napier Marque, this convened under the NPHT banner. Clive Boothman chaired the event for the Trust, while John Pulford of Brooklands Museum hosted the rally, which included great racing Napiers from Beaulieu and Holland, as well as the famous four-cylinder 50hp 1902 Gordon Bennett Cup-winning Napier, rebuilt and entered by former member Johnny Thomas of Carmarthen. The Napier Railton was disappointingly not mobile that day, but the red Napier Bentley with a similar 24-litre Sea Lion engine, by that time owned and driven by member Chris Williams, raised the echoes as he drove around the banking and shot up the test hill, much to everyone's delight. Chris was able to demonstrate that the slogan 'The Ultimate Laxative', printed in white along her bonnet sides, was for real!

The solid brass radiator-style plaques presented to attending drivers read: 'June 2000 – Napier Motor Carriage Centenary, BROOKLANDS – Lambeth and Acton works.'

A great assortment of Napier-based historical material was eventually to be sourced from the vaults of Napier Turbochargers in Lincoln, after Mr Neil White had suggested that NPHT officers take charge of the DNS records and archives they held, since these had been transferred there from DNS at Liverpool in 1970. A priceless collection of early documents and fine, Napier-won, silver trophies had come from the Acton site before its closure three years earlier and now, thirty years later, the NPHT charity had been given responsibility for their safe custody for the future. Earliest was the 1832 Sales Ledger of David Napier when he first opened the new Lambeth factory. DNS Company minute books right down to the 1960s were also included, plus records of most twentieth-century DNS Company patents. Three great motoring trophies, including the magnificent 'Thomas Trophy' won at the Daytona Speed Week in 1905, have already been placed on loan to Brooklands Museum, while the remaining eleven car and marine trophies were cleaned and kept under secure storage conditions ready for when they again would be displayed.

A particularly regular visitor on the NPHT stand at the annual Brooklands Society Reunion meeting has been the most senior Napierian (so far), member Gilbert Smith who started at Acton works as a fitter way back in 1920. As this final chapter is being completed in 2005, his one-hundredth birthday has just been celebrated on 5 October. His knowledge of the conditions existing within the works of DNS in the 1920s is now unique, and his clear recollections of his days on gearbox assembly and 'Lion' work have been of great value to all his NPHT friends, who extend to Gilbert their most hearty Acton congratulations!

The concluding reference to be made in this book is one relating to the management, staff and works engineers at Siemens Industrial Turbomachinery Ltd at Lincoln, who now design, build and market worldwide the present-day range of their Napier-branded turbochargers. For instance, the latest Napier '7' series product spans engine outputs from 2 MW to 6.5 MW per single turbocharger and was based around the original Napier

Napier Turbocharger staff in 2001 at Lincoln works with Bill Hughes' 1911 'Colonial' tourer.

cartridge design, but now with a 5:1 pressure ratio and overall efficiency of up to 70%. Their Retrofit Turbocharger scheme has the latest products retrofitted on to engines, for example the twelve-cylinder Paxman Valenta diesel that powers the Class 43 Intercity HST Power cars now offers a 12% increase in blower efficiency and a 2.9% reduction in fuel consumption. Other types of diesel engines benefiting from this are: ALCO 251, Ruston RKC Series, Dresser Rand KVS and KVR units, Wartsila and Paxman Diesels; all these are used for marine power and power generation.

It has been NPHT's privilege to exhibit certain Napier history and former products at two public works open days in Lincoln, one in 2001 with Alstom and again in 2005 for Siemens. With the turbocharger manufacturing plant in operation on these Saturdays, it has been possible to see the latest methods of production for the rotating core assemblies of a modern design of turbocharger, all produced by large fully automated CNC machine tools. To watch the manufacture of a turbine wheel 'blisk', starting from a precision rotary investment casting in high strength non-ferrous alloy, made into a finished integral turbine bladed rotor, united with a steel shaft with great concentric precision, balance and high temperature strength, is a revelation to any methods engineer hailing from the DNS Acton era of the 1950s. The entirely suitable choice of spheroidal graphite SG Cast Iron for turbocharger casings, achieved with some weight penalty, has now moved the modern turbocharger away from the more costly aero gas turbine standards and ultra lightweight aluminium alloy design and construction techniques that had come to Lincoln from DNS Acton, via Liverpool works in the 1970s. One of the first research tasks that NPHT undertook, through its then Chairman Geoff McGarry, was to request that the late Lionel H. Elford, C.Eng. MIMechE MRAeS, write and compile *The History of Napier Turbo-Blowers*, from the first at Acton in the 1940s to the 1960s when he retired from the company. This booklet, bound by NPHT, has proved of interest to many, including the younger present-day staff at Lincoln who can see the origins of the precision product that they have refined and modified using the latest CAD techniques, to give even greater service and efficiency for their customers in the market of the twenty-first century.

The words and expectations for the future of NPHT, written by Lord Nelson in 1992, very closely describe the path that this educational trust has adopted since its foundation in 1993. The dearth of information relating to the products of the 200-year-old London DNS Company within the engineering institutions, museums and college libraries has been so far partially remedied, as outlined in the foregoing paragraphs. This educational task is as yet unfinished, but is ongoing. It is hoped that this volume will further assist in the dissemination of facts and figures relating to the DNS Company since the nineteenth century.

A prime example of how an earlier lack of information has been addressed, relates to the library and archives held by the Institution of Mechanical Engineers in Westminster. When the volume and value of Napier archive material covering two centuries became too great a burden for the NPHT officers to hold themselves, an almost perfect solution presented itself in 2002, when the archivist of that famous Institution, Mr Keith Moore, offered to accept for conservation, through transferred ownership, all of the prime-source Napier Company archives that had been recovered by that time. Following negotiations with the Institution of Mechanical Engineering (I. Mech. E.), and when full approval had been given to this offer by the NPHT Executive Committee, the transfer of the archive material was made to 1 Birdcage Walk in 2003. Their own commitment made to NPHT was that the archives should be available for examination and research within their library by NPHT members, senior engineering students, institution members and the public by appointment. Also that a representative number of documents and photographs should be entered on-line onto the Internet, for reference on the worldwide web. A special feature, coinciding with this development and taking place at 1 Birdcage Walk, was the creation there of a new Napier Room, with a display of artefacts, intended for committee work but also available for NPHT meetings.

One might now ask as a senior citizen member of NPHT, or as a twenty-first-century practising engineer, how much closer to the ideas of that Institution's former President, the 2nd Lord Nelson of Stafford, could such a late solution have come? That it was only just-in-time, there can be no doubt whatsoever. The old London firm of D. Napier & Son had finally arrived 'home' into the fine English oak-panelled I. Mech. E. headquarters in Westminster, and would remain 'in house' there, holding a welcome for all those who wish to learn of its illustrious engineering past, and the present-day performance of its successors.

NPHT has been able to witness some notable Napier power-based highlights since its inauguration, these ranging from the re-launch of Air Sea Rescue Launch '102' by the

Barrow Hill Depot opening day in 2003, with Chris Williams' 'Lion'-engined Napier-Bentley roaring at both the prototype and a production 'Deltic' locomotive.

Queen Mother in 1996, to a flight of 'Scorpion Canberra WK163' back at Luton Airport, to the eventual return to Brooklands of Cobb's Napier Railton racing car, both of these latter events occurring in 1997. Finally the inevitable resumption of mainline running by the preserved Class 55 Deltic locomotives on UK mainline railways came to pass in 1999, culminating in the opening of a new Deltic locomotive dedicated diesel depot in 2003 at Barrow Hill, Chesterfield.

The rapidly approaching year 2008 will also prove a further highlight, as well as a historical milestone reached by D. Napier & Son Ltd after 200 years. That year, both live and static displays will be organised with several national museums, some engineering institutions, present-day companies, and NPHT itself through its many supporters. These will, no doubt, be seen and appreciated worldwide, not only by those who had earlier founded their engineering careers upon the well established Napier standards of innate precision and irresistible power, but also those younger people now involved in the twenty-first-century industrial scene.

A NAPIER EPILOGUE

God of metals, God of steel
God of piston, God of wheel
God of pinion, God of steam
God of girder and of beam
God of atom, God of mine
All the world of power is Thine

Lord of runway, Lord of rail
Lord of dockyard and of sail
Lord of rocket, Lord of flight
Lord of records, Lord of might
Lord of precision driving line
All the world of speed is Thine

Hope of ages, Hope of sale
Hope of balance and of scale
Hope of furnace, Hope of bench
Hope of hammer and of wrench
Hope of draughtsman's pencil line
All the world of skill is Thine

Love of research, Love of test
Love of excellence manifest
Love of quality, Love of skill
Love of innovation's thrill
Love of performance, truly fine
All this creative world is Thine

By Alan Vessey, as inspired by two verses of the Revd R.G. Jones.

APPENDICES

APPENDIX I
EARLY NAPIER PRECISION ENGINEERING

Covering a ninety-year period in London, at Lloyds Court and Vine Street, Lambeth works until 1898 when, under M.S. Napier's new management, his early Internal Combustion Engines were tested in boats and cars.

a) Printing Presses and Machines

1815   Napier-built 'Stanhope Lever'-type printing presses – toggle-jointed, applied-pressure system.
1818   Napier-built 'Rutt' single-cylinder printing machines – later driven by Napier small steam engines.
1820   Napier-built 'Treadwell' printing presses – treadle-operated pressure.
1824   The single-cylinder 'Nay-peer' printing machine – over 100 built over a period of twenty years. These were powered either by a manually-operated, two-man 'Flywheel' or by a Napier-built steam engine gear, driven via pulleys.
1830   The 'Desideratum' single-cylinder printing machine – over 150 built – either manual or steam-driven.
1835   The 'Double Imperial' two-cylinder printing machine for 'perfecting' of sheets – over thirty built.
1837   The Napier 'Platen'-operated printing machines – single or double-ended – over sixty built up to 1890.
1853   The Napier-patented Bank Note Platen-type printing machine – two inking rolls and toggle pressure.

b) A Selection of Steam and Other Engines Supplied from Lambeth over a Forty-Five-Year Period

1840   A 2nhp (nominal horse power) high-pressure steam engine to power a Quadruple Printing Press.
1843   Small 'Vacuum Engine', using atmospheric pressure, to drive 3 Automaton machines at the Bank of England.

1845   A 2nhp steam engine with Flywheel for printing compositors, plus boiler also giving room-heating.

1845   An 8nhp non-condensing steam engine with two boilers, with shafting and hangers in working order.

1855   An Ericsson hot-air engine supplied to Spain.

1856   A 40nhp horizontal steam engine with boiler and mountings.

1857   A 15nhp horizontal non-condensing steam engine for expansive working with boiler. This engine to power a steam flour mill was supplied with four 4ft-diameter French Burr mill stones and shafting.

1862   A 4nhp non-condensing steam engine with expansive gear and shafting.

1862   A 25nhp condensing and expansive beam engine with two internal flue boilers.

1863   A 10nhp high-power, high-pressure steam engine and boiler.

1864   A 20nhp high-pressure horizontal steam engine with variable expansion gear.

1865   A 3nhp Ericsson calorific engine and shafting.

1866   A 2nhp steam engine to the 'Mercury' Office to drive a printing machine.

1867   A 10nhp high-pressure horizontal steam engine.

1874   A 12in bore x 20in stroke horizontal steam engine – variable expansion and a steam-jacketed cylinder.

1875   A 30nhp high-pressure horizontal steam engine – supplied to the Inland Revenue at Somerset House.

1885   An atmospheric steam engine to drive sixty Napier Automaton coin machines for the Mint of India.

c) Napier 'Moneyer' Machines

1840   Napier constructed Light Coin Rejecting Machine to a W. Cotton idea from within the Bank of England.

1843   Three Patent Automaton Coin Sorting Balances to the Bank of England, with vacuum drive engine.

1845   Automaton Coin Weighing Machine (Patent by Cotton) one each to Banks of England & Ireland.

1850   'Light Coin Rejector' Sorting Machines, powered 'electrically', for the Bank of England and branches.

1851   Napier Coin Defacing Machines – first order from the Royal Mint via the Master Sir John Herschell.

1851   Five Napier Coin Sorting Weighing Machines for Royal Mint – into too light, medium and too heavy.

1860   Onwards – Heavy Coining Presses and Double Strip Draw Benches supplied to various Mints.

1870   Hydraulic Bullion Balance *The Chancellor* 4ft beam to weigh 1,500 ounces for the Royal Mint.

1874   Another 'Chancellor' Type Balance for the Government of India to weigh up to 100 pounds.

1877   Balance *The Lord Chief Justice* with hydraulic motor beam lift, to the Bank of England.

1879   Bullion Balance *The Lord High Chancellor* to the Bank of England, weighing up to 1,200 ounces.

1885   A batch of sixty Napier 'Automaton' Coin Sorting Machines to the Government of India.

1888   Bullion Balance *The Chief Clerk* to the Bank of England, to weigh 2,000 ounces within one grain.

d) Napier-Designed Special Machinery

1835   Compressed bullet-making Machines. Apr-May 1839 Board of Ordnance received 300,000 rifle balls.

1843   Napier Gun-Barrel Boring Machines as supplied to the Board of Ordnance – Woolwich Arsenal.

1844   Hydraulic Overhead Travelling Crane for Great Western Railway – Swindon Locomotive works.

1845 Hydraulic Axle Presses and 10-ton hoists for GWR – Swindon works. Also for Great Northern Railway.

1846 Hydraulic Coach/Wagon Traversers for GWR, used at Bristol, Cheltenham and Paddington Stations.

1847 'Captains Registering Compass' Instruments. One was given to Steamship *Great Western* in 1848.

1853 Prototype of Napier Stamp Perforating Machine. Two supplied to Hon. Commissioner for Stamps.

1866 Several Stamp Perforating Machines exported to France (2), Germany (4), Italy and India.

1884 Napier 'Showspeed' instruments, acting as tachometers or speedometers through a mercury column.

e) Examples of new General Engineering Work undertaken

1833 Supply of a machined large flywheel, complete with a driver, weight 6cwt, 1qtr, 21lb.

1840 Gearcutting – Spur wheels 18in diameter with 52 teeth, 3¾in diameter with 32 teeth and a 3½ in Bevel gear.

1841 Ratchet Wheel – 32in diameter x2½in width, with 250 teeth of ¼in pitch (charge £1-18-0).

1842 Holtzapffel & Co. – Work done on four cast-iron cross frames for an Engraving Machine.

1840 Cutting Cast Iron Wheel 18¾in diameter 56 teeth & Pinion 5¼in diameter 14 teeth, 2¹/₈ in wide, 1in pitch.

1844 Chucking and planing two cast-iron side frames for a lithographic press (charge £1-7-6).

1845 Two specially-built vertical drilling machines for the Small Arms Factory, Enfield.

1846 Planing and slotting a frame and slide for Maudslay, Son & Field (charge £34-19-0).

1854 Lathes for Spain – Woodturning 13ft centres x 2ft diameter. Specials for drilling and screwcutting.

1857 Three spur wheels for the London South Western Railway. Turntable at Nine Elms locomotive depot.

1862 Six various turret clocks – one the timepiece for the 1862 International Exhibition in London.

1879 Dynamometer with driving and guide pulleys, built to the contract of Mr Schwendler.

1879 Standard Metre for Paris – the planing of three platinum iridium 'H' section rules for Johnson Matthey & Co. done in Lambeth works, to the order of La Commission Internationale du Metre, Paris.

APPENDIX II
NAPIER MOTOR CARRIAGES, BUSINESS VEHICLES AND COMPETITION CARS

D. Napier & Son designed, developed and manufactured engines and chassis for 'Pleasure Cars' and 'Business Vehicles' for just twenty-five years. This appendix divides itself between motor carriages, racing cars, general business vehicles and World Land Speed Record setting 'specials', powered by adapted Napier engines.

Before 1904 at Lambeth works, vehicle and engine reference numbers were seldom 'sequential', but then in 1903 at the new Acton works a fresh orderly system for both was begun. Now, motor carriage chassis types were given 'T' code numbers (between T20 and T80) while business vehicle chassis types had 'B' prefix numbers. All vehicle engine designs of various sizes were registered by 'E' prefix numbers, from E1 to E57. This 'E' No. sequence was then continued for ALL Napier engines to 1970 (Appendix III).

Selected vehicle chassis numbers are here listed in date order, with cubic capacity in litres, engine 'E' No., No. of cylinders, bore and stroke, valve gear, details of vehicle type and performance, & approximate No. built.

Date	Type No.	C. Capacity.	'E' No.	No. cylinders / Bore & stroke	Valve type	Detail of vehicle in use	No. built

a) Napier Motor Carriages

Date	Type No.	C. Capacity.	'E' No.	No. cylinders / Bore & stroke	Valve type	Detail of vehicle in use	No. built
1900	G20 8hp	2.47 litre	–	2 cylinder / 4in x 6in	Oat.I/SE	Awarded second in 1,000 Mile Trial	5
1900	H70 16hp	4.94 litre	–	4 cylinder / 4in x 6in	Oat.I/SE	One raced in 1900 all Phaetons	5
1902	D45 12hp	2.52 litre	–	4 cylinder / 3½in x 4in	Oat.I/SE	Various coachbuilt Tonneaus	180
1902	H8 12hp	2.52 litre	–	4 cylinder / 3½in x 4in	Oat.I/SE	Centre-engined 'Brougham'	5
1903	L49 30hp	4.95 litre	E1	6 cylinder / 4in x 4in	O.I./SE	First production six cylinder Car	65
1904	T20/A 40hp	4.95 litre	E1	6 cylinder / 4in x 4in	O.I./SE	Acton developed until 1908	270
1907	T21 60hp	7.72 litre	E2	6 cylinder / 5in x 4in	O.I./SE	Set the 24hr record in 1907	105
1912	T23 40hp	6.10 litre	E4	6 cylinder / 4in x 5in	O.I./SE	Landaulettes & Tourers	200
1908	T24 65hp	9.65 litre	E5	6 cylinder / 5in x 5in	O.I./SE	Sporting 'Grand Tourers'	80
1908	T26 30hp	4.10 litre	E6	6 cylinder / 3¼in x 5in	Side V.	Limousines & Light Tourers	200
1911	T28 15hp	2.75 litre	E8	4 cylinder / 3¼in x 5in	Side V.	Power unit for 'Colonials'	765
1908	T29 10hp	1.38 litre	E9	2 cylinder / 3¼in x 5in	Side V.	Power unit for light Taxicabs	100
1910	T31/A/B 15hp	2.75 litre	E14	4 cylinder / 3¼in x 5in	Side V.	Most numerous, often used as Taxicabs	890
1911	T36 30hp	4.10 litre	E23	6 cylinder / 3¼in x 5in	Side V.	Tourers & Limousines	50
1911	T38 15hp	2.75 litre	E25	4 cylinder / 3¼in x 5in	Side V.	Tourers & Light Saloons	200
1912	T43 30hp	4.10 litre	E29	6 cylinder / 3¼in x 5in	Side V.	Colonial Tourers, Landaulettes	100
1913	T44 30/35hp	4.10 litre	E34	3¼in x 5in	Side V	Landaulettes	150
1913	T45/6/7 15hp	2.75 litre	E30	4 cylinder / 3½in x 5in	Piston V.	An Experimental valve gear	330
1912	T51 45hp	6.10 litre	E32	6 cylinder / 4in x 5in	Side V.	Empire Export Limousines	40
1913	T54 15hp	2.75 litre	E37	4 cylinder / 3¼in x 5in	Side V.	Carriages with three or four speeds	305

1913	T55/A 15hp	2.75 litre	E37	4 cylinder / 3¼in x 5in	Side V.	Also ideal 'Doctors' Coupes'	230
1915	T64 16/22hp	3.2 litre	E44	4 cylinder / 3½in x 5in	Sloping Side V.	Light Touring cars	205
1914	T67 30/35hp	4.7 litre	E46	6 cylinder / 3½in x 5in	Sloping Side V.	Torpedo & Ambulance	50
1914	T68 20hp	3.2 litre	E44	4 cylinder / 3½in x 5in	Sloping OHV.	Staff cars & Ambulances	100
1915	T69/70/16/22hp	3.2 litre	E50	4 cylinder / 3½in x 5in	Side V.	As Ambulances & 15cwt trucks	550

1920	T75 40/50hp	6.18 litre	E52	6 cylinder / 4in x 5in	SOHC	Final production motor chassis	120
1921	T79/80 40/50hp	6.18 litre	E52	6 cylinder / 4in x 5in	SOHC	With longer Wheelbase of 12ft	45

b) Napier Racing Cars

1900	H70R 16hp	4.94 litre	–	4 cylinder / 4in x 6in		First British-entered racing car 25 July 1900	–
1901	Special 50hp	16.3 litre	–	4 cylinder / 6½in x 7½in		British entry for 1901 Gordon Bennett Race	–
1902	D50 40hp	6.44 litre	–	4 cylinder / 5in x 5in	4xOatIV/ SEV.	Won 1902 Gordon Bennett Race	–
1903	E61 50hp	7.78 litre	–	4 cylinder / 5½in x 5in		Three built for 1903 Gordon Bennett Race	–
1903	K5 80hp	13.1 litre	–	4 cylinder / 6½in x 6in		S.F. Edge Special for 1904 Gordon Bennett Race	–
1904	L48 90hp	15.1 litre	E10	6 cylinder / 6¼in x 5in	OH Inlet/ SEV.	First six cylinder racing car	–
1905	L48R 100hp	18.1 litre	–	6 cylinder / 6¼in x 6in		Rebuilt engine & streamlined body 'Samson'	
1907	T21R 60hp	9.62 litre	E5	6 cylinder / 5in x 5in		Short frame car set 24hr record at a speed of 65.9mph	–
1908	T24R 65hp	11.58 litre	E11	6 cylinder / 5in x 6in		Sprint & hill-climb special, capable of 90mph	–
1908	T27 26hp	5.76 litre	E7	4 cylinder / 4in x 7in		'Hutton' racer won I.O.M 'TT' at a speed of 50.5mph	–
1908	T48 70hp	12 litre	–	6 cylinder / 6¼in x 4in		Streamlined 'Meteor' sprint racer – 102mph	–
1908	G.Prix 80hp	11.5 litre	E12	6 cylinder / 4 31/32in x 6in		First British G.P. racing car to be 'disqualified'	–
1933	Napier-Railton	24 litre	E89	24 cylinder / 5½in x 5⅛in		Thomson & Taylor racing car – Lion XIA	
1950	Napier-Bentley	24 litre	E92	24cylinder / 5½in x 5⅛in		'Sealion' engine in 8-litre Bentley chassis	–

c) Napier Business Vehicles

1901	G20 9hp	2.5 litre	–	2 cylinder / 4in x 6in	–	Delivery Van – Hyam Clothing of Colchester	–
1901	– 12hp	3.8 litre	–	2 cylinder / 5in x 6in	–	Fourteen-seat char-a-banc for Scarborough Autos	–
1902	– 12hp	3.8 litre	–	2 cylinder / 5in x 6in	–	Omnibus for Scarborough Motor Vehicle Co.	–
1904	B22 –		E3	4 cylinder	–	Acton works' first built Omnibus chassis	–
1911	B34 10hp	2.88 litre	E22	2 cylinder / 4in x 7in	–	Light delivery vans carrying 6/8 cwt	–
1912	B52 16/20hp	2.72 litre	E36	4 cylinder / 3¼in x 5in	–	Vans carrying 1 ton	–

1913	B56 15hp	2.72 litre	E30	4 cylinder / 3¼in x 5in	—	Vans carrying 1 ton	—
1913	B58 40hp	6.26 litre	E39	4 cylinder / 4½in x 6in	—	Truck or Van carrying 3½ tons	—
1913	B59 30hp	4.94 litre	E40	4 cylinder / 4in x 6in	—	Van carrying 2 tons or char-a-banc body	—
1913	B62/A 20/24hp	3.2 litre	E37	4 cylinder / 3½in x 5in	—	Vans carrying 1½ tons	—
1914	B65 50hp	-	E45	4 cylinder	-	Heavy Truck or Van carrying up to 5 tons	—
1915	B72 20/24hp	3.2 litre	E51	4 cylinder / 3½in x 5in	—	Vans carrying 1½ tons	—
1920	B72A 25/30hp	3.5 litre	E55	4 cylinder / 3 11/16 in x 5in	—	Vans carrying 1½ tons or Light char-a-banc	—
1916	B74 40hp	6.26 litre	E39	4 cylinder / 4½in x 6in	—	Truck or Van carrying 3½ / 4 tons	—

d) Napier-Powered World Land Speed Record Cars

Listed in order of record attempts, with detail of builders and Napier engine types and related 'E' numbers.

Date	Name of Record Car	Engine type	'E' No.	Capacity/ Cylinders	Power output	W.L.S. Record
1905	L48 Racing car – 'Samson'	First Racing Six	E10	15 litre/ 6 cylinder	150bhp	104.65mph
1927	Napier-Campbell 'Bluebird'	Racing Lion VII	E74	24 litre/ 12 cylinder	700bhp	174.88mph
1928	Napier-Campbell 'Bluebird'	Racing Lion VIIA	E86	24 litre/ 12 cylinder	900bhp	206.96mph
1929	Irving-Napier Special G.A.	Racing Lion VIIA	E86	24 litre/ 12 cylinder	900bhp	231.44mph
1931	Napier-Campbell 'Bluebird'	Racing Lion VIID	E91	24 litre/ 12 cylinder	1,350bhp	246.09mph
1931	Harkness 'Enterprise'-Aust.	Racing Lion VIID	E91	24 litre/ 12 cylinder	1,350bhp	10 miles at a speed of 164mph
1932	Napier-Campbell 'Bluebird'	Racing Lion VIID	E91	24 litre/ 12 cylinder	1,350bhp	253.97mph
1938	'Railton-Napier Special'	2 x Racing Lion VIID	E91	48 litre/2x 12 cylinder	2,600bhp	350.20mph
1939	'Railton-Mobil Special'	2 x Racing Lion VIID	E91	48 litre/2x 12 cylinder	2,700bhp	369.70mph
1947	'Dunlop-Mobil Special'	2 x Racing Lion VIID	E91	48 litre/2x 12 cylinder	2,800bhp	394.20mph

(Note: in 1947 John Cobb drove this car in one direction over the measured mile at 403mph.)

APPENDIX III
EXTRACTS FROM THE NAPIER ENGINE DESIGN 'E' NUMBER REGISTER

Originally the 'E' Number Register was started on arrival at Acton works in 1903 by Chief Draughtsman A.J. Rowledge. The numbering sequence runs unbroken from 'E1' for a six-cylinder car engine of 1903, on to 'E296' of sixty-five years later for an 18-cylinder marine engine. Between these two dates, a fifty-year period covers the varied Napier aero-engine era, running intermittently from the 'Triple-four' twelve-cylinder 'E61' of 1916, to a free-turbine 'Gazelle' variant 'E257' of 1966. Napier Luton-developed Rocket engines have a separate NRE list.

Due to the vast array of mixed engine technologies contained in that register, this appendix is arranged with selected 'families' of similar engines, from the prototypes on test, down to often exotic developments within that family group designed many years later, but sometimes not ever constructed. As far as possible, 'E' numbers within an engine 'family' are arranged both in numerical as well as in date order.

Note: The road vehicle and power boat 'family' of 'In-line power units' from 'E1' to 'E60', will be found in Appendices 2 & 4, these relating to Motor Cars, Business Vehicles, Racing Cars and Marine Craft.

Date	'E Nos	Name & Mk	No. Cylinders-Bore & Stroke (or No. of Turbines)	Power Output (in shp/ ehp/ghp)	Special features of engine

a) The 'W' or Broad Arrow, Water Cooled – 'LION'

Date	'E Nos	Name & Mk	No. Cylinders-Bore & Stroke	Power Output	Special features of engine
1916	E 59	Triple Six	18 – 5in x 6¼in	–	Only Napier 6 x 6 x 6 single-crank
1916	E 61	Triple Four	12 – 4½in x 6½in	320	Prototype 4 x 4 x 4 cylinder aero-engine
1917	E 62	Triple Four	12 – 47/8 in x 5⅛in	400	Short stroke experimental engine
1918	E 64/ T	Lion I	12 – 5½in x 5⅛in	450	Prototype and single-test engine
1919	E 65	Lion I	12 – 5½in x 5⅛in	450	Low Red/G for 'Bodmin' wing-drive
1922	E 67	Lion II	12 – 5½in x 5⅛in	450	Low Red/G case within crankcase
1923	E 68/71	Lioness	12 – 5½in x 5⅛in	450	Inverted Lion, more forward view
1924	E 70	Lion V	12 – 5½in x 5⅛in	525	Similar to the 'II' engine in layout
1925	E 72/T	Lioness	12 – 5¾in x 5⅛in	500	Bored-out Commercial 3-cylinder test engine
1923	E 74	Racing Lion VII	12 – 5½in x 5⅛in	700	Direct-drive, 7.0:1 Comp Ratio
1924	E 75	Lion VI	12 – 5½in x 5⅛in	500	Direct drive, 5.8:1 C.R, hand start
1925	E 76	Blown Race Lion	12 – 5½in x 5⅛in	800	Direct-drive, new camshaft drive

1926	E 78	Lioness	12 – 5½in x 5⅛in	500	Inverted direct-drive test engine
1925	E 79	Lion VS	12 – 5½in x 5⅛in	500	Turbo-blown unit for high altitude
1925	E 83	Lion VIII	12 – 5½in x 5⅛in	535	Direct-drive, rear carburettor 6.25:1 C.R
1925	E 85	Lion IX	12 – 5½in x 5⅛in	550	Direct-drive, rear carburetors, front magnetos
1926	E 85B	Gear driven blower unit for E 85 Lion engine.	–	–	Mechanical Aero Supercharger
1927	E 86	Race Lion VII A	12 – 5½in x 5⅛in	900	Direct-drive, 10.0:1 comp ratio
1927	E 89	Lion XI	12 – 5½in x 5⅛in	520	Low gear, carburetor and magnetos at the rear
1927	E 90	Race Lion VIIB	12 – 5½in x 5⅛in	875	Double reduction gear, 10.0:1 C.R
1929	E 91	Race Lion VIID	12 – 5½in x 5⅛in	1,360	Prized supercharged racing engine
1929	E 92	Lion XIA	12 – 5½in x 5⅛in	560	Basis for the marinised 'Sea Lion'
1931	E 94	Race Lion VIIC	12 – 5½in x 5⅛in	975	Unsupercharged, 11:1 Comp ratio

b) The 'H' air-cooled 'Rapier'

1930	E 93	Rapier I	16 – 3½in x 3½in	300	Air-cooled, supercharged engines
1932	E 95	Rapier II	16 – 3½in x 3½in	325	Compact, 7.0:1 compression ratio
1935	E 100	Rapier V	16 – 3½in x 3½in	340	Push rod-operated overhead valves

c) The In-line engines – 'Javelin'

1931	E 97T	Test Engine	4– 4½in x 5¼in	100	Air-cooled inverted engine SOHC
1933	E 97	Javelin III	6– 4½in x 5½in	170	Valve operation giving 2,100rpm
1931	E99	Road Tractor Unit	4– 2½in x 3½in	RAC 10hp	Engine of the 'Mechanical Horse'

d) The 'H' air-cooled – 'Dagger'

1934	E 98T	Test Engine	2– 3¹³⁄₁₆in x 3¾in	–	Two cylinder air-cooled test unit
1934	E 98	Dagger I	24 – 3¹³⁄₁₆in x 3¾in	630	24-cylinder supercharged, 4 x SOHC
1934	E 104./T	Dagger	24 – 4in bore x 3¾in	–	Test of '4in cylinder spl. Parts'on E 98 T
1935	E 105	Dagger 800	24 – 3¹³⁄₁₆in x 3¾in	725	Double entry supercharger fitted

Year	Code	Name	Cylinders	Power	Notes
1937	E 108	Dagger/H10	24 – 3¹³⁄₁₆ in x 3¾in	935	Rated 935bhp at 4,100rpm at an altitude of 9,750ft
1939	E 110	Dagger VIII	24 – 3¹³⁄₁₆ in x 3¾in	1,000	2-speed supercharger & hydromatic propeller
1939	E 112	Enlarged Dagger	24 – 4¹⁄₁₆ in x 3¹⁵⁄₁₆in	–	With a 2-speed supercharger

e) The opposed piston, diesel, in-line – 'Culverin'

Year	Code	Name	Cylinders	Power	Notes
1934	E 102	Culverin	6 cylinder – 4¾in x 8¼in	720	Napier licence-built Junkers Jumo 4
1934	E 103	Cutlass	6 cylinder – 4⅛in x 6⁵⁄₁₆in	540	Napier/Junkers Jumo 5A – not flown
1955	E 164	In-line 6-19	6 cylinder – 5⅛in x 7¼in	575	2-stroke diesel (Deltic) R/T generator engine
1956	E 197	In-line T6-35	6 cylinder – 5⅛in x 7¼in	735	Turbocharged for Rail traction 1,600rpm
1956	E 207	In-line T6-38	6 cylinder – 5⅛in x 7¼in	835	Turbo/ch R/T diesel 1,600rpm output

f) The horizontal 'H' water-cooled – 'Sabre' Series

Year	Code	Name	Cylinders	Power	Notes
1931	E 101T	Two-cylinder diesel test	2 cylinder – 5in x 4¾in	–	Twin Sleeve valve bench test unit
1932	E 101	'H' diesel prototype	24 cylinder – 5in x 4¾in	–	24-cylinder Sleeve valve diesel engine
1932	E 101/6T	Six cylinder test unit.	6 cylinder – 5in x 4¾in	–	6-cylinder block mounted E101 crankcase
1935	E 107/T	Single cylinder	1 cylinder – 5in x 4¾in	–	Petrol conversion of E 101T unit
1935	E 107/2T	Two-cylinder	2 cylinder – 5in x 4¾in	–	Petrol Sleeve valve test unit
1936	E 107/6T	Six-cylinder test unit	6 cylinder – 5in x 4¾in	–	Petrol Sleeve valve test engine
1937	E 107	Sabre I engine	24 cylinder – 5in x 4¾in	2055	Prototype, twin-crankshaft engine
1939	E 109	Semi-Sabre	12 cylinder – 5in x 4¾in	–	Liquid-cooled, single crankshaft
1939	E 113T	Petrol injection unit	2 cylinder – 5in x 4¾in	–	2-stroke cycle, sleeve valve unit
1939	E 114	Air cooled H' unit	24 cylinder – 4¾in x 4¾in	–	Engine based on Sabre design
1939	E 115	Sabre Series IIA	24 cylinder – 5in x 4¾in	2235	'100 Octane' engine for Hawkers
1940	E 107A	Sabre Series IIB	24 cylinder – 5in x 4¾in	2420	New supercharger version of E107
1940	E 107B	Sabre Series IIC	24 cylinder – 5in x 4¾in	2420	Last use of 4 choke SU carburettor
1941	E 107C	Sabre Series V	24 cylinder – 5in x 4¾in	2,600	RAE-Hobson injection carburettor

1940	E 116	Contra-prop 'Sabre'	24 cylinder – 5in x 4¾in	–	Conversion of an E 107C engine
1941	E 118	Contra-prop 'Sabre'	24 cylinder – 5in x 4¾in	–	E 116 with 2 stage, 3-speed supercharger
1942	E 119	Contra-prop 'Sabre'	24 cylinder – 5in x 4¾in	–	E 118 strengthened & higher performance
1942	E 120	A stretched 'Sabre'	32 cylinder – 5in x 4¾in	–	An 'H'-type engine with 8 throw c/s
1943	E 121	'Sabre' Series VII	24 cylinder – 5in x 4¾in	3,055	With petrol & water- methanol injection
1943	E 122	'Sabre' Series VIII with Contra-props.	24 cylinder – 5in x 4¾in	3,350	25 lb/sq.in max boost, charge-cooled
1943	E 123	'H' Type 24 cylinders for 2 Stroke cycle	24 cylinder – 5in x 4¾in	4,000	Petrol-fuelled, high-speed project

g) The Compound Aero Engine – 'Nomad' Series

1944	E124	'Tilted H' 2 Stroke Diesel power unit	24 cylinder	6,000	Centrifugal & Axial Compressors and Recovery Turbine. Also 2-cylinder Test units, a) Loop Scavenge, b) Sleeve Valve, and a 6-cylinder unit for (a) or (b)
1945	E 125	Nomad I Compound.	12 cylinder – 6in x 7⅜ in	3135	Centrifugal and Axial compressor, twin turbines
1945	E 126	A Free Piston Engine	–	–	based on associated items as used on E 124/ E 125 Compound Units
1951	E 145	Nomad II Compound	12 cylinder– 6in x 7⅜ in	3580	Twelve-stage Axial compressor, 3 stage turbine
1955	E 173	Nomad III' Compound	12 cylinder– 6in x 7⅜ in	4500	Air-cooled Intercooler & Exhaust Reheat

h) Small Output Aero Gas Turbine – Turbo-props

1945	E 127	'Nymph' Turbo- propeller engine	–	500shp	First single- shaft gas-turbine type
1958	E 224	Single shaft Turbo- prop project	–	1,050shp	Take-off rating and small diameter
1956	E 226	Single shaft Turbo- prop project	3 stage turbine	715shp	Direct conversion from an E 146 Otyx

i) Turbo-prop Aero Gas Turbine – 'Naiad' Series

1945	E 128	'Naiad' I Turbo-prop	2 stage turbine	1,590ehp	Axial compressor as for E 125
1946	E 128D	'Double Naiad'	2 x 2 stage turbine	3,100ehp	Joint gearbox out to contra-props
1949	E 135	'Naiad' II Turbo-prop	2 stage turbine	2,000shp	Plus 560lb thrust at 14,500rpm
1949	E 136	'Naiad' II Developed	2 stage turbine	2,600shp	Plus 700lb thrust, E 124 Compressor

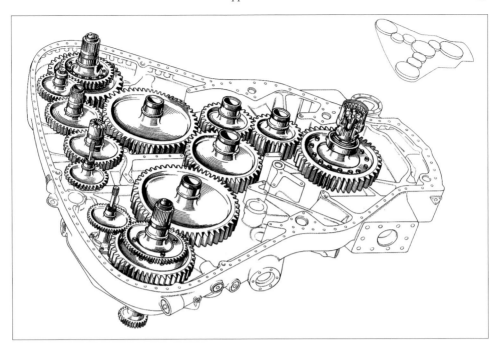

j) Napier Pure Jet Design Projects – from 1947 to 1955

1947	E 131	Compound (2 shaft) Jet Engine	2 stage turbine	5,000lb thrust	Two-spool Axial compressor
1948	E 132	Compound Jet Engine	2 stage turbine	7,000lb thrust	–
1948	E 133/134	Compound Jet Engine	2 stage turbine	9,000lb thrust	E134 had modified compressor blades
1949	E 137	Single Shaft Jet Engine	2 stage turbine	10,000lb thrust	7:1 pressure ratio Axial compressor
1949	E 138	Turbo Ram Jet Engine	–	–	3 units discharging into one reheat chamber to give 15,000lb total thrust
1950	E 140	Short Life Jet Engine based on the E 124 Compressor	–	–	Designed for an Australian project
1950	E 142	Turbo-jet Engine for a supersonic application	–	10,000lb thrust	For air mass flow to 140lb/sec
1951	E 143	Turbo-jet Engine	–	–	for supersonic flight to D.E.R.D Spec TE 6/50 for air mass flow to 125lb/sec
1952	E 148	Single Shaft Turbo-jet Engine	–	20,000lb thrust	Single axial compressor
1952	E 149	Compound (2 shaft) Turbo-jet Engine	–	20,000lb thrust	Two stage axial compressors
1955	E 181	Small Single- Shaft Turbo-jet Engine	2 stage turbine	1,100lb thrust	Based on the 'E 156' engine

k) The Turbo-prop Aero Gas Turbine – 'Eland' Series

1950	E 139	Big Turbo-prop Prototype	2 stage turbine	2,600ehp	Epicyclic Gears, E 124 Compressor
1950	E 141	'Eland' I Turbo-prop	3 stage turbine	3,000ehp	7:1 Press. Ratio Axial compressor
1951	E 141A/B	Eland up-ratings	3 stage turbine	3,500/3,250ehp	Higher turbine inlet temperature
1952	E 147	'Eland' design up-rated	3 stage turbine	3,750ehp	Higher power output of engine
1953	E 150	Double Eland	2 x 3 stage turbine	6,440ehp	Co-axial-type propeller engine
1953	E 151	Eland – Rotodyne	3 stage turbine	3,000ehp	Auxiliary compressor at rear
1954	E 151A	Eland-Rotodyne	3 stage turbine	3,500ehp	Higher turbine inlet temperature
1953	E 153	Eland power up-rated	3 stage turbine	4,000ehp	Turbine inlet temp. of 1,300K
1954	E 153A	Eland- more power	3 stage turbine	4,200ehp	8:1 Press. Ratio Axial Compressor
1953	E 154	Eland type Turbo-prop	3 stage turbine	5,000ehp	This power rating for take-off
1955	E 180	Eland-Rotodyne	3 stage turbine	4,000ehp	Conversion of E153 into E151
1955	E 187	Eland Single shaft T/P	3 stage turbine	5,500ehp	8.5:1 Press Ratio Axial Compressor
1957	E 208	Eland type Turbo-prop	3 stage turbine	–	Based on the Eland RG Compressor
1958	E 209	Eland for Helicopters	3 stage turbine	–	Based on the E 208 engine build
1958	E 210	Eland for Helicopters	3 stage turbine	–	Based on the 'N.El.6' Eland
1958	E 211	Eland–Westminster rear-drive unit	3 stage turbine	3,650shp	These had a 2½ minute rating
1956	E 229	Eland–drive taken from rear of turbine	3 stage turbine	2,400shp	Reduction gear & prop removed
1957	E 229A	Eland 503 for Westminster helicopter	3 stage turbine	2,400shp	Take-off rating as for E 229
1958	E 245	Eland Turbo-prop	3 stage turbine	3,500ehp	With take-off Torque limitation
1959	E 248	Eland Turbo-prop	3 stage turbine	3,750ehp	Final stage of Eland development
1959	E 249	Eland-Westminster	3 stage turbine	4,000shp	This a Maximum Contingency Rating

l) The Gas Producer Turbine – 'Oryx' Series

1951	E 144	Prototype Gas Producer	3 stage turbine	600ghp	Driving Auxiliary Compressor to Collector
1952	E 146	Oryx Gas Producer	3 stage turbine	825ghp	For helicopter rotor-tip propulsion

1953	E 152	Oryx Free Turbine	3 stage turbine	650shp	For horizontal installation
1953	E 155	Oryx Free Turbine	3 stage turbine	900shp	For vertical installation
1956	E 220	Oryx Free Turbine Unit	3 stage turbine	700shp	For helicopter applications
1956	E 221	Oryx Free Turbine Unit	3 stage turbine	900shp	Helicopter one-hour rating
1957	E 223	Turbo-prop Oryx Free Turbine	3 stage turbine	920ehp	Conversion of gas producer unit
1958	E 226	Single shaft 'Oryx' Turbo-prop	3 stage turbine	715shp	Fixed wing unit take-off rating

m) The Free Turbine – 'Gazelle' Series

1954	E 156	Gazelle-2 Free Turbine	2+1 stage turbines	1,260shp	Horizontal to vertical installation
1953	E 157	Large Free Turbine turbo-prop engine	–	5,000ehp	Not developed or flown
1956	E 200	Light Free Turbine turbo-prop engine	–	1,350ehp	Based on the E 156 Gazelle
1956	E 201	Gazelle Free Turbine	2+1 stage turbines	1,260shp	Opposite rotation to E 156 unit
1956	E202/ 203/204	Free Turbine 'Twin-prop' engines	–	1,650/1,800/ 2,000shp	Based on Gazelle
1956	E 213	Gazelle-13	With 7.0:1 Reduction Gear	1,450shp at Sea Level	One-hour rating
1958	E 216	Gazelle	An up-rated engine	1,525shp	With one-hour rating
1959	E 217	Gazelle-7	Modified axial intake & exhaust	1,650shp Rating	Maximum Contingency
1958	E 217A/B	Gazelle helicopter engines applications	2+1 stage turbines	1,600shp 1,675shp	Maximum Contingency Rating
1959	E218	Gazelle-21	Enlarged 'RB' Compressor	2,400shp	With one-hour rating
1959	E 219	Gazelle-18	An up-rated engine	1,750shp	With one-hour rating
1957	E 222	Light Free Turbine for a helicopter application	–	900shp	With one-hour rating
1960	E 225	Modified Gazelle as an Industrial Power Pack	2+1 stage turbines	1,200shp	Over a 1,000-hour overall life
1959	E 251	'Gazelle' developed coolant injection system	2+1 stage turbines	1,735shp	Take-off rating – 1,300shp contingency
1959	E 252	Gazelle – Uprated material for stage 1 rotor	2+1 stage turbines	1,735shp	Take-off & 1,300shp Maximum contingency
1960	E 254	Gazelle developed with 'O' stage in compressor	2+1 stage turbines	2,120shp	Max power at Sea Level
1961	E 257	Free Turbine based on E 225 Industrial Engine	2+1 stage turbines	–	See Drawing in Napier Technical Pub.10570

n) The Two-stroke High Speed Diesel – 'Deltic' Series

The following have been selected for their importance from the one hundred 'Deltic' variants listed by Napier. All 'Deltic' E 130 based, opposed piston engines had a 5^1/$_8$ in bore and a 7¼in stroke, so these dimensions have not been repeated or included in the following engine listing. The engine design number 'E 130' only was used for the first eight engine types, with Series numbers following based on the number of opposed piston cylinders, e.g. '9' and then the series type number/letter to follow, e.g. '18-7A'. The full 'Deltic E No.' listing includes engines with 1, 3, 6, 9, 15, 18 and 24 double ended uniflow Compression Ignition cylinders.

1946	E 130 T Single Cylinder Test Unit – with two flywheels, phasing gears and a central output shaft	
1946	E 130 /3 T Three Cylinder Test Unit & Central output, equivalent to 'One Bank' of the main engine	
1946	E 130 /18-1 Prototype design for the Deltic 18	2,500bhp at 2,000rpm-Mechanical Blower
1949	E 130 /18-4 Deltic MTB engine 946rpm out	2,500bhp at 2,000rpm – Ahead & astern g/box
1952	E 130 /18-11B Deltic MTB engine 950rpm out	2,500bhp at 2,000rpm – Twin plate clutch
1950	E 130 /18-7A Deltic Minesweeper at 400rpm out	1,500bhp at 1,400rpm – De-rated 18-11B
1950	E 158 Deltic Rail Traction – 18-12A prototype	1,650bhp at 1,500rpm – Mechanical Blower
1950	E 159 Deltic Minesweeper pulse generator – 9-5A	857bhp at 1,400rpm – Mechanical Blower
1954	E 162 Deltic for Rail Traction – '15'-23 engine	1,420bhp at 1,500rpm – Mechanically blown project
1955	E 164 In-line Generator drive – the '6'-19 engine	575bhp at 1,500rpm–Mechanically blown project
1955	E 165 Deltic Marine propulsion – 9-5B engine	825bhp at 1,500rpm – Ahead & astern g/box
1955	E 169 Deltic Cl.55 Rail Traction – 18-25 engine	1,725bhp at 1,500rpm – Mechanical Blower
1955	E 171 Deltic Rail Traction – T18-27 engine	2,200bhp at 1,600rpm – Geared Turboblower
1955	E 172 Deltic Cl.23 Rail Traction – T9-29 engine	1,100bhp at 1,600rpm – Geared Turboblower
1955	E 185 Deltic Marine Compound – C18-5 engine	5,500bhp at 2,000rpm – Turbo-compressor set
1955	E 189 Deltic Marine Compound – C18-5B engine	5,500bhp at 2,000rpm – Twin output shafts
1955	E 196 Deltic Marine 'Sprint' – 9-32B engine	1,250bhp at 2,000rpm – Mechanically blown
1956	E 197 In-line Rail Traction – Light 'T6'-35 engine	735bhp at 1,600rpm – Turbo-blown project
1956	E 198 Deltic Rail Traction – T9-33 engine	1,250bhp at 1,600rpm – Uprated turboblown
1956	E 239 Deltic Marine MTB – T18-37K engine	3,100bhp at 2,100rpm – Geared turbo-blown

1957	E 242 Deltic Gas Generator – G18-1 engine	3,700ghp at 1,500rpm – Axial compressor
1957	E 244 Deltic 2 Howden compressors – 18-25M	1,750bhp at 1,500rpm – Twin output shafts
1957	E 246 Deltic Alternator drive – T18-27B engine	2,200bhp at 1,600rpm – Output sht. ratio 1:1
1961	E 260 Square 24-cylinder engine Turboblown/Charge Cooled	5,400bhp at 2,100rpm – Reversing Gearbox
1961	E 263 Deltic MTB Turbocharged- CT18-42K	3,700bhp at 2,100rpm – Charge cooling
1965	E 276 Deltic Mine C.M.V. Pulse gen.-9-55B	-750bhp at 1,400rpm – 4 Hydraulic motors
1965	E280 'Deltic' MCMV Propulsion Engine-9-59K	950bhp at 1,700rpm – Mechanical blower

APPENDIX IV
NAPIER MARINE ENGINE APPLICATIONS

a) Racing Powerboats and Hydroplanes

Date	Length	Builder	Name	Engine(s) Output	Speed	Main Performances
1903	40ft	G.M. Tanner	*Napier I*	1 x 4 cyl. = 75bhp	20 knots	1903 Harmsworth Trophy won by E. Campbell-Muir at 19.53mph
1904	35ft	Saunders	*Napier Minor*	1 x 4 cyl. = 80bhp	21 knots	The Kaiser's Cup winner (first home in 1904 Harmsworth Trophy race, but technically disqualified in favour of the French entry
1904	40ft	Yarrow & Co.	*Napier II*	2 x 4 cyl. = 120bhp	22 knots	1905 Harmsworth Trophy won by Hon. John Scott-Montagu at 24.30mph
1905	40ft	Saunders (Linton Hope des)	*Napier III* (then *Siola*)	1 x 6 cyl. = 150bhp	–	For Hon. John Scott-Montagu & Lionel de Rothschild
1905	40ft	Saunders	*Napier 'Bulb'* (then *Dylan*)	1 x 4 cyl. = 80bhp	23 knots	(with 'wave piercing' bow)
1906	40ft	Saunders	*Yarrow Napier* (then *Flying Fish*)	1 x 6 cyl. = 140bhp	23 knots	1906 Harmsworth Trophy won by Lord Montague of Beaulieu
1906	40ft	Saunders	*Fiat San Giorgio*	4 x 4 cyl. = 280bhp	32 knots	Destroyed by fire on trials in Genoa

1911	40ft	Saunders	*Nigella*	2 x 6 cyl. = 180bhp	25 knots	For Lionel de Rothschild
1928	78ft	Saunders	*Jack Stripes*	4 x 12 cyl. Lion VII = 3,500bhp	–	For Trans-Atlantic Crossing attempt by Betty Carstairs
1928	26ft	Saunders Hydroplane	*Estelle I*	1 x 12 cyl. Lion VII = 875bhp	54 knots	For Betty Carstairs

1928	21ft	Saunders Hydroplane	*Estelle II*	1 x 12 cyl. Lion VII = 875bhp	75.5 knots	For Betty Carstairs
1928	27.5ft	British P.B. Co.	*Miss England*	1 x 12 cyl. Lion VIIA = 900bhp	–	91.9mph for Henry Segrave at Venice in 1929
1929	35ft	Sylvia Yard E. Cowes	*Estelle IV*	3 x 12 cyl. Lion VIID = 3,800bhp	-	Had 70mph crash in Detroit with Betty Carstairs
1930	28ft	Sylvia Yard Carstairs	*Estelle V*	2 x 12 cyl. Lion VIID = 2,600bhp	–	95mph (engines to J. Cobb)
1932	24ft	B.P.B. Co. Hythe	*Miss Britain III*	1 x 12 cyl. Lion VIID = 1,375bhp	–	World Sea Speed Record of 112mph, Hubert Scott-Paine won Venice Race at 110.1mph
1932	30ft	Saunders 'Puma'	*Whizz-Bang*	1 x 12 cyl. Lion XIA = 500bhp	–	Prototype for the 'Sealion'
1932	27.5ft	B.P.B. Co.h/plane	*Heliopolis*	1 x 12 cyl. 'Sealion' = 500bhp	–	Yacht tender with 63mph
1933	30ft	Saunders/BPB	*White Cloud II*	1 x 12 cyl. 'Sealion' = 500bhp	–	1hr Channel double crossing

b) Cruisers and Launches

1901	30ft	Saunders	Mr S.F. Edge's launch	1 x 16hp 4-cyl. Napier	-	Run Southampton to Cowes (Saunders Patent Launch Building Syndicate Ltd)
1903	27ft	Saunders	*A Pinnace*	1 x 35hp 4-cyl. Napier	–	Royal Navy coastal use
1905	40ft	Saunders (Saunders Patent Construction Co.)	*King of Siam*	1 x 45hp 4-cyl. Napier	–	Owned by the King of Siam
1905	35ft	Saunders	*Banzai*	1 x 35hp 4-cyl. Napier	–	Owned by S.F. Edge
1905	30ft	Summers & Payne	*Revolution*	1 x 20hp 4-cyl. Napier	12 knots	To Viscount Royston
1905	45ft	F. Miller & Co. (Lowestoft)	*Napier Major*	1 x 20hp 4-cyl. Napier	7 knots	Inshore Motor Yacht that gained many endurance trophies for Mr S.F Edge
1906	40ft	Saunders	*A Fast Cruiser*	2 x 4 cyl. Napier = 140bhp	–	For the Egyptian Government
1907	30ft	Fast launch	*Napier IV*	1 x 35hp 4-cyl. Napier	–	Inshore demonstrator boat
1907	40ft	Various Yards	*River Launches*	1 x 4 or 6-cyl. Napier	–	Many built for UK rivers and exported overseas within Europe and the British Empire
1912	42ft	Saunders	*Cygnet*	1 x 50hp 6-cyl. Napier	12 knots	For S.F. Edge
1938	–	B.P.B. Co.	*Kalan* Luxury Cruiser	2 x 12-cyl. Sealion=1,000bhp	–	Used in Scottish waters

c) Military Services Craft

1905	60ft	Yarrow-Napier Poplar Yard	Royal Navy MTB 1176 (later *Mercury II*)	5 x 4 cyl. Napier = 360bhp(driving three propellers)	26knots	Admiralty sold model to Russia
1908	100ft	Yarrow-Napier Scotstoun Yard	Royal Navy MTB	4 x 6 cyl. Napier= 600bhp (driving four propellers)	–	More built for Austrian, Brazilian & Australian navies
1909	110ft	Yarrow-Napier	RN H.Speed MGB 1225	4 x 6 cyl. Napier = 500bhp	–	Built for coastal defence
1934	60ft	B.P.B. Co.	RN MTB Nos 01-12./ 14-19	3 x 12 cyl. Sealion = 1,500bhp	40knots	Three flotillas of six
1937	63ft	B.P.B. Co.	RN MASB. Anti-sub boat	2 x 12 cyl. Sealion = 1,000bhp	30 knots	Total of sixty built
1937	63ft	B.P.B. Co.	RAF ASR Nos 100-121	3 x 12 cyl. Sealion = 1,500bhp	35 knots	Total of twenty-two built
1940	63ft	B.P.B. Co.	RAF ASR 'Whaleback'	3 x 12 cyl. Sealion = 1,500bhp	35 knots	Total of sixty-eight built
1942	67ft	Thornycroft	RAF H.S Launch MkII	3 x 12 cyl. Sealion = 1,500bhp	25.5 knots	Total of sixty built
1942	68ft	B.P.B. Co.	RAF HSL 'Hants & Dorset'	3 x 12 cyl. Sealion = 1,500bhp	28.5knots	Total of 120 built
1942	65ft	Walton	RAF High Speed Launch	2 x 12 cyl. Sealion = 1,000bhp	26.5knots	One built
1947	68ft	B.P.B. Co.	RAF Target Towing Launch	3 x 12 cyl. Sealion = 1,500bhp	25knots	Forty rebuilds (RTTL Conversion of 'Hants & Dorset')
1948	68ft	B.P.B. Co.	Radio-controlled target-launch	2 x 12 cyl. Sealion = 1,000bhp	19 knots	Total of four built
1953	68ft	Vosper	RAF Rescue TTL Mk 1A	3 x 12 cyl. Sealion = 1,500bhp	24knots	Total of four built
1956	68ft	Vosper	RAF Rescue TTL Mk 1B	3 x 12 cyl. Sealion = 1,500bhp	25 knots	Total of five built
1935	Various Yards	–	RASC Landing Craft Tank II	2 x 12 cyl Sealion = 1,000bhp	12 knots	Total of seventy-three built
1937	16ft	Spurr Co.	Empire Day MTB H./Plane	1 x 12 cyl Lion VIIC = 960bhp	80mph	Prototype tests
1938	63ft	B.P.B. Co.	RASC Battlefield Class HSL Launch	2 x 12 cyl. Sealion = 1,000bhp	19 knots	Total of twenty-one built
1945	111ft	B.P.B. Co.	Long-range rescue-launch	4 x Marine Sabre = 9,000bhp	–	Prototype built & tested

d) Deltic diesel powered Military Fast Patrol Boats and Minesweepers

Year	Boat Class/ Type of Action	User	Builder & No. built	Deltics fitted & Power/	Speed
1953	Bold Class, two experimental FPBs	Royal Navy	Vosper Ltd/ Metr GTs	2 x D18-11B = 5,000bhp (Plus Metravick Gas Turbines	43 knots

				= 9,000bhp)	
1954	'E-boat' P5212 conversion for Royal Navy	Royal Navy	D. Napier & Son	2 x D18-11B = 5,000bhp	36 knots (Hulls were Ex Levsen, Vegesack)
1957	'E-boat' P5208 conversion for Bundesmarine	Bundesmarine	D Napier & Son.	3 x D18-11B = 7500bhp	39 knots
1955	'Ton' Class Coastal Minesweeper	Royal Navy	Thornycroft-47 (By other yards 40)	2 x D18-7A = 3,100bhp (Plus 1xD9-5A sweep generator)	15 knots
1955	'Dark' Class 'A Boat' MTBs	Royal Navy	Saunders-Roe-18	2 x D18-11B= 5,000bhp	43 knots
1956	'Ton' Class C.M.S	Royal Indian Navy	Various-4	2 x D18-7A = 3,100bhp (Plus 1xD9-5A sweep generator)	16 knots
1956	'A Boat' MTB	Burma Navy	Saunders-Roe-5	2 x D18-11B= 5,000bhp	43 knots
1956	'Ayah' MTB	Israel Navy	Chantiers de Meulan-6	2 x D18-11B= 4,600bhp	42 knots
1957	'A Boat' MTB *Vasama*	Finland Navy	Saunders-Roe-2	2 x D18-11B= 5,000bhp	43 knots
1957	'A Boat' MTB	Japan Defenses	Saunders-Roe-1	2 x D18-11B= 5,000bhp	43 knots
1959	*Fort Steele* 118ft MPB	Royal Canadian Mounted Police (on the Great Lakes)	Canadian Yard-1	2 x D18-11B= 5,000bhp	25 knots
1961	PT 10 MTB	Japan Defenses	Mitsubishi-1	3 x T18-37K= 9,300bhp	48 knots
1960	'Nasty' MPB Prototype	Norway	Boatservice, Oslo-1	2 x D18-11B= 5,000bhp	43 knots
1960	'Hugin' Class MTB Type 152	Germany	Boatservice-2	2 x T18-37K = 6,200bhp	45 knots
1962	'Tjeld' Class MTB	Norwegian Navy	Boatservice-20	2 x T18-37K = 6,200bhp	45 knots
1962	'Nasty' PTF MTB	US Navy	Boatservice-16	2 x T18-37K = 6,200bhp	45 knots
1964	Vosper Type MTB	Peru Navy	Vosper Ltd-6	2 x T18-37K = 6,200bhp	30 knots
1964	Ex 'Hugin' Class MTB	Turkish Navy	Boatservice-2	2 x T18-37K = 6,200bhp	43 knots
1967	'Tjeld' Class MTB	Greek Navy	Boatservice-6	2 x T18-37K = 6,200bhp	43 knots
1967	'Osprey' Class PTF 23	US Navy	Sewart Seacraft-4	2 x T18-37K = 6,200bhp	40 knots
1967	PTF 17 Class MTB	US Navy	John Trumpy-6	2 x T18-37K = 6,200bhp	45 knots
1971	MGB P10XX Class ex-ton	Royal Navy	Various Yards-5	2 x D18-7A = 3,100bhp	16 knots
1972	Mine C.M Wilton in GRP	Royal Navy	Vosper-Thornycroft	2 x D18-7A = 3,100bhp (Plus 1 x D9-5A sweep generator)	18 knots

| 1980 | MTB Seawards Defence | Indian Navy | Calcutta Yard-4 | 2 x CT18-42K= 7,400bhp | 40 knots |
| 1982/89 | 'Hunt' Class Mine C.M | Royal Navy | Various UK Yards-13 | 2x D9-59K= 2,360bhp (Plus 1xD9-55B Hydraulics & sweep generator) | 17 knots |

e) Deltic-powered Ferries, Yachts and Ships.

1957	FPB/ Ferry 67.5ft	Shell Exploration Venezuela	Thornycroft-3	3 2 x D9-5B= 1,620bhp	31 knots
1958	*Bahama King* 1,700 ton 'Ore Carrier'	Deltic conversion by DNS	DNS	4 x D18-25K=7,400bhp	14 knots
1959	FPB/ Ferry 80ft	Shell Exploration	Venezuela-1 Vosper Ltd	1 2 x D18-25K= 3,700bhp	35 knots
1959	*Bass Trader* 3,685 tons	Tasmania	For Australian National Line	2xT18-27C= 4,400bhp	15 knots
1961	Motor Yacht *Naief*	Qatar Royal Family	Burmeister	2xD18-25K= 3,500bhp	18 knots
1963	Motor Yacht *l'Esterel*	French owner	Chantier Yard	2xT18-37K= 6,200bhp	34 knots
1964	Motor Yacht *Carinthia VI*	German owner	Chantier Yard	2xT18-37K= 6,200bhp	36 knots
1983	125ft Yacht *Blue Magic*	British flag	Sea Jets International, Italy	2xT18-37K= 6,200bhp	30 knots

APPENDIX V
NAPIER AERO ENGINE APPLICATIONS

a) British Aircraft Builders (Arranged Alphabetically)

Date	Aircraft Type or Name	User	Engine(s) & Total Power	Main Features & Records

AIRSPEED LTD

| 1934 | Courier – AS 5C | Racer | 1 x 16cylinderRapier IV=340bhp | Kings Cup race 166mp |
| 1956 | Elizabethan G-ALFR | BEA | 2 x T/Prop ElandI =5,400ehp | Conversion prototype |

ALLIANCE A/C of ACTON.

| 1918 | Endeavour – P1 | – | 1 x 12 cylinder Lion IB=450bhp | Commercial passenger |
| 1919 | Seabird – P2 | – | 1 x 12 cylinder Lion IB=450bhp | 1st London-Madrid record |

(A single-engine trans-Atlantic flight contender)

ARMSTRONG-WHITWORTH

| 1921 | Sinai I–103 | RAF | 2 x 12 cylinder Lion II=900bhp | Medium Bomber |
| 1923 | Awana–105 | RAF | 2 x 12 cylinder Lion II=900bhp | Troop Carrier–97mph |

AVRO

1920	Baby Racer–539B	Racer	1 x 12cylinder Lion II=480bhp	For 1921 Aerial Derby
1920/5	Bison I /II–555	FAA	1 x 12cylinder Lion II/V=500bhp	Carrier-borne Fleet spotter
1922	Aldershot II – 549	RAF	1 x 16cylinder Cub = 1,000bhp	Single-engine Bomber
1925	Buffalo I /II–571	FAA	1 x 12cylinder LionVA=500bhp	Torpedo Bomber/Seaplane
1925	Avenger I–566	RAF	1 x 12 cylinder LionVIII=525bhp	Fastest fighter plane of its time
1928	Avenger II–567	–	1 x 12cylinder Lion IX =535bhp	Kings Cup race at 180mph.
1948	Lincoln	DNS	1xT/Prop.Naiad =1,450ehp	Flying test bed
1951	Lincoln	DNS	1 x 12 cylinder Nomad I=3,100bhp	Flying test bed
1955	Lancaster	DNS	1 x 12 cylinder Nomad II=3,150bhp	Flying test bed

BEARDMORE

1924	Rohrbach-Napier	–	2 x 12cylinder Lion III=920bhp	All-metal sea monoplane
1926	Inverness Be R02	–	2 x 12cylinder Lion III=920bhp	A flying boat

BLACKBURN

1920	Swift–T1	FAA	1 x 12 cylinder Lion IB=450bhp	Torpedo bomber–131mph
1922	Dart I /II–T2	FAA	1 x 12 cylinder Lion IIB=480bhp	Torpedo bomber
1922	Bull	FAA	1 x 12cylinder Lion=450bhp	Two-seat trainer
1922	Cubaroo	RAF	1 x 16 cylinder Cub =1,000bhp	Single-engine bomber–122mph
1925	Velos–T3	FAA	1 x 12 cylinder Lion V=500bhp	Torpedo seaplane
1923	Pellet	Racer	1 x 12cylinder Lion IIB=480bhp	Flying boat–161mph
1923	Blackburn–R1	FAA	1 x 12 cylinder Lion IIB=480bhp	Fleet spotter biplane
1928/33	Ripon I/ II/III–T5	FAA	1 x 12 cylinder LionV/XIA=570bhp	Torpedo bomber
1937	Iris Mk V	MAEE	3 x 6 cylinder Culverin =1,650bhp	Flying boat diesel test bed
1935	H.S.T. 10	–	2 x 16 cylinder Rapier =790bhp	Ten seater–200mph
1942	Firebrand I /II	Royal Navy	1 x 24 cylinder Sabre III=2,300bhp	Fighter/Torpedo bomber

BOULTON & PAUL LTD

1919	Atlantic - P8	Twin Civil Airliner	2 x 12 cylinder Lion IB=900bhp	Trans-Atlantic flight record contenda
1920	Type P 11	–	Prototype 1 x 12 cylinder Lion IB=450bhp	Projected Amphibian mock-up
1921	Bodmin-P12	–	Prototype 2 x 12 cylinder Lion IB=900bhp	Both engines in steel fuselage driving two pairs of tractor and pusher propellers via chain drives
1922	Bolton–P15	RAF	2 x 12 cylinder Lion IB=900bhp	A Medium bomber
1922	Bourges Mk. IIIA & IIIB	RAF	2 x 12 cylinder Lion IB=900bhp	Day Bomber development
1925	Bugle Mk II	RAF	2 x 12 cylinder Lion IIB=900bhp	Three-seat Day Bomber
1926	Sidestrand–P29	RAF	2 x 12 cylinder Lion IIB = 940bhp	Before conversion to Jupiters

BRISTOL AEROPLANE Co.

1920	Ten Seater–Type 62	Instone	1 x 12 cylinder Lion II = 450bhp	Croydon-Paris route July 1921
1922	Bristol Type 71	DNS	1 x 16 cylinder Cub = 1,000bhp	Prototype Flying test bed
1931	Bulldog F2B Fighter	DNS	1 x 16 cylinder Rapier = 350bhp	Flying test bed – J6721
1936	Type 124	RAE	1 x 24 cylinder Dagger=850bhp	Flying test bed
1958	Belvedere Type 192 HC Mk1	RAF	2 x Free T. Gazelle = 3,300bhp	Tandem rotor helicopter

BRITISH KLEMM – B.A.

1933	Eagle	Racer	1 x 6 cylinder Javelin =170bhp	With retracting undercarriage

DE HAVILLAND – (AIRCO)

1918	DH Type 4G	RAF	1 x 12 cylinder x Lion IB = 450bhp	Altitude record at 30,500ft
1919	DH Type 4R	Racer	1 x 12 cylinder Lion IB = 450bhp	Won Aerial Derby at 129mph
1918	DH Type 9A/C/ R by Westland	RAF	1 x 12 cylinder Lion IB = 450bhp	Day bomber from 18/03/1918
1919	DH Type 16	ATT Ltd	1 x 12 cylinder Lion IB = 450bhp	First commercial four-seater
1920	DH Type 18A	ATT/ Instone	1 x 12 cylinder Lion II = 470bhp	Eight-seat commercial
1920	DH Type 23	Instone	1 x 12 cylinder Lion IB = 450bhp	Four-seat commercial
1920	DH Type 14A Okapi	Racer	1 x 12 cylinder Lion II = 470bhp	Two-seat racer/long distances
1921	DH Type 25	ATT Ltd	1 x 12 cylinder Lion II = 470bhp	–
1922	DH Type 25 Doncaster	–	1 x 12 cylinder Lion II = 470bhp	Ten-seat Cantilever Monoplane
1922	DH Type 34B	Imperial Airways	1 x 12 cylinder Lion II = 470bhp	–
1927	DH Type 65A Hound	RAF	1 x 12 cylinder Lion XA = 540bhp	Two-seat + 1000kg at 161mph
1929	DH Type 77	RAF	1 x 16 cylinder Rapier II = 340bhp	Braced monoplane Fighter Interceptor

ENGLISH ELECTRIC

1918	Phoenix-Cork	–	2 x 12 cylinder Lion IB = 900bhp	Flyingboat
1924	Ayr	–	1 x 12 cylinder Lion II = 470bhp	–
1924	Kingston I /II	FAA	2 x 12 cylinder Lion V = 940bhp	A Biplane Flyingboat
1956	English Electric Canberra B2	DNS/RAF	1x N.Sc.1-2 Rocket = 4000lb thrust	Two flying test beds

(Napier Scorpion Canberra' WK163 gained the World Altitude Record of 70,310ft on 28 August.)

FAIREY AVIATION

1919	R.A.F XXI	RAF	1 x 12 cylinder Lion IB = 450bhp	Seaplane
1919	Fairey III (N10)	–	1 x 12 cylinder Lion IA = 450bhp	Only Schneider Cup finisher
1920/24	Pintail I/II/III	FAA	1 x 12 cylinder Lion V = 530bhp	Floatplane, three to Japanese Navy
1924	Fairey III D	RAF&FAA	1 x 12 cylinder Lion V = 530bhp	Land or Floatplane–200 plus
1927	Fairey III F	RAF& FAA	1 x 12 cylinder Lion XIA = 570bhp	Land or Floatplane – 600 plus
1935	Gordon/ IIIF	–	1 x 6 cylinder Culverin = 720bhp	Diesel engine test bed
1924	Fawn II/III	RAF	1 x 12 cylinder Lion V = 530bhp	Day bomber/ reconnassiance
1924	Fawn III	RAE	1 x 12 cylinder Lion IV = 500bhp	Turbo-supercharger test bed
1929	Postal Mk I	RAF	1 x 12 cylinder Lion XIANS = 570bhp	Long-range monoplane
1931	Postal Mk II	RAF	1 x 12 cylinder Lion XIANS = 570bhp	5,309 mile flight Feb.1933
1933	Fairey Queen	FAA	1 x 12 cylinder Lion XIA = 570bhp	Radio control target aircraft
1936	Seafox	FAA	1 x 16 cylinder Rapier VI = 395bhp	Reconnaissance seaplane
1938	Battle	RAE	1 x 24 cylinder Dagger VIII = 1,000bhp	Engine flying test bed
1939	Battle	DNS/RAE	1 x 24 cylinder Sabre I /II = 2,200bhp	Engine flying test bed
1957	Rotodyne	DNS/Fairey	2 x Aux.Comp.T/ Prop Eland NEI.3 = 5,600bhp	Convertiplane prototype

(First VTOL gas turbine helicopter airliner – then Holder of the closed circuit speed record at 191mph.)

FOLLAND

1940	Type 43 /37	DNS/Luton	1 x 24 cylinder Sabre II /V = 2,400bhp	Spl. engine flying test beds
1946	Type Fo 108	–	1 x 24 cylinder SabreVII = 3,050bhp	Development fighter design

GLOSTER AIRCRAFT

1921	'Bamel' Mars I/II	Racer	1 x 12 cylinder Lion IIB = 470bhp	Kings Cup Air Race Winner

(Became known as the 'Lion-Hearted' racing biplane, while it created four air-speed records)

1922	Gloster I	Racer/RAF	1 x 12 cylinder Lion V = 530bhp	1921/2/3 Aerial Derby winner
1925	Gloster III A	RAF/Racer	1 x 12 cylinder Lion VII = 670bhp	Second in Schneider Cup at 199mph
1926	Guan	DNS/RAE	1 x 12 cylinder Lion IV/VI/Lioness	Turbocharger engine test bed

1926	Gorcock	RAF/RAE	1 x 12 cylinder Lion IV = 525bhp	First all metal, 185mph fighter.
1926	Gloster IV A	RAF/Racer	1 x 12 cylinder Lion VIIA = 900bhp	Direct-Max Speed of 310mph
1927	Gloster IV B	RAF/Racer	1 x 12 cylinder Lion VIIB = 875bhp	Retired lying second in Schneider Cup
1929	Gloster VI- 'Golden Arrow'	Racer	1 x 12 cylinder Lion VIID = 1,380bhp	Air speed record 336.3mph

GRAHAME WHITE

191	Type GWE9 'Ganymede'	RAF	2 x 12 cylinder Lion IB = 900bhp	Twelve-seat convertible to a bomber

HANDLEY PAGE

1919	Type W 8	Imperial Airways	2 x 12 cylinder Lion IB = 900bhp	Britains first new twin-engined airliner. In 1921, Lion IIBs replaced those built with 'Eagles'.
1920	Type O 400	–	2 x 12cylinder Lion IB = 900bhp	Ex-Bombers fitted with twelve seats
1920	Type W 10	Imperial Airways	2 x 12 cylinder Lion IIB = 940bhp	Fourteen-seat passenger airliner
1920	Type V 1500 (Type 15)	–	4 x 12 cylinder Lion II = 1,800bhp	Test development for passengers
1921	Type 18 'Hannibal'	RAF	4 x 12 cylinder Lion II = 1,800bhp	Troop-carrier and/ or passengers
1921	Type 19 Hanley I	–	1 x 12 cylinder Lion IIB = 470bhp	115mph in level flight
1923	Type W 8D Hyderabad	RAF	2 x 12 cylinder Lion IIB = 940bhp	Night Bomber of 109mph
1923	Type HP 25 Hendon	–	1 x 12 cylinder Lion IIB = 470bhp	108mph in level flight
1924	Type HP Handcross	RAF	1 x 12 cylinder Lion VI = 500bhp	Day bomber
1926	Type HP 21 Harrow II/IVA	FAA	1 x 12 cylinder Lion VA = 525bhp	Torpedo bomber – 115mph
1929	Type HP 38 biplane	RAF	2 x 12 cylinder Lion VA = 1,050bhp	Night bomber prototype
1937	Hampden	DNS/RAE	2 x 24 cylinder Dagger VIII = 1,800bhp	Twin-engine flying test bed
1938	Hereford (built Short & Harland)	RAF	2 x 24 cylinder Dagger VIII = 2,000bhp	Bomber-crew trainer

HAWKER AIRCRAFT

1925	Horsley biplane	RAE	1 x 12 cylinder Lion V = 580bhp	Engine flying test bed
1934	Hart	RAE	1 x 24 cylinder Dagger III = 750bhp	Flight development bomber
1936	Hector	RAF	1 x 24 cylinder Dagger IIIMS = 805bhp	Army support bomber
1940	Typhoon IB	RAF	1 x 24 cylinder Sabre IIA = 2,180bhp	Ground attack fighter bomber (capable of 412mph in level

				flight at 19,000ft, then the world's fastest and most powerful fighter)
1941	Tempest I (Typhoon II)	RAF	1 x 24 cylinder Sabre IV=2,400bhp	Max Level speed 440mph
1943	Tempest V	RAF	1 x 24 cylinder Sabre IIB = 2,420bhp	Low altitude interceptor
1944	Tempest VI	RAF	1 x 24 cylinder Sabre VA = 2,600bhp	Max Level speed 466mph
1946	Fury Mk I (Tempest III)	R.A.E	1 x 24 cylinder Sabre VII = 3,050bhp	Max Level speed 490mph (this had a water-methanol injected Sabre VII engine, cooled by both annular and wing root radiators)

HESTON AIRCRAFT

1939	Type 5	Napier_Heston Nuffield Racer	1 x 24 cylinder Sabre I S = 2,300bhp	For World air-speed record attempt

MARTIN-BAKER AIRCRAFT

1935	Type MB-1	DNS/M-BA	1 x 6 cylinder Javelin = 160bhp	Prototype installation
1937	Type MB-2	DNS/M-BA	1 x 24 cylinder Dagger = 800bhp	Fighter prototype
1942	Type MB-3	DNS/RAF	1 x 24 cylinder Sabre II =2,100bhp	Prototype fighter – crashed

PARNALL

1923	Possum Triplane	–	1 x 12 cylinder Lion II = 450bhp	Two geared-in propellers
1926	Pike Biplane	FAA	1 x 12 cylinder Lion IIB = 470bhp	Fleet reconnaissance plane
1926	Puffin Floatplane	–	1 x 12 cylinder Lion IIB = 470bhp	An Amphibian biplane

PERCIVAL AIRCRAFT

1932	D2 Gull Four Mk II	–	1 x 6 cylinder Javelin III = 160bhp	Three seat fast monoplane
1933	P2 Mew Gull I	Racer	1 x 6 cylinder Javelin IA = 170bhp	Single seat racing monoplane
1935	P14 (project)	–	4 x 16 cylinder Rapier = 1,560bhp	Fourteen-seat transport
1938	P26 (project)	–	1 x 24 cylinder Sabre I = 2,000bhp	Engine flying test bed
1953	P74 Helicopter (built & tested)	–	2 x Oryx Gas Producer = 1,360ghp	Research tip-jet helicopter
1957	P105 Helicopter (project)	–	2 x Oryx Gas Producer = 1,400ghp	Ten passenger version of P74

ROYAL AIRCRAFT FACTORY

1916	RE 7 Biplane	RFC	1 x 12 cylinder Napier/ RAF 3A = 300bhp	Acton works built 50 RE 7s

SAUNDERS-ROE

1925	A14 Flying boat	–	2 x 12 cylinder Lion VA = 1,000bhp	Metal hull type
1934	A19 Saro Cloud	–	2 x 16 cylinder Rapier IV = 680bhp	Re-engined Flying boat
1956	Saro Skeeter 6 Helicopter	DNS/Army	3 x NRE 19 steam Rotor Tip Units	Rate of climb rocket-boosted

SHORT BROTHERS

1921	N 3 Cromarty	FAA	2 x 12 cylinder Lion II = 900bhp	Metal hull flying boat
1937	S 20 Mercury boat	RAF	4 x 16 cylinder Rapier V = 1,360bhp	High-speed postal flying
1938	S 20 Mercury	RAF	4 x 16 cylinder Rapier VI = 1,480bhp	Atlantic crossing at 177mph
1952	Empire-Shetland (project)	–	4 x 12 cylinder Nomad II = 13,000bhp	Long-range flying boat

SOPWITH AVIATION

| 1920 | Cuckoo | RAF | 1 x 12 cylinder Lion IB = 450bhp | Land-based torpedo-bomber |

SPARTON

| 1933 | Arrow–Single seat biplane | – | 1 x 6 cylinder Javelin III = 160bhp | Engine flying test bed |

SUPERMARINE

1919	Type S1- Sealion I	–	1 x 12 cylinder Lion IA = 450bhp	R.Mitchell Flying boat-147mph
1922	Sealion II	Racer	1 x 12 cylinder Lion II = 470bhp	Won Schneider Cup – 145.6mph
1923	Sealion III	Racer	1 x 12 cylinder Lion III = 525bhp	Third in Schneider Cup-at 151.6mph
1922	Seal II	FAA	1 x 12 cylinder Lion IA = 450bhp	Fleet-spotter flying boat
1923-6	Seagull I/ II/III	FAA	1 x 12 cylinder Lion V = 490bhp	Amphibian – Royal Australian Air Force
1924	Swan II	–	2 x 12 cylinder Lion IIB = 980bhp	Amphibian Flying boat
1925	Sheldrake	–	1 x 12 cylinder Lion V = 490bhp	Amphibian for Spanish Navy
1925/7	Southampton	RAF I/ II/ III	2 x 12 cylinder Lion VA = 1,050bhp	Long life and range flying boat
1925	Type S4	RAF/HSF	1 x 12 cylinder Lion VII = 700bhp	Air speed record – 226.5mph
1927	Type S5-21	RAF/HSF	1 x 12 cylinder Lion VIIA = 900bhp	Direct drive – second Schneider Cup race
1927	Type S5-25	RAF/HSF	1 x 12 cylinder Lion VIIB = 875bhp	Won Schneider Cup – 281.6mph

TARRANT

| 1919 | Tabor Triplane bomber | RAE | 6 x 12 cylinder Lion IB = 2,700bhp | Prototype crashed on take-off |

VICKERS AVIATION

1920	Viking III Amphibian N147	FAA	1 x 12 cylinder Lion IB = 450bhp	Won B.A.M. £10K competition
1921	Viking IV– Laurentide	R.C.A.F	1 x 12 cylinder Lion IB = 450bhp	Flying boat-Canadian Vickers
1922	Viking V–N157	FAA	1 x 12 cylinder Lion II = 470bhp	Amphibian Flying boat
1924	Vulture (Viking VI)	–	1 x 12 cylinder Lion II = 470bhp	Amphibian
1925	Vanellus (Viking VII) N169	R.A.E	1 x 12 cylinder Lion V = 490bhp	'Round the world' amphibian
1921	Vernon II/III	RAF	2 x 12 cylinder Lion II = 940bhp	Troop transport
1922	Virginia I/VII/ VIIIA/X/IX	RAF	2 x 12 cylinder Lion V= 980bhp	Heavy Night bomber – 108mph
1922	Vimy Commercial	–	2 x 12 cylinder Lion IB = 900bhp	Also ambulance version in 1921

1922	Vulcan- 'Flying Pig'	Imperial Airways	1 x 12 cylinder Lion IIB = 470bhp	Eight-seat commercial biplane
1923/8	Vanguard - T 170	A.M./Imperial Airways	2 x 12 cylinder Lion V = 980bhp	Unique twenty-two seat transport/airliner
1928	Victoria I/ III/V–T 56	RAF	2 x 12 cylinder Lion XI = 1,140bhp	Twenty-five man troop carrier-110mph
1923	Vivid– T 142	Racer	1 x 12 cylinder Lion XI = 570bhp	Chin radiator, all metal biplane
1923	Valparaiso I – T 93	–	1 x 12 cylinder Lion VA = 486bhp	Chilean height record 20,000ft
1923/26	Vixen I/II/III	RAF/FAA	1 x 12 cylinder Lion V = 500bhp	Two-seat fighter and floatplane
1925	Venture	R.A.E	1 x 12 cylinder Lion V = 490bhp	Combined Vixen Types 71/87/91
1927	Vickers 121 Wibault Scout	C.A.F	1 x 12cylinder Lion XI = 570bhp	Metal parasol monoplane- Chile
1941	Vickers B1/35	Design	2 x 24 cylinder Sabre II = 4,400bhp	Twin-engine Bomber project
1944	Warwick C Mk III	DNS/VA	2 x 24 cylinder Sabre VI = 5,200bhp	Annular radiator devt. a/c
1947	Wellington	DNS/VA	2 x T/Prop Naiad = 3,200bhp	Engine flying test bed
1948	Viscount V 640	DNS/VA	4 x T/Prop Naiad = 6,400bhp	Prototype built, but not flown
1954	Varsity	DNS	2 x T/Prop Eland = 6,250bhp	Assymetric engine flying test bed

WESTLAND AIRCRAFT

1920	Limousine III	Instone	1 x 12 cylinder Lion IB = 450bhp	Six-seat airliner –Won £7,500 prize
1920	Walrus I (DH 9A)	FAA	1 x 12 cylinder Lion II = 450bhp	Three-seat carrier-based spotter reconnaissance
1923	Dreadnought	A.M.	1 x 12 cylinder Lion IIB = 470bhp	Expl. metal 'aerofoil monoplane'
1957	Sikorsky HSS-I	DNS	1 x Free Turbine Gazelle = 1,100bhp	Helicopter engine flying test bed
1958	Wessex WS 58	DNS/WA	1 x Free T.Gazelle 161 = 1450bhp	Prototype gas turbine helicopter
1958	Whirlwind	DNS/WA	3 x NRE 19 Rotor Tip-jet Units	Rate of climb rocket- boosters
1958	Westminster S 56	DNS/WA	2 x T/Drive Eland 229A = 6,300bhp	A forty-seat/six-ton lift helicopter
1960	Wiltshire	DNS/WA	2 x Free T/Drive Gazelle = 3,100bhp	Civil helicopter, project only
1959	Wessex WS 60	Royal Navy	1 x Free T. NGa. 3 Gazelle = 1,450bhp	Twelve-passenger helicopter
1961	Wessex HAS Mk I	Royal Navy	1 x Free T. Gazelle 161 = 1,450bhp	Anti-submarine helicopter
1962	Wessex HAS3/31	R.N./R.A.N.	1 x Free T. Gazelle 160 = 1,650bhp	Anti-submarine/Rescue for Australia

b) Overseas Aircraft Builders

AICHI (Japan)

| 1935 | AB– 4b | J.A.F | 1x12 cylinder Lion XV = 555bhp | Six-seat, biplane flying reconnaissance |

CANADAIR (Canada)

| 1959 | Airliner CL66A/ CV540A | – | 2 x T/Prop.Eland 504A = 7,000bhp | A forty-eight to sixty-eight-seat new airliner |
| 1960 | Cosmopolitan CL66B | – | 2 x T/Prop.Eland 504A = 7,000bhp | A cargo/passenger CV540B |

(Ten aircraft, as CC109s, were supplied to Royal Canadian Air Force Transport Command.)

| 1959 | CC66C/CV440 | P.Eng. conversions | 2 x T/Prop.Eland 504=6,600bhp | Flew with Quebecair airlines |

DORNIER (Germany)

1924	Komet III	–	1 x 12 cylinder Lion V = 500bhp	–
1926	Wal (whale)– Tandem engines	–	2 x 12 cylinder Lion V = 1,000bhp	Flying boat, first to cross the South Atlantic
1929	Superwal – Tandem pairs	–	4 x 12 cylinder Lion VIII = 1,940bhp	20-passenger long-range flying boat of 135mph

FOKKER (Netherlands)

1922	Type B I	–	1 x 12 cylinder Lion II = 450bhp	Amphibian flying boat
1924	Type C IV	–	1 x 12 cylinder Lion II = 450bhp	Round-world flight biplane 159 built
1925	Type DC I	–	1 x 12 cylinder Lion II = 450bhp	Reconnaissance biplane
1925	Type D XIII	–	1 x 12 cylinder Lion IIB = 470bhp	Fighter aircraft–171mph
1926	Type F VII	–	1 x 12 cylinder Lion IIB = 470bhp	Ten-seat Amphibian
1926	Type F XII	–	1 x 12 cylinder Lion IIB = 470bhp	Anti-stall Safety High-Wing Monoplane
1927	Type L 66	–	1 x 12 cylinder Lion IIB = 470bhp	Postal Biplane
1928	Type T III	–	2 x 12 cylinder Lion IIB = 940bhp	Monoplane bomber

GENERAL DYNAMICS– CONVAIR (United States)

1954	Convair 540	DNS	2 x T/Prop. Eland 503 = 6,500bhp	Prototype conversion of a Convair. CV 340, by replacement of its Pratt & Witney R2800 piston engines
1958	Convair 540	Allegheny	2 x T/Prop. Eland NEl 6 = 7,000bhp	Six CV440 converted-aircraft used
1960	Convair 540	RCAF	2 x T/Prop. Eland 504 = 6,600bhp	Four conversions from CV440 a/c

HEINKEL (Germany).

1923	Type HD 17	–	1 x 12 cylinder Lion II = 470bhp	Reconnaissance Biplane
1923	Heinkel-Napier HE 5	–	1 x 12 cylinder Lion II = 470bhp	25,000ft reconnaissance seaplane
1925	Type HD 23	–	1 x 12 cylinder Lion II = 470bhp	Built for the Japanese A.F.
1926	Type HD 25	–	1 x 12 cylinder Lion V = 500bhp	–

HENDY (United States)

1934	Hendy 308	–	1 x 6 cylinder Javelin = 160bhp	Witney Straight's long-wing monoplane

JUNKERS (Germany)

1925	Type G 23	–	1 x 12 cylinder Lion IIB = 490bhp	An Anti-stall 'Safety Plane'
1926	Type G 24	–	3 x 12 cylinder Lion IIB = 1,470bhp	Ten seat all-metal monoplane

KIRKHAM (Harold Vandebilt, New York USA)

1925	Kirkham Air Yacht	–	1 x 12 cylinder Lion IIB = 490bhp	Five-seat monoplane flying -boat

LETOV (Czechoslovakia)

1926	Smolik-Napier	Racer	1 x 12 cylinder Lion V = 500bhp	Racing Monoplane–225mph

LOCKEED (United States)

1955	Electra CL 303	Civil	4 x T/Prop.Eland = 13,000bhp	High wing airliner -project only

MITSUBISHI (Japan)

1921	Type 1 MF 1	–	1 x 12 cylinder Lion II = 470bhp	Carrier-borne Biplane
1922	Type 1 MT	–	1 x 12 cylinder Lion II = 470bhp	Triplane torpedo bomber
1924	Type 2 MT	–	1 x 12 cylinder Lion IIB = 490bhp	Torpedo bomber-450 built

TUPOLEV (Central Aero-Hydrodynamic Institute -Russia)

| 1926 | Type ANT 3 | – | 1 x 12 cylinder Lion II = 470bhp | All-metal Biplane RR-SOV |

WACKETT (Cockatoo Islands Dockyard, Aircraft Dept. N.S.W. Australia)

| 1936 | Codock | – | 2 x 6 cylinder Javelin = 340bhp | Light Monoplane Air Ferry |

INDEX